African Histories and Modernities

Series Editors
Toyin Falola
The University of Texas at Austin
Austin, TX, USA

Matthew M. Heaton
Virginia Tech
Blacksburg, VA, USA

This book series serves as a scholarly forum on African contributions to and negotiations of diverse modernities over time and space, with a particular emphasis on historical developments. Specifically, it aims to refute the hegemonic conception of a singular modernity, Western in origin, spreading out to encompass the globe over the last several decades. Indeed, rather than reinforcing conceptual boundaries or parameters, the series instead looks to receive and respond to changing perspectives on an important but inherently nebulous idea, deliberately creating a space in which multiple modernities can interact, overlap, and conflict. While privileging works that emphasize historical change over time, the series will also feature scholarship that blurs the lines between the historical and the contemporary, recognizing the ways in which our changing understandings of modernity in the present have the capacity to affect the way we think about African and global histories.

Vusi Gumede • Santos Bila
Mduduzi Biyase • Shonisani Chauke
Sodiq Arogundade

South African Economy

Trails and Possibilities

palgrave
macmillan

Vusi Gumede
University of Mpumalanga
Mbombela, South Africa

Santos Bila
University of Johannesburg
Auckland Park, South Africa

Mduduzi Biyase
University of Johannesburg
Auckland Park, South Africa

Shonisani Chauke
University of Mpumalanga
Mbombela, South Africa

Sodiq Arogundade
University of Johannesburg
Auckland Park, South Africa

ISSN 2634-5773 ISSN 2634-5781 (electronic)
African Histories and Modernities
ISBN 978-3-031-54179-7 ISBN 978-3-031-54180-3 (eBook)
https://doi.org/10.1007/978-3-031-54180-3

Cover image credit line: Tanatat pongphibool, thailand/Getty Images

This Palgrave Macmillan imprint is published by the registered company Springer Nature Switzerland AG.
The registered company address is: Gewerbestrasse 11, 6330 Cham, Switzerland

Paper in this product is recyclable.

Foreword

The South African society and its economy require all those concerned about the wellbeing of the country to not only better understand the socio-economic status of the country but to come up with possible solutions. Understanding South Africa's economy in a historical context as the book guides is critical in our endeavour to bring about an inclusive economy and the kind of society that our Constitution promises. As we continue to build an effective developmental state, we must grow the economy and ensure that everyone especially those who were sidelined by the apartheid system benefit if not play roles in growing our economy and society.

The various government interventions to grow the South African economy and to ensure inclusive socio-economic development have not worked well of late. The government is implementing many economic reforms and addressing inefficiencies and dealing with corruption. The book welcomes and encourages the endeavours by the government. However, the book makes a convincing case for what it calls a clear economic policy for South Africa. It also argues for a comprehensive social policy that must work in tandem with economic policy for inclusive socio-economic development in South Africa.

We are confident that this book will help policy makers while it empowers students of economics and researchers on the South African economy. Among its major contributions is the combination of advanced econometric methods and incisive policy analysis. It is also commendable that the book examines the South African economy in a comparative context, comparing South Africa with selected emerging market economies (i.e. Brazil, Nigeria, Malaysia and Poland) given that South Africa is an emerging market economy. This is an insightful approach because many comparative studies of the South African economy compare South Africa mainly with middle-income countries or the broad category of the developing world. In this book, South Africa is compared with a country in each of the important regions from the perspective of emerging economies culminating in important lessons for us in South Africa particularly as far as our economy and the role of the government are concerned.

I commend and congratulate the authors. I recommend this book to all those concerned about South Africa and its future.

Pretoria, South Africa Enoch Godongwana

Preface

The South African economy performed relatively well in the 1990s to the late 2000s after the democratic government stabilised the economy in the 1990s. During apartheid, the economy served mainly the minority white at the detriment of the African majority. In the dying years of apartheid, the South African economy was in recession. The various economic indicators improved in the 1990s and there was job creation until late 2000s. Wellbeing of the majority improved, at least when measured by the human development index (HDI) and by the gross domestic product (GDP) per capita. GDP per capita in particular increased at an impressive rate in the 1990s and 2000s.

With regard to GDP, during the 1994–2004 period, the growth averaged at about 3% which is a considerable improvement on the decade prior to 1994 when the growth averaged at 1% per year. However, from about 2013, GDP growth started to decline. GDP per capita has declined to negative growth of late. Similarly, socio-economic development has been deteriorating. Relative to comparable economies, South Africa's economy has performed poorly although its size has significantly expanded since 1994. Notwithstanding external factors that have negatively affected the South African economy in the democratic dispensation, a combination of internal factors have negatively affected the South African economy.

Our main argument is that lack of (or an unclear) economic policy is the main reason for poor economic performance of late, if not since the mid-2000s. Granted, the challenges such as load shedding, logistics bottlenecks, generally deteriorating quality of infrastructure, crime and corruption as well as constraints to the economy associated with global economic recessions and Covid-19 cannot be overlooked. However, the deterioration in the economy and the subsequent worsening of socio-economic development can be attributed to the lack of or unclear economic policy starting around the mid-2000s. Economic policy was relatively clear during 1996 to late 2000s. Indeed, this coincided with the period when the South African economy benefited from the commodity boom.

This book contributes to the study of the South African economy. It is an attempt at a comprehensive analysis of the South African economy, culminating to the argument presented above (viz. that South Africa needs a clear economic policy that is relevant for South Africa and its context if the economy is to grow, and wellbeing improved). It was/is necessary to undertake a more detailed and contextual study of an economy in order to have a better understanding of its components. The book takes into account the history that has shaped the South African economy which has for many decades mainly served the white minority and is shaped by the mineral-energy complex. The mismanagement of the South African economy in the dying years of apartheid required macroeconomic stabilisation, which arguably was well done through the Growth, Employment and Redistribution (GEAR) economic policy inaugurated in 1996.

GEAR however should have been replaced by a more appropriate economic policy after the economy was sufficiently stabilised. It was not until 2005 that the Accelerated and Shared Growth Initiative for South Africa (AsgiSA) economic policy was unveiled. AsgiSA was promising as an economic policy, but it was never fully implemented. It was abruptly replaced by the New Growth Path (NGP) which was also replaced by the National Development Plan (NDP) in a short space of time. Although there have been numerous efforts to come up with a clear economic policy since 2005, there is no clear economic policy in South Africa. The economic reforms pursued as far as network industries and other areas are commendable but that cannot take a space of an economic policy.

Building on the research of the authors over the years, the book analyses economic policies and political economy interventions that South Africa has implemented since 1994. Based on that analysis, the book concludes that South Africa needs a clear economic policy because the various interventions in the economy should be guided by a clear economic policy. The micro- and macroeconomic reforms as well as other reforms pertaining the South African economy would have greater positive impact if guided by a robust economic policy.

To come up with a clear or comprehensive economic policy, it is important that the nature and the performance of the South African economy, including how the South African economy has evolved since 1994 taking into account how it was structured and performed during the apartheid dispensation, are well understood. Our analysis of the nature and the performance of the South African economy confirms that the structure of the South African economy has not changed much in the democratic period compared to the apartheid era. It also shows that South Africa's economic performance is lower than that of comparable economies. In the book, we compare South Africa with selected emerging economies and other comparable countries. We have used various econometric techniques, also to understand what drives economic growth in South Africa. Not surprisingly, consumption, government spending and exports are the key determinants of economic growth in South Africa. That said, we cannot discount the role of other factors such as foreign exchange, savings and investment. These factors should be playing more role in economic growth, especially investments in the form of capital formation to put it simplistically.

It is not enough to understand what drives a particular economy. It is critical to analyse the link between economic growth and social development. Our analysis suggests that the decline in the performance of the South African economy has resulted in the deterioration in wellbeing. The HDI has not been increasing of late, particularly since 2015. The decline in economic growth started around 2013. Compounded by other challenges such as the global economic recession from which South Africa never fully recovered and the recent Covid-19 pandemic, wellbeing in South Africa has been compromised as GDP per capita data and poverty rates show. There are many mistakes that have resulted in weakening wellbeing in South Africa. Even if the economy continued to perform at the pre-Covid levels, wellbeing would have weakened and inequalities increased because of the mismanagement of public funds and laxity in the public sector, among other factors.

It is also important to understand how a particular economy responds to shocks. In other words, what is an economy's macroeconomic resilience? It is in this context that the book also examines shocks transmission mechanisms for the South African economy and comparable economies. It should be more useful to see how a particular economy responds to shocks relative to comparable economies. In our case, we study South Africa and other emerging market economies. We find that South Africa experienced different shocks compared to the economies we compare South Africa with. We also find that there is macroeconomic resilience albeit minuscule compared to other economies. Regarding transmission mechanisms, we find that although most of the variables considered played some role, consumption was found to be a high transmission factor of the shock. This can be explained. Rather, it makes sense because consumption (as indicated earlier) is among critical factors driving the South African economy. In addition, exports are shock absorbers in assisting the South African economy handle external shocks.

The study of an economy, for it to be comprehensive, must also examine the interface between the government and the market. Put differently, to what extent should a government intervene in a particular economy? The book searches for that equilibrium, empirically. In addition, the book examines the impact of State-Owned Enterprises (SOEs) on the economy. Although the importance of SOEs for socio-economic development cannot be debated, the debt burden to the fiscus is something to be concerned with. We find that SOEs' debts have a negative effect on the economy in the short run. In the long run, the impact is positive. As far as the government size is concerned, empirical results indicate that the relationship between government size and economic growth is characterised by a non-linear relationship (i.e. a U-shape), implying that government intervention deteriorates economic growth initially before having a positive impact later on. We recommend, based on estimates, that the ratio of government spending to GDP should not be high. Results give a threshold of 17.9%.

Lastly, an economy is part of society and government plays a critical role hence the importance of an institutional architecture in relation to whether a government can be effective or not. In this context, we examined how the South African government is organised and structured. While there have been various public sector reforms since 1994, the implementation and effectiveness in the government remain weak. In fact, it is puzzling that the increase in the size of the government in terms of numbers of employees coinciding with the increase in the wage bill, measured by the compensation of employees as a share of consolidated government expenditure and of GDP, but socio-economic development declines.

Our analysis confirms that the government can play a much better role in the economy and society. One of the areas we deal with is social policy. Although our focus is on the economy, we estimate the impact of social policy on economic development because social policy should play a critical role in any society. We find that indeed social policy can significantly contribute to economic development. This supports the argument for a comprehensive social policy in South Africa or in any society for that matter. It is however critical that a correct balance or proper interface between economic and social policies is ensured because social policy should work in tandem with economic policy.

The book is wide ranging, attempting to cover all critical areas of the South African economy from a macroeconomic perspective. We put a high premium on the need to restructure the South African economy. However, while focusing on the restructuring of the South African economy, there are specific areas that are critical aspects of an inclusive economic policy that we argue for or recommend. In particular, the small, micro- and medium enterprises (SMMEs) as well as the informal sector and cooperatives have potential to grow the economy while ensuring inclusive development. Another area that has great potential for economic growth and inclusive development is agricultural development and the associated subsectors and agrarian reforms that contribute to economic development. Thirdly, needless to say, an inclusive industrial development strategy will go a long way in facilitating economic development for South Africa. Such a strategy has to take into account climate change implications and the envisaged energy transition.

We are emphasising an inclusive industrial development strategy because we believe that such a strategy (not a policy per se) would have to encompass various aspects of industrial development that can ensure economic growth and inclusive development. For all associated interventions—be it for SMMEs or for agricultural development—Black African youth and women should be prioritised, given the political history of the country.

Mbombela, South Africa Vusi Gumede

Contents

About the Authors

Sodiq Arogundade holds a PhD in Economics from the School of Economics and Econometrics at the University of Johannesburg (UJ). He has more than six years of cognate experience in financial markets, public policy advocacy and management consulting. He works as a research fellow and a part-time assistant lecturer at the School of Economics and Econometrics at UJ. He has authored several scientific papers in international peer-reviewed journals and has been involved in several professional consulting projects.

Santos Bila worked as an assistant lecturer at the University of Johannesburg and as a PhD research fellow at the South African Institute for International Affairs (SAIIA). He is pursuing a PhD in Economics at the University of Johannesburg.

Mduduzi Biyase is a director of the Economic Development and Wellbeing Research Group (EDWRG) and Associate Professor of Economics at the University of Johannesburg. He is a researcher specialising in the field of development economics, with a particular focus on exploring remittance behaviour, poverty, unemployment, inequality, wellbeing economics and gender-related topics. In addition to his academic achievements, he has played a crucial role in coordinating and conducting research projects for the South African government and he has authored many journal papers.

Vusi Gumede is the Dean for the Faculty of Economics, Development & Business Sciences at the University of Mpumalanga, worked in the South

African government in various capacities for 12 years, after starting his career as researcher at the erstwhile National Institute of Economic Policy. He has been an academic since 2010 and he has held professorships at the University of Johannesburg, University of South Africa and University of Mpumalanga and he has also lectured at the Wits School of Governance, the University of Cape Town's Graduate School of Business and the National School of Government. Among his qualifications, he holds a PhD in Economics completed at the University of Natal (Durban) in 2003. His works have been widely published, including 18 books.

Shonisani Chauke is Lecturer in Economics at the University of Mpumalanga. Her research interests are in macroeconomic policy and political economics. She started her academic career as an associate lecturer at the Nelson Mandela University. Prior to her academic career, she worked in National Treasury's Budget Office.

List of Figures

List of Tables

CHAPTER 1

Introduction

1.1 Background

The South African economy has largely performed below its potential, even to a point that it got overtaken by the Nigerian economy as a biggest economy in Africa. Although the size of the South African economy has significantly increased since 1994 (the year in which South Africa became a democratic country), its performance has not been spectacular. In addition, unemployment, income inequality and poverty have remained high since 1994 although there is a period (i.e. 2002–2008) when data implied that unemployment and poverty were declining. Similarly, levels of human development have been increasing since 1994 but the increase has been slow. In the past ten years or so, the South African economy has performed rather badly even resulting in declining per capita incomes.

There have been many explanations for the manner in which the South African economy has performed since 1994. Equally, there are many books and journal articles that have attempted to explain the various parts of the puzzle. However, there has not been a comprehensive analysis of the South African economy that covers most of the important issues, ranging from its history and the impact of that history to its worsening performance. In order to come up with possible solutions (viz. to improve the performance of the South African economy) there is a need to examine the South African economy thoroughly.

V. Gumede et al., *South African Economy*, African Histories and Modernities, https://doi.org/10.1007/978-3-031-54180-3_1

It is in that context that this book attempts to explain the South African economy in detail through examining the South African economy prior to 1994 and after 1994. This book is arguably the only book yet that comprehensively analyses the South African economy and revisits economic policies as well as proposes aspects of an economic policy that could improve the South African economy. The other books on the South African economy, like journal articles, describe the various aspects of the economy instead of a comprehensive analysis of the entirety of the macroeconomy with a view of improving socio-economic development. The books referred to are made up of a collection of essays or chapters (i.e. edited volumes).

Policy makers formulate policies and make informed (or uniformed) decisions in real time using whatever information at their disposal on current economic conditions. However, statistical information is usually released with lags and is subject to frequent revisions. This book tries to help policy makers and practitioners in economic policy decision making. Of paramount importance is that our book examines the performance of government on the one hand and that of the market on the other hand, and we suggest optimal levels of government and the market if the South African economy is to perform well.

Post 1994, government intervention in the South Africa remained relatively high by international standards via greater government spending as a percentage of gross domestic product (GDP). What we now know is that too much government intervention can be costly—might impact negatively on economic growth after a certain point—'optimal level'—of government involvement in the economy is attained—usually brought about by inefficiencies inherent in government participation. By the same token leaving everything in the hands of the markets is equally costly due to market failures. Thus, this book contributes and improves upon the existing books and other publications by shedding more light on the potential optimal levels of government and the market for the South African economy.

We have endeavoured to undertake some comparative analysis. In particular, the book compares South Africa with selected emerging economies; a country in South America (Brazil), a country in Asia (Malaysia) and a country in Europe (Poland) as well as the biggest economy in Africa (Nigeria). Availability of data shaped the extent of comparative analysis conducted. Nigeria, Poland, Malaysia and Brazil are all classified as emerging market economies because of their respective markets which are relatively developed, and these countries are increasingly engaging with global markets.

Brazil was an obvious choice of countries to compare South Africa with in the South American region because it is also viewed as an emerging developmental state, like South Africa (although South Africa appears to have drifted away from becoming a developmental state). Although there is no single agreed upon definition, developmental states are countries that have a clear development agenda or programme based on a robust long-term plan and have sufficient requisite capacity to implement that agenda or programme in partnership with other role players in that society. Malaysia was selected because it has similarities with South Africa and South Africa used the Malaysian development experience in crafting some of the policies and programmes. Poland was the only obvious choice in Europe because it has a larger population size compared to other emerging markets in Europe. With regard to Nigeria, our view is that it is important to also include the biggest economy in Africa when undertaking comparative analysis that involves an African country (i.e. South Africa in the context of this book).

1.2 The South African Economy in a Historical Perspective

Historically, the South African economy was guided by inwardly focused policies and the industrialisation efforts were supported by import substitution (Clark, 1994). This, together with exploitation of the labour of Africans in the southern African region, resulted in a relatively diversified economy but predominantly based on mining and minerals. It is in this context that there is a notion of Mineral-Energy-Complex in South Africa. It is a historical creation than a coincidence. The colonial and apartheid economy in South Africa survived on the link between minerals and energy. This has not changed much, and it has become a constraint because the structure of the post-apartheid South African economy limits economic growth and job creation as well as exacerbates economic inequality or makes it difficult to reduce economic inequality.

During apartheid, many South African companies were protected from international competition and foreign market pressures.[1] The inward orientation allowed domestic industries to grow in such a manner that could not have been economically feasible in the absence of the import

[1] Clark, N. L. 1994. Manufacturing Apartheid State Corporations in South Africa. Yale University Press.

protection. This worked then and the focus was ensuring livelihoods for the white population group. In the post-apartheid dispensation, the apartheid economic structure and logic have become a problem for the economy. It is in this context that many people argue that restructuring the South African economy so that it benefits more people is critical, actually overdue. This would require that the government leads in ensuring that the structure of the South African economy is changed for better.

The apartheid government mainly assisted the Afrikaner and British capital through the support to capital-intensive industries which were linked to minerals, primary consumer products and the defence.[2] As Clark (1994) explains, the apartheid government invested heavily and set the foundation of the Mineral-Energy-Complex referred to earlier. In addition, there were significant subsidies for commercial white farmers. They received tax subsidies, rail transport subsidies, special credit facilities and grants and extension services (i.e. veterinary and horticulture services). Critical to the success of this model was the 1913 Land Act that ensured that 87% of the land belonged to white people and institutions such as the Land Bank, the Marketing Boards and the Cooperatives. At the core of the apartheid agenda was the disempowerment and dispossession of the majority black population in order to produce a dual labour market, cheap labour and labour reserves to serve the needs of the white farming community, mines and other industries that were aimed at benefiting the white population group.

The colonial and apartheid dispensations shaped the kind of society and economy that the post-apartheid dispensation is experiencing. There are three key periods in the history that have shaped the current post-apartheid society, namely, *1652–1795*, *1795–1870* and *1948–1994*. The first period *(1652–1795)* represents colonial exploits of the Dutch kingdom and its particular type of colonialism, which used commercial entities like the Dutch East Indian Company (DEIC). It was during this time the Cape of Good Hope (present-day Cape Town) slowly began to be used as a place of trade and stop overs on the way to get to Asian colonies and spice markets.[3] The second period 1795–1870 represents the ascent and eventual colonialism of the British Empire of the Cape initially and eventually South

[2] Op.Cit.

[3] South African History Online. *Dutch East India Company (DEIC)/VOC*. Accessed on the 29 November 2014, http://www.sahistory.org.za/topic/dutch-east-india-company-deicvoc.

Africa. It was during this period the development of mining, financial institutions and other activities evolved (Aartsma, 2008).

The third period 1948–1994 represents the period in South Africa's history where the Afrikaner nationalists were in power and formally installed the apartheid system. It was during this period that the majority of Afrikaner people would like the English citizens of South Africa benefit from the usage of the State to gain not only political but economic power (Mathebula, 2012). The end result of this white minority rule was that eventually African peoples' land was confiscated (through the Land Act of 1913), their movement across the country was restricted and were legally forced to live in Bantu areas based on their ethnic classification (Population Registration Act of 1950, Group Areas Act of 1950, Prohibition of Mixed Marriages Act of 1949, Black Homeland Citizenship Act of 1970 and Reservation of Separate Amenities Act of 1953) and the education system of South Africa was configured to favour white (Bantu Authorities Act of 1951 and Bantu Education Act 1953).

It is therefore important to understand the fact that when discussing the post-apartheid South Africa and the South African economy, one is attempting to understand and analyse a system of 350 years of systematic oppression and dispossession.

As discussed in Gumede (2008),

> *The era of apartheid, its legislation and institutions through which the ideology was implemented, produced and left a legacy of persistent poverty and extreme inequality that spans 300 years. So, the society is confronted with massive 'accumulated disadvantages', particularly for the majority of South Africans, which can only be sustainably addressed collectively.* (Gumede, 2008, p. 10)

Gumede (2016) characterises this as apartheid colonialism—a shorthand capturing 350 years of colonial and apartheid dispensations of systemic dispossession and oppression of the African majority by the white minority.

It is in this context that the critical intervention for the economy is to change its structure and reverse the Mineral-Energy-Complex. The structure of an economy needs to be changed in order to ensure effective social and economic inclusion. In brief, as discussed in Gumede (2015), the structure of an economy entails (1) the sectors and their contribution to economic growth, (2) respective capital and labour intensity of the sectors and (3) the dominant sectors and their linkages. The third issue in particular about the structure of an economy is about the major sectors, say mining and mineral sectors, and linkages to other big sectors, say energy sector. As indicated above, the structure of South Africa's economy has been the main obstacle to social and economic transformation on two levels. The structure of the South African economy has remained relatively unchanged from the predominantly Mineral-Energy-Complex bias and in terms of ownership patterns.

This book makes a contribution to understanding the post-apartheid South African economy and possibilities for its growth and job creation as well as the reduction of poverty and inequalities. The book should help policy makers in decision making about the South African economy. It should be useful to everyone interested in better understanding the South African economy, its traces so far and possibilities going forward.

1.3 Economic Growth and Socio-economic Development

The fundamental question that the book deals with relates to economic performance and wellbeing in the South African economy. It is important that the economy grows, and it is critical that there is socio-economic development, particularly for a society with the history that South Africa has. Since 1994, and especially in the last two decades, the South African economy has not performed well as indicated in the opening sentences in this chapter. It is in this context that we have undertaken a comprehensive study of the South African economy which has culminated to this book. We have tried to avoid temptation to also deal with a whole variety of issues that many economists end up talking about (e.g. crime, corruption, load shedding, etc.). Many of such factors indeed have a negative impact on the economy, but it is important to focus on the economy itself and less on ancillary issues. Arguably, even if crime, corruption and load shedding were low, it would still be critical to examine the performance of the South African economy in relation to the balance between government and the market as well as related issues covered in the book.

It is worth highlighting the findings from the different studies that are relevant for this book. To start with, the International Monetary Fund (IMF) (2023a) emphasises how, in addition to the well-known domestic and international shocks that plunged the South African economy into severe recessions in different years, a decline in the contribution of total factor productivity, load shedding and the decline in private investment have also significantly contributed to low growth in South Africa. Furthermore, according to the IMF, this was made worse by the decline in both human and physical capital as well as the drop in commodity prices that occurred in or around 2015.

These factors have been behind the low growth rates along with other structural challenges such as high unemployment rate, high inequality as well as poverty. In its recent consultation report, the IMF (2023a) highlights that South Africa is still battling with economic and social challenges such as poverty, unemployment and inequality that remain high. This indicates that far-reaching reforms are needed to address the said social problems and unleash growth which in turn will be translated into job creation especially for the most vulnerable people such as youth and those that are discouraged from looking for a job. For the IMF, if the necessary reforms are not implemented, the economy would face different downside risks such as a sharp decline of GDP growth to about 0.1% mainly due to an increase in the electricity crisis, external environment and weak commodity prices. To have shock buffers, the IMF argues for fiscal consolidation to decrease public debt and build resilience. Many if not all economists agree with this view. However, in our view, it is important to undertake a thorough examination of the South African economy to ensure that there is proper understanding what fundamentally constrains and what should be done. Our view is that even if structural transformation or economic reforms are undertaken, as government has been trying, the economy may still perform below its potential. Our research attempts to quantify the interface between the government and the market and we study the policies pursued since 1994 as well as estimate what can be viewed as an equilibrium in the South African economy. It is in that context that we argue that structural transformation or economic reforms (that many argue for) would not be sufficient to grow the South African economy and advance wellbeing (i.e. improve the levels of human development).

As we were concluding this book, Hausmann et al. (2023) in what is known as the Growth Lab at Harvard University released a report on the South African economy that is of relevance for our book. The Growth Lab report highlights different growth impediments that have negative spillover effect to the development. According to Hausmann et al. (2023), the country's path regarding fighting the major social challenges is not encouraging. In other words, the country is failing to achieve growth through inclusion. Miyajima (2023) concurs that policy makers need to make reforms and find pro-poor and pro-vulnerable solutions as priority towards building resilience as the Growth Lab report argues. The report documents that to achieve growth through inclusion, this has to be done in a way that the excluded population, especially black people, are included in the modern economy given that the Black Africans in South Africa remain the majority population: 81.4% as a percentage of the total population according to Statistics South Africa (2022).

Similar to other reports or studies on the South African economy, the Growth Lab report tries to deal with a whole range of issues. Among the areas that occupy the Growth Lab report is the poor performance of State-Owned Enterprises (SOEs) and the challenge of load shedding. These issues have become standard concerns by anyone or any institution that examines the South African economy. In our view, a more robust analysis of the South African economy is critical. For instance, our research demonstrates that among the crucial issues for the South African economy is the need for a comprehensive economic policy, working in tandem with a robust social policy.

The World Bank (2018), like the Growth Lab, understands the current exclusion as an incomplete racial inclusion transition. As the World Bank explains, addressing this systematic exclusion is crucial in order to address the triple challenge of poverty, unemployment and inequality while building resilience in population and in the economy as a whole, and this requires strong and effective institutions. Environment-related disasters are also at the core of the downside growth risk (Qu et al., 2023). As per the World Bank (2018), because the new growth path and the National Development Plan (NDP) commit to sustainable economic growth, setting a course for climate resilience and low-carbon development is an imperative. This issue is being debated in South Africa, particularly the pace of the energy transition that can be fair and just. For the World Bank (2018), as far as growth is concerned, the World Bank argues that different uncertainties impede growth, and these include policy/institutions uncertainties, slow or inconsistent policy making and social fragilities associated with low or even structural low growth rates. Hence, building resilience includes first ensuring that these uncertainties are adequately resolved.

With regard to the relationship between government, economic growth and socio-economic development (which is our focus in this book), there are many recent studies although none has done as a comprehensive study on an economy as we have done in the context of South Africa. To start with, Chindengwike and Tyagi (2022), for instance, examined the government expenditure policy impact on sustainable economic development in Uganda. The study discovered that the level of public spending on infrastructure, communication and energy has a direct impact on the rate at which Uganda's economy is developing. Similarly, Onwuka (2022) disaggregated government expenditure and economic development in Nigeria and discovered that 70.9% of Nigeria's short-run human development index (HDI) shocks are corrected annually. In a similar vein, Montenegro and Shenai (2019) employed the Ordinary Least Square technique to examine the relationship between government spending, economic development and economic growth in Brazil and found that government spending contributes to economic development and economic growth.

Some studies have also argued against the role of the government on the economy. Starting with the study by Barilee and Christain (2021) which assesses the relationship between federal government expenditures and economic development in Nigeria, the study concludes that government recurrent expenditures do not boost development in the long run. Likewise, Barilee and Benvolio (2021) evaluated the government expenditure on transportation and economic development in Nigeria, and their findings indicate that the government's recurrent expenditures do not promote development significantly in the long run. Rugeiyamu et al. (2021) analysed the contribution of local government to Tanzania's economic development and service delivery to local communities; the study concludes that the local government authorities boost local investment, improve corporate infrastructure and promote local economic development by offering subsidised loans.

Sulakshna and Singh (2018) looked at how the government affects economic development and found that it has a crucial role to play in accelerating the rate of growth both directly by engaging in economic activity and indirectly by pursuing suitable financial institutions, providing economic and social overhead capital or building the necessary infrastructure. Relatively similar studies have been conducted in South Africa (see, e.g. Khambule, 2018; Khambule & Mmtapuri, 2018; Mashamaite, 2018; Pretorius & Blaauw, 2010). Khambule (2018), for instance, studied how local economic development agencies fit into South Africa's plans for a developmental state and found that while the roles and responsibilities of South African local economic development agencies align with the aspiration of a developmental state, the lack of coordination among local institutions undermines their ability to fulfil their developmental mandate. Along the same lines, Khambule and Mmtapuri (2018) in their study on the role of local economic development agencies in KwaZulu-Natal (a province in South Africa) confirm that the lack of institutions jeopardises the impact that this would have if the institutions were strong. Mashamaite (2018) examined the role of South African local government in local economic development and concluded that local government plays an important role.

The empirical literature on the role of privatisation and nationalisation entities in the economy is mixed. Zhang (1995) and Szarzec et al. (2021) are of the view that SOEs are inefficient, are a burden to the fiscus and are politically influenced halting economic growth. On the other hand, Qi and Kotz (2020), who looked at the role of SOEs on economic growth in China, found that SOEs have had a positive impact on growth through the large-scale investments undertaken. According to Kikeri (2022), government intervention does not have to be through to have full control such as SOEs, but can be through Public-Private Partnerships, which would require some level of administrative capacity.

Some studies have also been conducted on the nexus between the size of government and economic development outcomes. While studies such as Stiglitz (2021), Chen (2020), Kimaro et al. (2017), and Ghose and Das (2013) provide empirical support on the positive relationship between government size and macroeconomic outcomes, other studies discovered that government intervention crowds-out domestic investment and discovered a negative relationship between government size and economic growth. These studies also conclude that larger government requires more taxes, which can reduce market incentives and be detrimental to economic growth (see Heitger, 2018; Hauptmeier et al., 2018; Makhoba et al., 2019; Nuru & Gereziher, 2020). However, some studies have identified a specific threshold of government size that an economy must maintain to achieve sustainable and inclusive growth (Altunc & Aydın, 2013; Chen & Lee, 2005; El Husseiny, 2011; Nouira & Kouni, 2021; Zungu & Greyling, 2022).

Undoubtedly, South Africa has experienced numerous socio-economic pathologies in the post-apartheid period, including poverty, unemployment and inequality (which are largely ramifications of the apartheid system and colonialism). While these pathologies became quite noticeable during the apartheid regime, they are still very much with us today, with some worse than they were before. The Mapungubwe Institute for Strategic Reflection (MISTRA) released a book on the structure of South Africa's economy as we were finalising our book. The MISTRA book sheds some light on the link between economic development and structural transformation. It proposes a broad-based economic transformation which not only looks at specific sectors of the economy but also focuses on financialised mineral energy finance complex system of accumulation.

The authors make an argument that heterodox economics is quite practical compared to mainstream economics which is based on the invisible hand and rational behaviour by economic agents. Heterodox economics takes into account the interaction between institutions, financial markets and economic uncertainties. Moreover, heterodox economics provides a connection between income and distribution, emphasising the role of government intervention in the market economy. This literary foundation forms the basis to understanding African National Congress' (ANC) policy making overtime. The initial post-apartheid strategy was based on heterodox, Keynesian welfare economics to stimulate economic growth and address past inequities. However, the ANC did not seem to be confident enough that an unorthodox policy was the best for South Africa. Adehlzadeh (2023) makes a statement on what could explain why the ANC did not have a robust plan to turnaround the economy post-apartheid:

> *when the ANC was banned (1960–1990), the fight to defeat the apartheid state and realise universal suffrage overshadowed the discussion on post-apartheid socioeconomic policies.* (Adehlzadeh, 2023, p. 91)

The party later focused on policy issues after it was unbanned. The ANC envisioned to establish a mixed economy that would allow the economy to grow in a sustainable manner. Although the Reconstruction and Development Programme (RDP) was a Keynesian policy, the signing of the International Monetary Fund (IMF) medium-term policy package in 1993 compelled the ANC to side with mainstream economic views. In as much as the RDP was the ANC's campaigning policy on the 1994 democratic elections, it was later abandoned two years after it was released. According to the authors, the shift of ANC policies from heterodox to orthodox economics is the main reason South Africa is the most unequal country in the world, characterised by high unemployment, high poverty levels and stagnant growth rates.

After disregarding the Macroeconomic Research Group report of 1993, the ANC government continued to implement mainstream economic policies (as argued in the MISTRA book). This is despite the recommendations of the report that South Africa requires a neoclassical approach that proved to have yielded positive results in countries such as Brazil, Malaysia and Taiwan (Swilling et al., 2023). The effortless way through which the ANC-led government could redress past imbalances was to capacitate the State-Owned Enterprises (SOEs) to cater for the collective population. However, Swilling et al. posits that:

> *The African National Congress came to power in 1994 without a clearly articulated vision for the future of SOEs and DFIs within a non-racial, developmentally oriented democracy.* (Swilling et al., p. 520)

Instead of SOEs being the vehicle to foster economic growth and redress past inequities, they have become corruption dens. The report of the Zondo Commission on State Capture revealed that major SOEs and Development Finance Institutions (DFIs) such as Transnet, Eskom, Denel and Industrial Development Corporation (IDC) were looted billions of rands, which has resulted in compromising economic growth. The mismanagement of SOEs and DFIs has raised questions about the involvement of the state in the economy of South Africa.

The editors of the MISTRA book stress that "today more than ever the state must play a developmental role to ensure both environmental and economic sustainability, while also fulfilling the vision of just and equitable transformation, which informed the Freedom Charter and formed the basis of the struggle against apartheid" (Mohamed et al., 2023, p. 11). Our book shares this sentiment and attempts to quantify the role that the state can play in the economy. The MISTRA book identifies among other things the significance of state's role, thereby leaning more heavily towards supporting state-driven way out. The view taken by the contributors in the MISTRA book, while crucial in emphasising the prominence of effective governance, somewhat tones down the potential drawbacks and state failures. There is a need for a more balanced approach which ought to encompass a thorough consideration of the strengths and limitations of both state and market mechanisms. Striking an optimal balance between these forces could be key to addressing the complex challenges facing South

Africa's economic landscape, ensuring a more comprehensive and adaptable framework for sustainable development. Our book puts forward a more nuanced approach, considering among other things, both state and market mechanisms, in order to contribute to a more effective understanding of socio-economic development in South Africa.

1.4 Scope of the Book

The next chapter (i.e. Chap. 2) examines the nature and the performance of the South African economy. The South African economy exhibited a comparatively favourable performance from the mid-1990s to the mid-2000s, albeit with growth that lagged behind that of comparable economies. This is due to a variety of factors, including inadequate levels of savings and investment, as well as the economic structure of South Africa (briefly discussed above). The chapter examines the impact of the primary drivers of the South African economy by employing the autoregressive distributed lag (ARDL) econometric method and data spanning from 1980 to 2019, in accordance with the macroeconomic identity. We utilised the cointegration test and the vector error correction (VEC) model to examine the long-run relationship. The primary findings indicate that exports, investment and consumption are crucial determinants of economic development in South Africa. Regardless of the time horizon, this remains true. In order to validate the existence of a long-term relationship between the variables, we conducted additional robust bound tests; the outcomes support the hypothesis that such a relationship exists. From a policy standpoint, it is advisable for the government to take measures to stimulate increased exports and investment in the economy. Additionally, the findings indicate that aside from national income identity variables, other factors that have the potential to impede economic development should be taken into consideration.

Chapter 3 analyses social and economic development since 1994, starting with looking at various social and economic indicators. Through describing trends in social and economic development both in broad terms and in relation to various aspects of socio-economic transformation, we lay the ground for problematising economic performance in democratic South Africa and making proposals regarding what can be done to further advance socio-economic transformation. The decline in social and economic development can be attributed to inefficiencies in the government which also explains the reversals in the economy. The chapter also briefly explains the policies that South Africa has implemented since 1994 aimed at socio-economic transformation. The chapter, based on analysis of various social and economic indicators, concludes that socio-economic transformation in South Africa was advancing in a commendable way since the mid-1990s until the late 2000s. The various measures of wellbeing were confirming that human development was improving. The economy had been performing relatively well and jobs were being created, albeit insufficiently. The deterioration in the economy and in inclusive development began to show signs prior to the global economic recession of 2009/10. Besides inefficiencies in the public sector, lack or unclear economic and social policies account for deterioration in socio-economic outcomes since the mid-2000s.

Chapter 4 deals with the macroeconomic resilience to shocks of South Africa and other emerging economies, including Brazil, Nigeria, Malaysia and Poland. South Africa has been wrestling with the multifaceted issues characterised by high levels of poverty, inequality and unemployment as indicated earlier. Moreover, South Africa must grapple with the issues of sluggish economic growth, poverty and inequality in the midst of domestic and global economic shocks. These challenges are rampant in numerous developing countries, especially emerging economies. As these emerging economies rise to prominence, they face an increasing exposure to a range of economic shocks, whether they originate locally, regionally or globally. In this context, the chapter explores their ability to withstand, recover from and prosper after facing such shocks during the period 1980 to 2023. The chapter uses descriptive statistics and Impulse Response Functions (IRFs) for a comprehensive analysis, revealing the evolving impact of economic shocks over time. This dynamic approach deepens our understanding of these economies' responses, providing policy makers and researchers with crucial insights into their economic dynamics.

Chapter 5 analyses the role of government in the economy in the context of State-Owned Enterprises. The point of departure is evaluating the role of government as a market participant. This chapter shows that the government is the biggest economic anchor through its role as the employer, producer and a consumer. For the longest time in the democratic South Africa, the government remained the biggest employer which has created fiscus burden through large public sector wage bill. Another way through which the government participate in the economy is through production of certain goods and services. There are several State-Owned Enterprises (SOEs) which were established to correct market failures. These SOEs however have been underperforming and even failing to render their primary services. The fiscus burden of these SOEs is enormous as they are struggling to stay afloat and must be bailed out through tax revenue. The impact of government failure seems to now outweigh that of market failure. In this chapter, the Bayesian vector autoregressive (BVAR) approach is used to estimate the role as well as the size of government in South Africa's economy. The BVAR results indicate that SOEs have a negative shock on economic growth, and there is also evidence of crowding out private investment. The suggestion would be that the government reinforces economic institutions, tackles corruption and promotes good governance. This is to lay a foundation conducive for the private sector to thrive, rather than having the government solve all economic challenges.

Chapter 6 is an attempt at finding an ideal interface between the government and the market. Despite the large fiscal redistribution, however, South Africa remains one of the most unequal countries in the world. The chapter examines the role of government intervention in the economy by drawing from the perspective of countries like Poland, Malaysia, Brazil and Nigeria, Venezuela and Singapore. This chapter also leans on cointegrating regression models and threshold autoregressive model. Empirical results support the view that the government size in South Africa is nonlinear (i.e., a U-shape) relationship between government intervention and the economy. This infers that at the initial stage, government intervention deteriorates economic growth up to a certain point before the impact is positive. Our analysis further suggests a threshold of about 18% of government spending to GDP (compared to 30% which has been the case in South Africa and is expected to remain the case). Our results suggest that while it is important for government to intervene in the economy in order to direct, regulate and act as a catalyst for economic prosperity, social justice and ecological sustainability, too much of government intervention may be detrimental to the economy.

Chapter 7 examines the extent to which South Africa can be viewed as achieving its developmental goals based on its institutional architecture and how the institutional set up has evolved since 1994. The analysis (linked to Chap. 3) examines the progress, challenges and prospects of South Africa in achieving its developmental goals. This analysis is undertaken in a comparative context and largely makes use of a developmental state framework. The chapter concludes that many mistakes have been made regarding the development approach pursued in South Africa so far. Among other issues, the way government is organised and capacitated has constrained its effective functioning which has resulted in weak socio-economic development. The analysis is supported by the quantification of the role of government in pursuing socio-economic development. The results confirm that government's intervention in the economy can yield positive development outcomes. This supports the argument that the capacity and the organisation of the South African government can be reconfigured to better pursue socio-economic development. The reorganisation of the government discussed in the chapter is about the institutional architecture and the functions of as well as relationships between institutions tasked with planning, monitoring and evaluation in order to ensure improvements in wellbeing in the country. In addition, the chapter supports the view that government must play an active role in the economy, and it further confirms the important role of social policy in economic development.

The book concludes—Chap. 8—with revisiting economic policies that have been implemented since 1994. The focus is on macroeconomic policies and the national development plan. Although the national development plan (viz. Vision 2030) is not an economic policy per se, it cannot be ignored because it has some aspects of economic policy. The same can be said about the Reconstruction and Development Programme (RDP). The chapter makes a case that the various economic policies implemented since 1994 have not worked well, with some exception in relation to the Growth, Employment and Redistribution (GEAR) Framework. In fact, the chapter argues that South Africa has not had a clear economic policy that is comparable to GEAR. The Accelerated and Shared Growth Initiative for South Africa (AsgiSA) had a potential to match GEAR but it was not fully implemented; AsgiSA was replaced with the New Growth Path within three years of its unveiling. GEAR achieved its overarching goal of macroeconomic stabilisation. It however took relatively long to replace it with an economic policy for inclusive growth that advances wellbeing. AsgiSA was arguably that kind of an economic policy but it was unveiled in 2005 when GEAR had achieved its main goal by late 1990s. Overall, the chapter proposes elements of an economic policy that would be ideal for South Africa. The chapter analyses various economic variables, based on stylised facts, and juxtaposes that against policies pursued. That informs the proposed aspects of an economic policy that South Africa should embrace if the economy is to perform well, and socio-economic development improves.

In addition, Chap. 8 synthesises main issues discussed in the book and discusses prospects for the South African economy. There are many complex issues that face the South African economy and society. The wage bill in government, as an example, has spiralled out of control. The government and its State-Owned Enterprises have not, seemingly, played an effective role in the economy. The market and the private sector have not contributed much on economic development. There is, arguably, no clear economic policy although *Towards an Economic Strategy for South Africa* (2019) is an attempt towards coming up with a comprehensive economic policy for South Africa. The South African society seems deteriorating in many respects and if the economy cannot play its part in addressing well-being, the danger is that the South African society will completely fall apart. The concluding chapter would wrestle with these issues, examine projections and propose what can be done to rescue the South African economy and society.

References

Aartsma, H. (2008). *Early History of the Cape Colony, South Africa.* Retrieved November 29, 2023, from www.south-africa-tours-and-travel.com.

Adehlzadeh, A. (2023). Why Is South Africa economy Stuck in Chronic Crises? In S. Mohamed, A. Ngoma, & B. Baloyi (Eds.), *The Evolving Structure of South Africa's Economy: Faultiness and Futures.* Johannesburg.

Altunc, O. F., & Aydin, C. (2013). The Relationship between Optimal Size of Government and Economic Growth: Empirical Evidence from Turkey, Romania and Bulgaria. *Social and Behavioral Sciences, 92*, 66–75.

Barilee, B. N., & Benvolio, J. (2021). Government Expenditure on Transportation and Economic Development in Nigeria. *World Bulletin of Management and Law.*. https://www.scholarexpress.netvolume-5, December-2021 ISSN: 2749-360

Barilee, B. N., & Christain, M. L. (2021). Government Expenditure and Economic Development: Evidence from Nigeria. *Social Science and Humanities Research, 4*, 40–58.

Chen, J. (2020). Research on the Relationship Between Government Size and Economic Growth. *Modern Economy, 11*(2), 209–219.

Chen, S. T., & Lee, C. C. (2005). Government Size and Economic Growth in Taiwan: A Threshold Regression Approach. *Journal of Policy Modelling, 27*(9), 1051–1066.

Chindengwike, J., & Tyagi, R. (2022). The Vector Auto Regressive Analysis Identifying Government Expenditure Policy Impact on Sustainable Economic Development. *Journal of Global Economy, 18*(2), 110–122.

Clark, N. L. (1994). *Manufacturing Apartheid State Corporations in South Africa*. Yale University Press.
El Husseiny, I. A. (2011). The Optimal Size of Government in Egypt: An Empirical Investigation. *Journal of North African studies, 24*(2), 271–299.
Ghose, A., & Das, S. (2013). Government Size and Economic Growth in Emerging Market Economies: A Panel Co-integration Approach. *Macroeconomics and Finance in Emerging Market Economies, 6*(1), 14–38.
Gumede, V. (2008). Public Policy Making in a Post-apartheid South Africa: A Preliminary Perspective. *Africanus: Journal of Development Studies., 38*(2), 7–23.
Gumede, V. (2015). *Political Economy of Post-apartheid South Africa*. CODESRIA Press.
Gumede, V. (2016). *Post-apartheid South Africa: Economic and Social Inclusion*. Cambria Press.
Hauptmeier, S., Martin, H., & Ludger, S. (2018). Expenditure Reform in Industrialized Countries: A Case Study Approach. *Journal of Economic Studies, 18*, 3–30.
Hausmann, R., Lochmann, F., Venturi, S. K. L., Enciso-Valdivia, S., Vashkinskaya, E., Ahuja, K., Klinger, B., Sturzenegger, F., & Tokman, M. (2023). *Growth Through Inclusion in South Africa*. WP, Growth Lab, Harvard University.
Heitger, B. (2018). The Scope of Government and Its Impact on Economic Growth in OECD Countries. *Journal of Economic Literature, 22*, 38–39.
International Monetary Fund. (2023a). Article IV Consultation – Press Release; Staff Report; And Statement by The Executive Director for South Africa. IMF Country Report No. 23/194.
International Monetary Fund. (2023b). The Link Between Social Grants and Employment in South Africa. IMF Country Report No. 23/195.
International Monetary Fund. (2023c). *Regional Economic Outlook. Sub-Saharan Africa: Light on the Horizon?* International Monetary Fund.
Khambule, I. (2018). The Role of Local Economic Development Agencies in South Africa's Developmental State Ambitions. *Local Economy, 33*(3), 287–306.
Khambule, I., & Mmtapuri, O. (2018). Assessing the Role of Local Economic Development Agencies in KwaZulu-Natal, South Africa. *Local Economy, 33*(4), 438–455.
Kikeri, S. (2022). Privatization of State-Owned Enterprises: A Summary of Experience.
Kimaro, E. L., Keong, C. C., & Sea, L. L. (2017). Government Expenditure, Efficiency and Economic Growth: A Panel Analysis of Sub-Saharan African Low Income Countries. *African Journal of Economic Review, V No. II*, 34–54.
Makhoba, B. P., Kaseeram, I., & Greyling, L. (2019). Assessing the Impact of Fiscal Policy on Economic Growth in South Africa. *African Journal of Business and Economic Research, 14*(1), 7–29.

Mashamaite, K. (2018). Role of the South African Local Government in Local Economic Development. *International Journal of Ebusiness and Egovernment Studies, 10(1). ISSN*, 2146–0744. (online).

Mathebula, F. M. (2012). *Imagining Governance in a Post-liberation Struggle Context: A Public Administration Perspective.* Paper Delivered at the 12th Annual Conference of the South African Association of Public Administration and Management (SAAPAM) on the State of Governance in Africa at the Turn of the Centenary of the African National Congress: Reflective Perspectives from Scholarship and Practice. Bloemfontein: University of Free State.

Miyajima, K. (2023). *The Link Between Social Grants and Employment in South Africa* (IMF Selected Issues Paper (SIP/2023/039)). International Monetary Fund.

Mohamed, S., Ngoma, A., & Baloyi, B. (Eds.). (2023). *The Evolving Structure of South Africa's Economy: Faultiness and Futures.* MISTRA.

Montenegro, F., & Shenai, V. (2019). Government Expenditure, Economic Development and Economic Growth in Brazil. *International Journal of Business Marketing and Management, 4*(10), 35–58.

Nouira, R., & Kouni, M. (2021). Optimal Government Size and Economic Growth in Developing and MENA Countries: A Dynamic Panel Threshold Analysis, Middle East. *Development Journal, 13*(1), 59–77.

Nuru, N. Y., & Gereziher, H. Y. (2020). The Effect of Fiscal Policy on Economic Growth in South Africa: A Nonlinear ARDL Model Analysis. *Journal of Economic and Administrative Sciences.* https://doi.org/10.1108/JEAS-06-2020-0088

Onwuka, C. E. (2022). Disaggregated Government Expenditure and Economic Development in Nigeria: An Econometric Analysis. (1981–2020). *Journal of Economic Research & Reviews, 2*(3), 206–216. University of Benin-Department of Economics & Statistics, Nigeria Keywords: Disaggregated Government Expenditure, Human Development Index, VECM, Nigeria. JEL Classification Code: C22, H50, O15. *Introduction The Economy of Nigeria Has Been Forecast to Become a Developed Economy by, 2050.*

Pretorius, A. M., & Blaauw, P. F. (2010). Local Economic Development Agencies in South Africa Six Years Later. *South African Journal of Economic History, 23*(1-2), 155–183.

Qi, H., & Kotz, D. M. (2020). The Impact of State-Owned Enterprises on China's Economic Growth. *Review of Radical Political Economics, 52*(1), 96–114.

Qu, H., Thube, S., & Walker, S. (2023). *South Africa Carbon Pricing and Climate Mitigation Policy* (IMF Selected Issues Paper (SIP/2023/040)). International Monetary Fund.

Rugeiyamu, R., Kashonda, E., Shayi, A., & Mohamed, B. (2021). Role of Local Government Authorities in Promoting Local Economic Development and Service Delivery to Local Communities in Tanzania. *Local Administration Journal, 14*(2), 123–144.

Stiglitz, J. E. (2021). The Proper Role of Government in the Market Economy: The Case of the Post-COVID Recovery. *Journal of Government and Economics, 1*, 100004.

Sulakshna, & Singh, S. (2018). Role of Government in Economic Development. *Journal Global Values, IX*(1), 2018.

Swilling, M., Callaghan, N., & McCallum, W. (2023). *Political Settlements and the Rebuilding of South Africa's State-Owned Enterprises.* In S. Mohamed, A. Ngoma, & B. Baloyi (Eds.), *The Evolving Structure of South Africa's Economy: Faultiness and Futures.* Johannesburg.

Szarzec, K., Totleben, B., & Piątek, D. (2021). How Do Politicians Capture a State? Evidence from State-Owned Enterprises. *East European Politics and Societies, 36*(1), 141–172.

World Bank. (2018). *An Incomplete Transition Overcoming the Legacy of Exclusion in South Africa* (Report No: 125838-ZA). World Bank.

Zhang, C. (1995). Reform of SOE's Corporate Governance: A Financial Perspective. *Journal of Reform* (3).

Zungu, L. T., & Greyling, L. (2022). Government Size and Economic Growth in African Emerging Economies: Does the BARS Curve Exist? *International Journal of Social Economics*, 1–17.

CHAPTER 2

Nature and Performance of the South African Economy

2.1 Introduction

The democratic transition in South Africa was followed by a turnaround in its growth performance, a growth acceleration that lasted into the 2000s before being interrupted by several economic shocks, such as the financial crisis and the recent Covid-19 outbreak. Since the onset of the crisis, South African growth has regressed to substantially lower levels and shows few prospects of revival on a trend basis (Fedderke & Mengisteab, 2017). This has forced the government to undertake a number of programmes designed to promote aggregate demand. This and subsequent efforts to reverse budget deficits, raise investment and expand exports have coincided with a resurgence in economic research on the efficacy of aggregate demand policies. It has also been recognised in economic growth and development theories that changes in discretionary spending impact the economy (Barro, 1990). Studies such as Naimzada and Nicolo (2017) and Pusch (2012) have estimated the autonomous expenditure multiplier in the context of economic crises.

There is no agreement on the leading factors behind economic growth, despite the fact that a significant number of research have looked at the effects of various macroeconomic factors on growth. As indicated in Gumede and Bila (2022), this can be because different studies employed different methods and sets of data. Mo (2007), Goldsmith (2008),

V. Gumede et al., *South African Economy*, African Histories and Modernities, https://doi.org/10.1007/978-3-031-54180-3_2

Mabugu et al. (2013), Jooste et al. (2013), Kneller and Misch (2014) and Kavese and Erero (2018) examined the relationship between government expenditures and economic growth and discovered a positive correlation. The level of government spending, according to Romero and Strauch (2003) and Schaltegger and Benno (2006), is harmful to economic growth. While Day and Yang (2011) contend that this will only produce the expected results depending on the marginal propensity to consume along with the marginal propensity to save which will then increase investment. Ghani and Din (2006) find that only public investment has a positive correlation with economic growth. In the same vein, growth and investment were examined, and a long-run relationship between the two variables was discovered (Qin et al., 2006; Roman & Padureanu, 2012). The contribution of consumption to economic growth has also been examined (Radulescu et al., 2019; Pegkas, 2018; Wang & Wen, 2017). The findings indicate a favourable correlation between consumption and economic growth. This suggests that, ceteris paribus, economic growth is driven by consumer spending. This is not shocking considering that private consumption drives around 60% of practically all global economies.

However, although a great deal has been done, the lack of consensus in the existing studies and the persistent poor economic growth leaves a big room for contribution in the body of the existing knowledge. Therefore, the chapter will explain the South African economy in detail, paying attention to the components of total output or gross domestic product (GDP). Economists refer to the National Income Identity which is made up of Consumption (C), Investment (I), Government Expenditure (G) and Exports (EX) less Imports (IM). This (i.e. C+I+G+EX-IM) represents the total economy. When imports and exports are included (without subtracting imports), that is gross domestic expenditure which is useful for estimating price elasticities for imports and exports.

Linked to this is what constrains growth in an economy. As such, the chapter will deal with the binding constraints to the South African economy so that there is a clear understanding of what could be done to improve economic development (not just economic growth) in South Africa. It will discuss in detail the sectoral and sub-sectoral contribution of the various sectors and subsectors in the South African economy. The chapter also summarises the evolution of economic policies in the South African economy since 1994. The chapter largely draws from Gumede and Bila (2022).[1]

[1] Gumede, V. & Bila, S. 2022. Applying the National Income Identity Approach in Examining Determinants of Economic Growth in South Africa, *African Journal of Economic Review*, 10 (2), 166–181.

2.2 Theoretical and Empirical Perspectives

An alternative theoretical approach demonstrates that the components of demand, such as consumption (C), investment (I), government spending (G), as well as net exports (X-M), play a significant role in determining economic growth, as originally proposed by Serrano (1996) and later developed in Freitas and Serrano (2015). It is crucial to test these factors' empirical importance despite the fact that they are critical for economic growth. While some studies (such as Mo, 2007; Goldsmith, 2008; Qazizada & Stockhammer, 2015) have primarily focused on the impact of the consumption variable, other studies (such as Qin et al., 2006; Ghani & Din, 2006; Tsen, 2008; Day & Yang, 2011; Wang & Wen, 2017; Pegkas, 2018; Radulescu et al., 2019 and Hsu et al., 2019) have gone one step further by including other components of the aggregate demand. For example, Mo (2007) examined the effect of government spending on economic growth and discovered a positive correlation between government spending and economic growth. This is different from past findings that showed a negative link between government spending and economic development by Romero and Strauch (2003) and Schaltegger and Benno (2006). Romero and Strauch (2003) showed that government expenditure had a detrimental effect on economic growth while using a distributed lag model to examine whether or not the persistent pattern between growth and fiscal policy had been noticed. Schaltegger and Benno (2006) empirically tested the relationship between growth and government size using a large data set of wealthy countries, and their results demonstrate that in wealthy countries, the magnitude of government spending inhibits economic growth. However, Ghani and Din (2006) employed the vector autoregressive (VAR) model to examine the effect of public investment on economic growth in Pakistan, and their findings indicate that, in contrast to public investment, private investment is more important for economic growth. In addition, Qin et al. (2006) used the impulse response to investigate the empirical effects of investment on economic growth in China and came to the conclusion that there is a long-term positive association between investment and economic growth.

According to Goldsmith's (2008) research, economic growth is correlated in the short run with rising public investment and consumption. Long term, however, the rises in public consumption and investment will cause an increase in interest rates, which will drive away private investment and slow economic growth. Later studies by Roman and Padureanu corroborated this finding (2012). This is not linear, though. For instance, neither the short-term nor the long-term impact caused by this component is typical. Production drives the demand for investment at specific points, Roman and Padureanu (2012).

Tsen (2008) examined how exports and domestic demand (total consumption, government spending and investment) affected Malaysia's GDP using Granger causality and cointegration techniques and came to the conclusion that there was only weak Granger causality between exports, domestic demand and real GDP per capita. Government spending and investment, on the other hand, vary from consumption expenditure in that they both have a greater impact on real GDP per capita. This suggests that only these two aspects of aggregate demand appear to be crucial for economic expansion. But because there is a significant linear correlation between export and real GDP per capita, this is also significant for real GDP per capita.

In a similar vein, Qazizada and Stockhammer (2015) investigated the government spending multiplier in contraction and expansion using panel data from 21 nations and found that during the expansion, it was approximately 1, as opposed to 3, during the contraction. In light of this, a countercyclical macroeconomic policy is justified. In other words, the authors compared the government spending multiplier effect for two different economic cycles (i.e. expansion and contraction) and they found that during the recession/contraction government spending had higher multiplier effect as compared to expansion. In other words, the authors compared the government spending multiplier effect for two different economic cycles (i.e. expansion and contraction) and they found that during the recession/contraction government spending had higher multiplier effect as compared to expansion.

Additionally, Akalpler (2017) examined the effect of net export on growth using the VEC model and discovered that net exports are highly influential on the performance of economic growth. On the other hand, Day and Yang (2011) conclude that the effect of a rise in government expenditure relies on the size of the marginal propensity to invest and consume. In contrast, Wang and Wen (2017) found that there is a general causal relationship between government expenditure, consumption, investment and economic growth after using Monte Carlo studies to examine the macroeconomic consequences of government spending in China. Pegkas (2018) used the autoregressive distributed lag (ARDL) method to examine the connections between economic growth and a variety of factors in Greece, including investment, consumption, government spending, trade openness, population growth and government debt. He discovered that while there is a long-term relationship between the variables, only investment, government spending and trade openness had a positive impact on growth. More recently, Radulescu et al. (2019) and Hsu et al. (2019) investigated various GDP responses to various economic shocks using various econometric techniques. For instance, Radulescu et al. (2019) used the panel least squares and pool least squares methods to determine whether investment or consumption was the primary driver of the high economic growth in Central Eastern European countries. As their findings show, consumption has a long-term positive impact on growth. Additionally, Hsu et al. (2019) analysed the economic fluctuations in China using the dynamic stochastic general equilibrium (DSGE) model, and their findings coincided with those of the preceding studies. For instance, they discovered that government expenditure is what causes economic volatility in China. In contrast to these studies, Girardi and Pariboni (2016) focused on empirically assessing the Sraffian super multiplier in their research. The results of this analysis, which used a cointegration technique using US macroeconomic data, showed that all demand components and output are cointegrated and, over time, they have a considerable impact on output.

Similar ambiguous findings on how government expenditure affects growth are also shown in the stylised data acquired in South Africa. According to certain researchers, government expenditure has a favourable effect on economic growth (Mabugu et al., 2013, Jooste et al., 2013, Kneller & Misch, 2014, Kavese & Erero, 2018; Makrelov et al., 2018). Mabugu et al. (2013) used an intertemporal Computable General Equilibrium (CGE) model to study the effects of South Africa's fiscal policy, and their results point to the extension of the fiscal policy having a favourable effect on growth. Jooste et al. (2013) employed a time-varying parameter vector autoregressive model, a structural vector error correction model and a dynamic stochastic general equilibrium (DSGE) model. The analysis discovered that while South Africa's countercyclical fiscal strategy has been successful, its effects vary over time. Kavese and Erero (2018) examined the effects of fiscal expansion in the South African province of the Eastern Cape using the Social Accounting Matrix (SAM-Leontief Model). The findings imply that one rand (R1) increase in government spending is related to an increase in economic growth, a decrease in poverty and the creation of new jobs. When Kneller and Misch

(2014) looked at the similar effect of government expenditure at the business level, they came to the conclusion that expansionary fiscal policy had a beneficial influence on firm productivity (see also Makrelov et al., 2018).

2.3 The Evolution of South African Economic Structure Since 1994

The South African economy is still underperforming, at least relative to its peers. Higher interest rates, increasing inflation, high unemployment, ongoing power cuts together with high debt levels and limited fiscal space, against a backdrop of an unstable global growth environment (largely due to persisting supply bottlenecks, economic disruptions caused by the Ukraine crisis, higher food and energy prices and rising policy rates globally), are affecting South Africa's investment and net export. If left unaddressed, these risks could prolong the stagnant growth path the country has found itself on for more than a decade. Figure 2.1 shows the various components of GDP and how that has evolved over many decades.

On investment, gross fixed capital formation contracted in the third quarter of 2021. As a result, investment remains about R84.6 billion below pre-pandemic levels—with private investment, the largest component of fixed-capital formation, accounting for 84% of the shortfall. Renewed investment in fixed capital is vital to economic recovery and growth. Higher and more effective public-sector investment, specifically in network industries such as transport and energy, is needed to catalyse a sustained recovery. Structural constraints, weak demand and low confidence are expected to weigh on private investment prospects in the short to medium term. As government stabilises and reduces its debt, real interest rates are likely to decline, creating more space for private investment. The rollout of energy infrastructure planned through the Renewable Independent Power Producer Programme (REIPPP), embedded generation projects and investment in bulk infrastructure will support both public and private investment over the medium term.

Concerning international trade, the country is anticipated to maintain a robust trade performance due to the rise in the value of merchandise exports over imports. This was mainly due to a strong performance in mining, which accounts for just over 60% of total exports—particularly iron ore, rhodium and coal. The current account is expected to moderate to a marginal surplus in 2022 before moving into a deficit of 1.2% and 1.5% of GDP in 2023 and 2024, respectively.

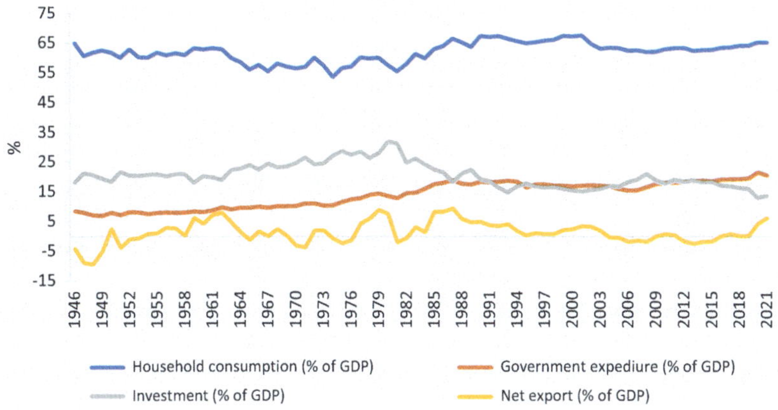

Fig. 2.1 Structural evolution of the South African economy. (Source: Based on National Treasury data)

2.4 Economic Sectors

It is important to explain in more detail the extent to which South Africa's primary, manufacturing and tertiary sectors have contributed to GDP over time. We discuss trends in real output, real value-added, employment, skills composition, labour productivity, as well as an international comparison of the share of services in the economy during this period. What stands out is that the South African economy (like many other emerging economies) showed a classic pattern of dwindling primary (includes any industry involved in the extraction and production of raw materials, such as farming, logging, fishing, forestry and mining) and secondary sectors (covers all those activities consisting in varying degrees of processing of raw materials, manufacturing and construction industries)—transformed from the production of primary products to the production of services. In 2021 the tertiary industry generated roughly 66.3% of South Africa's GDP. Judging by the size of the economic sectors, the tertiary sector was undoubtedly the biggest contributor to the GDP in 2021, followed by the secondary sector which was responsible for 18.8% and the primary sector which produced 7.8% of South Africa's economic activity. From 1993 to 2021, the contribution of the tertiary sector to GDP increased from 56% to 66.3%, while the share of the secondary and primary sectors decreased over the same period, from 20.6% to 18.8% and from 12.6% to 7.8%, respectively.

Table 2.1 gives the descriptive statistics for each key economic growth variable. The real value added has a mean of about 1.55 million with minimum and maximum values of about 292,958 and 4.04 million, respectively. Employment appears to have a mean of 5,296,337 with minimum and maximum values of 1.2 million and 12.43 million, respectively.

Splitting into skilled and semi-skilled, we find that while skilled labour formal ranged from 4.8 to 27.20 as a share of the total employment, the semi-skilled is found to be ranging from 48.2 to 80.9, also as a share of the total employment. Moreover, although not graphically represented at this stage, other indicators such as the real output, export as a % of the total output, exports and imports of goods and services, fixed capital productivity and the real fixed capital stock seem to be well distributed with good means.

According to theories on the structure of an economy, in the early stage of development, the primary sector dominates the economy. As the economy progresses, the secondary sector dominates. The tertiary sector dominates the economy at advanced knowledge economy. The structural evolution of the South African economy over the years reveals that the economy has evolved away from the dominance of primary activity

Table 2.1 Descriptive stats

Variables	*Mean*	*Min*	*Max*
Real output	3,345,986.5938	688,133.8300	9,092,698.3700
Real value added	1,553,544.5551	292,958.6300	4,048,276.1500
Employment formal	5,296,337.5841	1,157,008.5082	12,431,447.287
Export as a % of total output	21.9984	2.7800	66.3400
Exports of goods and services	497,794.9500	53,768.7700	1,260,422
Imports of goods and services	448,440.4545	54,685.5700	1,294,555
Labour productivity	92.2960	54.7400	120.8900
Fixed capital productivity	117.4471	90.1800	152.0600
Real fixed capital stock	3,245,459.0910	590,826.8900	8,703,755
Employment formal: skilled as a % of the total employees per sector	14.7222	4.3819	27.2033
Employment formal: semi- and unskilled as a % of the total employees per sector	66.9214	48.1913	80.8741

(Agriculture and Industry) to tertiary/services, which means the country is an advanced knowledge economy (see Fig. 2.2).

The labour market (employment trends) also changed during this period as displayed by a shift from the primary and secondary to tertiary sectors—employment more and more flowing to the tertiary sector. For example, Fig. 2.2 shows formal employment shares for each of the three sectors: primary, secondary and tertiary sectors. What emerges from Fig. 2.2 is that employment in the tertiary sector has been trending upward compared to the other sectors which saw a slight decline in formal employment during this period. Employment in the primary and secondary sectors appears to be indistinguishable from each other, while the gap between employment in the tertiary sector and the other sectors has been rising.

While Fig. 2.2 demonstrates that the tertiary industry far outstrips the other sectors regarding its share in employment, Figs. 2.3 and 2.4 confirm this trend/shifts in the employment distribution by occupation. We observe that there has been an upward trend (which was interrupted by the international financial crisis in 2008/2009) of the share of skilled employment in the tertiary sector, with a shrinking share of employment formal—semi- and unskilled during the same period. "Understanding these trends is crucial, as they should inform economic and labour market policies. Employment services and educational planning should be designed with these trends in mind, to successfully meet future skills needs. It is also essential for labour market entrants and jobseekers to be

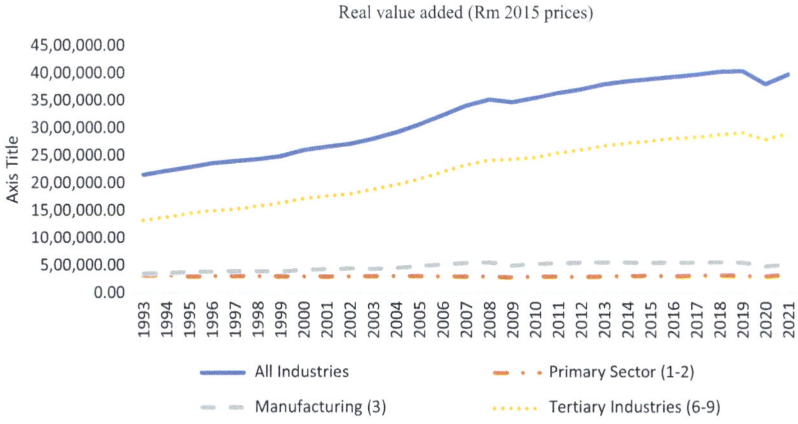

Fig. 2.2 Value added from 1993 to 2021. (Source: Authors' own plot)

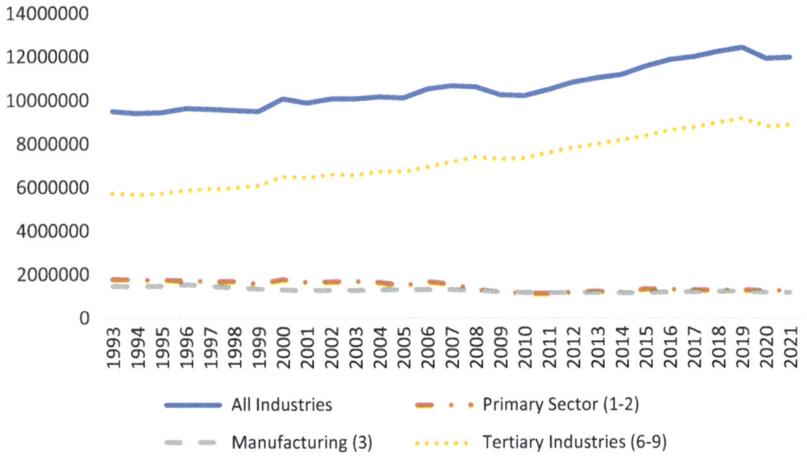

Fig. 2.3 Employment formal. (Source: Authors' own plot)

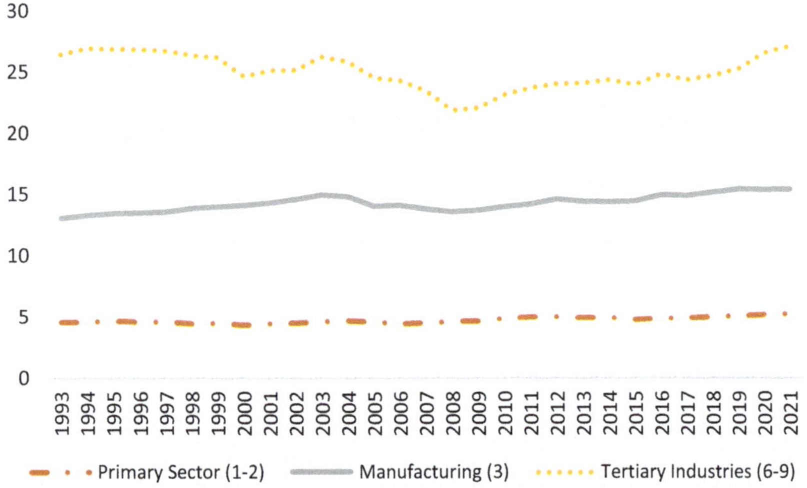

Fig. 2.4 Employment formal—skilled as a % of the total employees per sector. (Source: Authors' own plot)

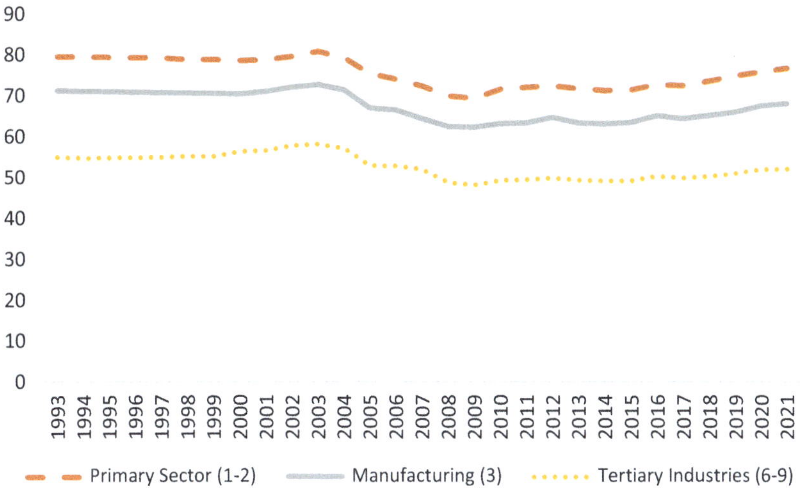

Fig. 2.5 Employment formal—semi- and unskilled as a % of the total employees per sector. (Source: Authors' own plot)

aware of the industries and occupations where the jobs of the future are likely to be" (ILO, 2018) (Fig. 2.5).

Figure 2.6 displays changes in labour productivity (proxied by total output) in the three sectors. Although the trends seem almost indistinguishable initially, there are episodes where productivity appears to increase in the primary sector.

The manufacturing value added (MVA) per capita for the selected emerging market countries (i.e. South Africa, Brazil, Malaysia, Poland and Nigeria) is shown in Table 2.2. As can be seen, in these countries, South Africa has lagged behind its peers except for Nigeria. Despite being ahead of Nigeria, South Africa's MVA per capita appears to be declining, a similar trend as that of Nigeria. Malaysia and Poland, on the other hand, have higher MVA per capita in this group of countries. This suggests that South Africa has not done enough to boost its manufacturing sector, causing economic growth to be driven more by the service sector in comparison to manufacturing. As previously stated, the service sector drives the South African economy, and its GDP per capita has been steadily decreasing since 2013, which is thought to be due to the fact that one of the most critical sectors has been performing poorly, with MVA per capita decreasing since 2013.

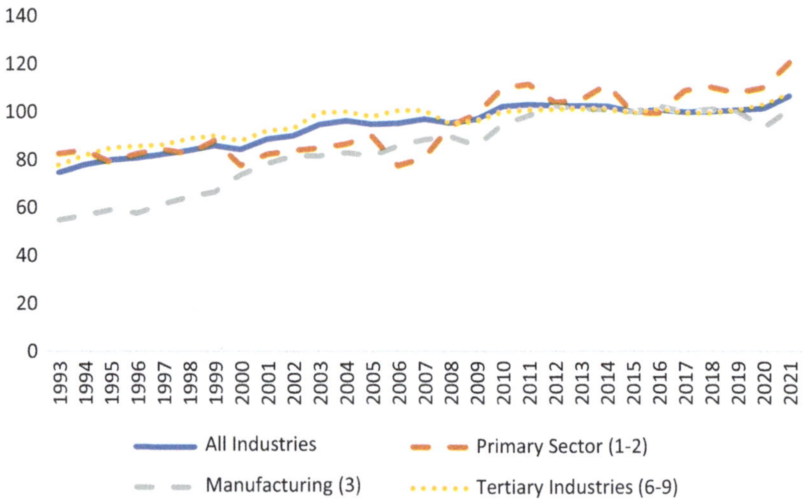

Fig. 2.6 Labour productivity. (Source: Authors' own plot)

Table 2.2 Manufacturing value added per capita

Year	*Brazil*	*Malaysia*	*South Africa*	*Poland*	*Nigeria*
2010	1080	1847.81	702	1729.67	160
2011	1094	1917.15	712	1824.62	183
2012	1059	1969.66	716	1873.98	203
2013	1081	2004.79	711	1809.52	240
2014	1022	2094.36	703	2021.34	268
2015	927	2162.36	689	2165.98	257
2016	876	2224.53	684	2281.29	240
2017	889	2325.9	674	2323.97	233
2018	894	2409.15	671	2459.4	232
2019	884	2468.72	657	2523.05	228
2020	840	2374.81	573	2474.89	216

Source: Based on United Nations Industrial Development Organization

2.5 South African Economic Performance at Macro Level

After the worst of the Covid-19 pandemic, the South African economy has taken a while to recover. South Africa's gross domestic product (GDP) recovered to pre-pandemic levels in the first quarter of 2022 after falling in the second quarter of 2020, when lockdown restrictions were at their strictest (Q1: 2022). In June 2022, Stats SA announced its most recent set of GDP figures, which underlined this (Fig. 2.7).[2] Compared with 51 other nations, South Africa's recovery has been sluggish, according to data from the International Monetary Fund (IMF).[3] The world economy started feeling the ill-effects of the pandemic in the first quarter of 2020. This was followed by a sharp downturn in global production in the second quarter as countries scrambled to impose hard lockdowns.

After a decade of slow growth, the South African economy was already in a precarious state when the pandemic hit. The resumption of load shedding brought on by operational and financial issues at the energy utility Eskom contributed to the economy's 0.1% growth in 2019 (see Fig. 2.7). The recovery is anticipated to last through 2022, with GDP growth projected to be 2.1% in 2022 and 1.7% on average over the next two years.

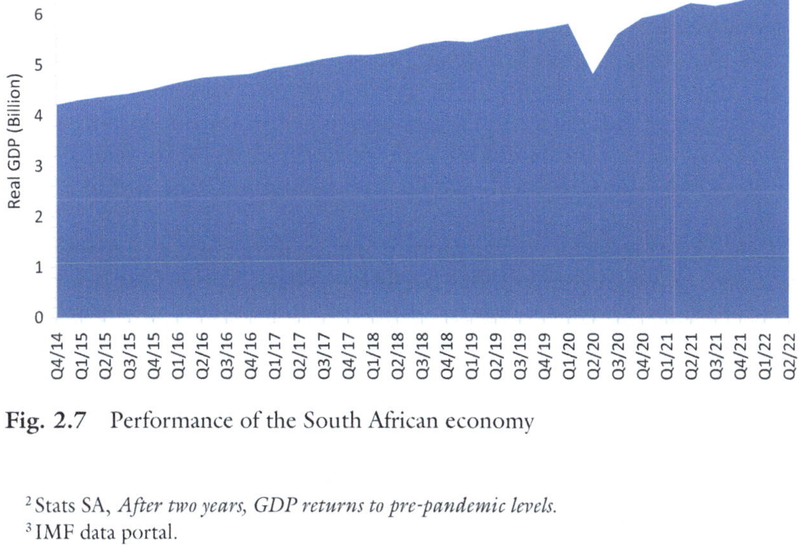

Fig. 2.7 Performance of the South African economy

[2] Stats SA, *After two years, GDP returns to pre-pandemic levels.*
[3] IMF data portal.

Long-standing structural restrictions, such as a lack of electricity, are still in place. In 2021, significant steps were taken to overcome structural barriers to growth that are present over the medium term, including raising the licensing threshold for embedded power generation. Although South Africa, a significant net exporter of minerals and a net importer of oil, still depends on commodity prices, increasing investment, particularly foreign direct investment (FDI), will be essential to boosting growth and generating jobs.

Consumption expenditure by households is one of the fundamental components of gross national product (GNP) and gross domestic product (GDP) and is generally considered to be a major variable in determining a country's growth. This is because, in most countries' consumption expenditure represents a large proportion of GDP, and to some extent, it reflects the country's productive success (Ladaique, 2006). The level of aggregate consumption expenditure, which includes expenditure on durable and nondurable goods, can therefore reflect the general position of a country's economy (Ezeji & Ajudua, 2015). The nature of the consumption function has engaged much of the macroeconomic debate dating back to Stuart Mills and the classical economists of the eighteenth and nineteenth centuries, which include economists such as John Maynard Keynes, Milton Friedman and Ando Modigliani (Ezeji & Ajudua, 2015). This ongoing debate is significant because of the important role played by consumption expenditure in any economy as consumption expenditure accounts for approximately two-thirds of aggregate expenditure in most economies across the world (Tapsin & Hepsag, 2014). Neoclassical economists generally consider consumption to be the final product of economic activity and thus argue that the level of consumption per person is seen as a central measure of an economy's success in productivity (Ezeji & Ajudua, 2015). In the South African context, aggregate consumption expenditure is vital to the economy as it represented more than 60% of GDP (SARB, 2021). The level of aggregate consumption expenditure greatly influences a country's growth rate, and this has been evident in the fluctuations in South Africa's growth rate due to changes in the country's aggregate consumption expenditure over the past years.

Household consumption, meanwhile, recovered in 2021 (estimated at 5.6%), but it is forecast to average only about 2% over the next three years (see Deloitte's Global Consumer Tracker[4]), households have taken on more debt and consumers are particularly concerned about rising prices, making upcoming payments, savings and credit card debt. Yet, of the 23 countries surveyed by Deloitte, South African consumers emerged as the most optimistic about their financial situation improving over the next three years.

2.6 Estimating the Performance of the South African Economy

2.6.1 Theoretical Review

Social and economic development is arguably what countries, especially in the developing world, should aspire for. Access to basic services and improvements in wellbeing for all have many advantages for societies. Healthy people and the population that live longer can ensure economic growth through productivity, among other possible factors. Governments have important roles to play in ensuring socio-economic development. Stiglitz (2021), for instance, uses the scenario of the post-Covid recovery to analyse the function that the government plays in a market economy. Many market inefficiencies are analysed along with their potential negative effects on the economy if there is insufficient government intervention. The author demonstrated that in a variety of nations, a growth slowdown and different economic development factors have been negatively induced by pure market forces. Moreover, Stiglitz argues also that, in addition to the fiscal stimulus package, the government should increase its economic intervention in several ways if economic development has to improve. These strategies include putting laws into effect (regulation), preserving full employment, fostering fierce competition, discouraging exploitation, limiting market power and offering social protection.

Many of the studies reviewed in Gumede and Bila (2022) confirm a positive relationship between government expenditures and economic growth. For instance, Mo (2007), Goldsmith (2008), Mabugu et al. (2013), Jooste et al. (2013), Kneller and Misch (2014) and Kavese and Erero (2018) examined the relationship between government expenditures and economic growth and discovered a positive correlation. On the

[4] https://www2.deloitte.com/za/en/insights/industry/retail-distribution/consumer-behavior-trends-state-of-the-consumer-tracker.html

other hand, the study by Ghani and Din (2006) finds that only public investment has a positive correlation with economic growth (see Gumede & Bila, 2022). In the context of multiplier effects, Qazizada and Stockhammer (2015) investigated the government spending multiplier in contraction and expansion using panel data from 21 nations and found that during the expansion, it was approximately 1, as opposed to 3, during the contraction. In other words, the authors compared the government spending multiplier effect for two different economic cycles (i.e. expansion and contraction) and they found that during the recession/contraction government spending had higher multiplier effect as compared to expansion.

There is sufficient recent literature that tries to establish the empirical relationship between government, economic growth and economic development worldwide. For example, Chindengwike and Tyagi (2022) investigated the government expenditure policy impact on sustainable economic development in Uganda and found that the level of public spending on infrastructure, communication and energy has a direct impact on the rate at which Uganda's economy is developing. Of critical importance is that the Johansen cointegration test results show that the correlation between the amount of money spent by the government on infrastructure, communication and energy and the level of financial development appears to be much more effective in the long more than in the short run. In addition, the outcomes of the Granger causality analysis indicate that there is an indirect relationship between the rate of economic development and all elements of public spending.

Onwuka (2022) investigated disaggregated government expenditure and economic development in Nigeria and found that 70.9% of Nigeria's short-run human development index (HDI) shocks are corrected annually. This suggests a long-term equilibrium between the HDI and government expenditures. In the long run, government expenditure on social security, education, health and agriculture has a positive and considerable impact on Nigeria's HDI, whereas infrastructure expenditure has a negative but significant impact. Nevertheless, in the short run, while government expenditure on infrastructure (GEI) has a significant effect on HDI at lag period two, education and agriculture were significant at lag period one. In the similar vein, Montenegro and Shenai (2019) employed the Ordinary Least Squares (OLS) technique to examine the relationship between government spending, economic development and economic growth in Brazil, found that government spending contributes to economic development and in economic growth. In addition, the correlation between government spending and economic development in Brazil lends credence to the notion that an increase in government spending can spur the HDI. The authors find that there is a strong connection between economic growth and human development in Brazil.

Barilee and Christian (2021), assessing the relationship between federal government expenditures and economic development in Nigeria, conclude that government recurrent expenditures do not boost development in the long run. Likewise, Barilee and Benvolio (2021) evaluated the government expenditure on transportation and economic development in Nigeria, and their findings indicate that the government's recurrent expenditures do not promote development significantly in the long run. Rugeiyamu et al. (2021) analysed the contribution that the local government authorities play in Tanzania's promotion of local economic development and service delivery to local communities and the authors conclude that the local government authorities boost local investment, improve corporate infrastructure and promote local economic development by offering subsidised loans. In addition, local government authorities enhance service delivery by ensuring water supply, assisting with energy supply and enhancing educational facilities. Hasdinawati and Wahid (2021) examined the village government's role in Pulau Harapan Village's fishermen's economic development. The study found that the village government in Pulau Harapan in Pulau Sembilan Subdistrict had not done enough to realise and develop production centres, processing industry centres, village transportation, community agribusiness, business facilities/business centres in rural areas, and information and communication technology, implying that the village government has not played the expected role towards economic development.

Shaldehi et al. (2020) examined the impact of attracting foreign direct investment (FDI) and government reforms on economic development in East and Southeast Asia and concluded that these two factors have been the most significant influences on both economic growth and the development of East and Southeast Asian societies. Sulakshna and Singh (2018) looked at how the government affects economic development and found that it has a crucial role to play in accelerating the rate of growth both directly by engaging in economic activity and indirectly by pursuing suitable financial institutions, providing economic and social overhead capital or building the necessary infrastructure.

As indicated in the Introduction chapter, relatively similar studies have been conducted in South Africa (see, e.g. Khambule, 2018). Khambule (2018), for instance, studied how local economic development agencies fit into South Africa's plans for a developmental state and found that while the roles and responsibilities of South African local economic development agencies align with the aspiration of a developmental state, the lack of coordination among local institutions undermines their ability to fulfil their developmental mandate. Along the same lines, Khambule and Mtapuri in their study on the role of local economic development agencies in KwaZulu-Natal (a province in South Africa) confirm that the lack of institutions jeopardises the impact that this would have if the institutions were strong. Mashamaite examined the role of South African local government in local economic development and concluded that local government plays an important role.

The chapter would delve deeper on various factors associated with the performance of the South African economy since 1994 and discuss the variables that are important for socio-economic development in South Africa.

2.6.2 *Empirical Analysis*

This section builds on the previous chapter (Chap. 1) and establishes an empirical determinant of economic growth. The idea is to understand whether factors that were deemed to be in the shock transmission mechanisms in fact do transmit or not. To do so, the chapter considers at the first stage all the national income identity indicators and later includes factors that are more likely to influence economic growth to ensure that there is no variable omitted bias. To do so, we use data from 1980 to 2019 collected from the World Development Indicators. In this study, we control for different variables such as consumption measured in 2010 constant prices, government spending measured as the general government final consumption (2010 constant prices), investment measured by the gross fixed capital formation, exports of goods and services (2010 constant prices), imports of goods and services (2010 constant prices) and later included inflation measured by the consumer price index (CPI), foreign direct investment, net inflow (%GDP) and social infrastructure proxied by the mobile phone subscribers per 100.

Model Specification

In a case where variables have a mixed stationarity process, for instance, some at I(0) and some at I(1), the recommended technique for the data analysis is the autoregressive distributed lag (ARDL) model; this model can also be utilised if all the variables have the same integration order and regardless of the sample size (Khan et al., 2015). The baseline output equation is defined as follows:

$$Y_t \equiv C_t + I_t + G_t + \left(X_t - M_t\right), \tag{2.1}$$

where

$$C_t = C_{0t} + cY_{dt}, \tag{2.2}$$

$$M_t = mY_t. \tag{2.3}$$

Equation (2.1) indicates the national identity equation thus we use ≡instead of the normal equality sign where Y is the level of output. On the right-hand side of the equation, we outline GDP components, such as consumption (C) measured by the sum of the autonomous (C_{0t}) and induced consumptions (cY_{dt}) (see Eq. 2.2 above), investment (I), government spending (G) and the trade balance or simply the net export (X-M). For simplicity, it is assumed a linear import and let m denote the marginal propensity to import (see Eq. 2.3).

The autoregressive distributed lag is a model of order p and n, ARDL (p, n), hence the model is of a scalar variable y_t as follows:

$$Y_t = \sum_{i=i}^{p} a_i Y_{t-i} + \sum_{i=0}^{n} c'_i X_{t-i} + u_t, \tag{2.4}$$

where

Y_t is the same as Eq. (2.1), X_t indicates the vector of autonomous components of the aggregate demand in time t and u_t is the error term. In Eq. (2.4) is included the constants, however, it is suppressed for simplicity. The coefficients a_i and c'_i are scalars and row vectors, respectively. It is also defined the lag polynomials $a(L)$ and $c(L)$ by employing the lag operator L applied to each vector's component, $L^k X_t = X_{t-k}$, formally expressed as follows:

$$a(L) = 1 - a_1 L - \ldots - a_1 L^p,$$
$$c(L) = c_0 + c_1 L + \ldots + c_n L^n.$$

Building from the above expressions, Eq. (2.4) can be re-written as shown below:

$$a(L)Y_t = c'(L)X_t + u_t.$$

Equation (2.4) can be easily estimated, however, to get parameters that can be economically interpretable, Eq. (2.4) must be transformed such that the $a^{-1}(L)$ gives an infinite distributed lag representation (for more details see Hassler & Wolters, 2005). As previously recommended, after some mathematical transformations by re-arranging the X's one obtains with Δ=1-L (see Eq. (2.5) below)

$$Y_t = \sum_{i=i}^{p} a_i Y_{t-i} + a(1)\beta' X_t - \sum_{i=0}^{n-1}\left(\sum_{j=i+1}^{n} c_j\right)' \Delta X_{t-i} + u_t, \tag{2.5}$$

where.

As previously recommended by Pesaran and Shin (1998), model (5) is suitable for cointegration analysis with Υ_t being a function of its lag values, current X_t and differences ΔX_{t-i}. To take into account further specification Υ_t to X_t and their differences we subtract $\left(\sum_{i=i}^{p} a_i\right)Y_t$. We further re-organise Eq. (2.5) and re-write it as exhibited below:

$$Y_t = \frac{-1}{a(1)} \Sigma_{i=0}^{p-1}\left(\Sigma_{j=i+1}^{p} a_j\right)\Delta Y_{t-i} + \beta' X_t - \frac{1}{a(1)} \Sigma_{i-0}^{n-1}\left(\Sigma_{j=i+1}^{n} c_j\right)' \Delta X_{t-i} + u_t \tag{2.6}$$

The correlation between $\Delta\Upsilon_t$ on the right-hand side of Eq. (2.6) and the error term u_t appears to be a shortcoming of the equation despite β's being the long-run coefficients of X_t. That in turn invalidates the OLS estimations (Bewley, 1979; Hassler & Wolters, 2005). To address this, one further transformation that will allow for cointegration estimation and testing is needed. Nonetheless, this can be done by allowing $\Upsilon_{t-1}, \ldots, \Upsilon_{t-p-1}$ and $X_t, \ldots, X_{t-n+1}$ to be consistent instruments in the IV estimation.

To demonstrate, we allow:

$$\sum_{i=1}^{p} a_i Y_{t-i} - Y_{t-1} = -a_i(1) Y_{t-1} - \sum_{i=1}^{p-1} \left(\sum_{j=i+1}^{p} a_j \right) \Delta Y_{t-i}.$$

Combining the equation above and the $X_t = X_{t-1} + X_t$ we get the error correction model. This shows the adjustment speed of Y_t through $a_i(1)$ to equilibrium deviations in the lagged period, $Y_{t-1} - \beta' X_{t-1}$, and this is shown below:

$$\Delta Y_t = \sigma Y_{t-1} + \delta' X_{t-1} + \sum_{i=1}^{p-1} a_i \Delta Y_{t-i} + \sum_{i=0}^{n-1} \pi'_i \Delta X_{t-i} + u_t, \quad (2.7)$$

where

$$\sigma = -\alpha(1), \delta = \alpha(1)\beta = -\sigma\beta. \quad (2.8)$$

The parameters a_i *and* π_i can be easily estimated.

For robustness check we add some variables into the specification. Therefore, in that particular model, we allow the vector X_t to contain also consumer price index (CPI), foreign direct investment (FDI) and infrastructures.

Unit Root Results

To ensure that spurious results are avoided, we employ the Augmented Dickey-Fuller (ADF) technique to conduct a unit root test and the results are summarised in Table 2.3. The results exhibit that only FDI is integrated of order I(0) showing no existence of unit root, and all other variables are cointegrated of order I(1). This implies that they become stationary at the first difference and none of them is cointegrated of order I(2), meeting in this case the fundamental condition of the autoregressive distributed lag (ARDL) approach.

2.7 ARDL Results

The key results of empirically regressing the national income identity determinants (C, I, G and NX) using the ARDL approach are shown in Table 2.4. R-squared and adjusted R-squared test model relevance, while t-stats and Prob. Values test coefficient significance. Modelling lag-length and specification criteria are chosen from Akaike information criterion

Table 2.3 Unit root test results (Augmented Dickey-Fuller)

	ADF Prob (level)	*Decision*	*ADF Prob (First difference)*	*Decision*	*Cointegration*
GDP	0.3603	Not stationary	0.0203**	Stationary	R(I)
Cons	0.5134	Not stationary	0.0325**	Stationary	R(I)
Gov	0.3811	Not stationary	0.0209**	Stationary	R(I)
Inv	0.2754	Not stationary	0.0228**	Stationary	R(I)
X	0.1564	Not stationary	0.0001**	Stationary	R(I)
M	0.3236	Not stationary	0.0004**	Stationary	R(I)
CPI	0.9987	Not stationary	0.0359**	Stationary	R(I)
FDI	0.0003**	Stationary	-----------	------------	R(0)
Infrastructure	0.7801	Not stationary	0.0001**	Stationary	R(I)

Critical value of ADF is selected at 5% significance level. (*) and (**) shows rejection of Null Hypothesis at 5% and 10%

(AIC) and Schwarz information criterion (SIC). Table 2.4 shows that the characteristics we examined affect national identity. Their effect to growth varies. Beyond the GDP of the previous era, which captures baseline conditions, consumption is a primary predictor of economic growth in South Africa, with a 1% rise in consumption increasing growth by 60%. The result validates Qin et al. (2006), and Roman and Padureanu (2012). This matches the role of consumption on economic growth in several economies, where private spending drives 70% of growth. If the government wants to boost economic growth, it must ensure that households actively participate in the economy so their income rises and their consumption expenditures rise. This supports the South African government's actions to boost family and individual economic activity.

Investment is also shown to stimulate economic growth in South Africa, as Ghani and Din (2006) discovered, and this is consistent with economic theory. Our findings indicate that investment is strongly linked to economic growth and that the relationship is statistically significant. However, its magnitude is less than that of consumption. For example, whereas

Table 2.4 ARDL regression results

	Model I		*Model II*	
Variable	*Coef.*	*Std.Err*	*Coef.*	*Std.Err*
Log(GDP(-1))	0.696**	0.1551	0.762**	0.0589
Log(Cons)	0.598**	0.1810	-0.122	0.0672
Log(Cons(-1))	-0.536**	0.2051	0.948**	0.1135
Log(Cons(-2))	0.136	0.2187	-0.934**	0.1032
Log(Cons(-3))	0.108	0.0867	1.811**	0.1201
Log(Gov)	-0.032	0.1089	0.404**	0.0485
Log(Gov(-1))	-0.172**	0.0927	-0.528**	0.0274
Log(Gov(-2))	0.104	0.0804	0.102**	0.0316
Log(Inv)	0.131**	0.0412	-0.367**	0.0365
Log(Inv(-1))	0.010**	0.0413	0.197**	0.0324
Log(Inv(-2))	0.052	0.0422	-0.748**	0.0400
Log(Inv(-3))	0.030	0.0370	0.060**	0.0098
Log(X)	-0.059**	0.0281	0.043**	0.0160
Log(X(-1))	-0.000	0.0483	-0.246**	0.0210
Log(X(-2))	-0.101**	0.033	0.182**	0.0148
Log(X(-3))	-0.051	0.0326	0.105**	0.0142
Log(M)		-6.8451	0.269**	0.0173
Log(M(-1))		-6.1485	-0.043**	0.0128
Log(M(-2))		-6.5996	0.320**	0.0224
Log(CPI)		0.9996	-0.212**	0.0651
Log(CPI(-1))		0.9994	-0.238**	0.0438
Log(CPI(-2))			-0.730**	0.0669
Log(CPI(-3))			0.681**	0.0580
FDI			-0.004**	0.0004
FDI(-1)			0.002**	0.0005
FDI(-2)			0.002**	0.0006
FDI(-3)			0.004**	0.0001
Infrastructure			0.000**	0.0001
Infrastructure(-1)			-0.002**	0.0001
Infrastructure(-2)			0.001**	8.79
Infrastructure(-3)			-001**	0.0001
AIC				-11.4298
SC				-9.9495
				-10.9080
				0.9999
				0.9999

(*) and (**) showing significance at 1% and 5%, respectively

consumption accounts for 60% of the whole economy, increasing investment by 1% boosts economic growth by 13%. Export, which has historically been seen as a growth engine by various scholars and policy makers, also plays an important role in stimulating economic growth, both empirically and theoretically.

The coefficient value in Table 2.4 is (0.010), implying that a 1% increase in export will result in a 1% rise in economic growth. Although statistically significant, its magnitude is tiny in comparison to the magnitude of consumption's impact on growth. This once again demonstrates that consumption trumps practically all other factors in determining national income identity. While consumption, investment and export have a considerable impact on economic growth, other variables in national income identity have been proven to be insignificant. According to Kavese and Erero (2018) and Makrelov et al. (2018), one possible explanation for the weak link between government spending and growth is that various shocks that drive the government to boost its expenditures increase the debt load. For example, aside from having a relatively tiny coefficient of 3%, government spending is really negative to economic growth. In other words, if this is significant, it means that a 1% increase in government expenditure reduces economic growth by 3% in the short run.

GDP can also be determined by some other factors different from those controlled for in the national income identity. Therefore we also included other regressors in the analysis. We include inflation, FDI and social infrastructures. As model II in Table 2.4 shows, these variables also play a role. For example, it is evident that although consumption is not statistically significant, it is detrimental to growth. This means that the impact of consumption or any other factor in the national income identity is sensitive to the model specification. Another thing to note is that investment also has become negative, and it is statistically significant. The inclusion of the variables in model II also had an impact on the export coefficient. Although this has remained statistically significant, its magnitude increased showing that not controlling for those factors can obscure the real picture of the impact of exports on economic growth. Furthermore, all the variables included in model II seem to be having a significant impact on growth as they are all statistically significant which is in line with economic theory and empirical literature. Attention should be paid to the social infrastructure, where although positive and statistically significant, its magnitude is small suggesting that it does not have a major impact on growth. This might be due to the measurement we have used. This is a tricky variable as

Table 2.5 ARDL-ECM

	Model I		*Model II*	
Variable	*Coef.*	*Std.Err*	*Coef.*	*Std.Err*
Dlog(Cons)	0.596***	0.0911	-0.122**	0.0177
Dlog(Cons(-1))	-0.244**	0.1202	-0.867***	0.0241
Dlog(Cons(-2))	-0.108	0.0711	-1.811***	0.0386
Dlog(Inv)	-0.033	0.0598	-0.367***	0.0083
Dlog(Inv(-1))	-0.105**	0.0534	0.687**	0.0120
Dlog(Inv(-2))	0.010**	0.0285	-0.060**	0.0027
Dlog(Gov)	0.028	0.0262	0.404***	0.0081
Dlog(Gov(-1))	0.059	0.0214	0.063**	0.0064
Dlog(Gov(-2))	-0.001	0.0217	0.165**	0.0073
Dlog(X)	0.051**	0.0198	0.043**	0.0042
Dlog(X(-1))	-0.3037***	0.0499	-0.287***	0.0074
Dlog(X(-2))		-7.1154	-0.105**	0.0051
Dlog(M)		-6.6365	0.269***	0.0049
Dlog(M(-1))		-6.9467	-0.302***	0.0053
Dlog(M(-2))		0.9381	0.018**	0.0027
Dlog(CPI)		0.9142	-0.212**	0.0102
Dlog(CPI(-1))			0.049**	0.0122
Dlog(CPI(-2))			-0.681***	0.0151
D(FDI)			-0.004***	0.0001
D(FDI(-1))			-0.006***	0.0001
D(FDI(-2))			-0.004***	0.0001
D(INFR)			0.000**	2.26
D(INFR(-1))			-0.000**	2.23
D(INFR(-2))			-0.001**	2.22
CointEq(-1)*			-0.2377***	0.0042
AIC				-11.9163
SC				-9.9495
HQC				-10.8279
				0.9997
				0.9993

(*), (**) and (***) indicate the rejection of the H0 at the 1% and 5% level of significance, respectively

it depends on availability of data. We employed an ARDL error correction model for long-run relationships. The results are summarised in Table 2.5.

The results of the ARDL cointegration test indicate that while certain variables exhibit substantial cointegration with one another according to their significance levels, others do not. It is noteworthy, among other factors, that consumption and export exhibit substantial cointegration, as evidenced by the cointegrating outcomes in Table 2.4. However, no

Table 2.6 Results of the bound test

F-Bounds test			*Null hypothesis: No levels relationship*				
Test statistic	*Value*		*Significance level*	*I(0)*		*I(1)*	
F-Statistic	4.9799	81.1816	10%	1.81	1.85	2.93	2.85
K	5	8	5%	2.14	2.11	3.34	3.15
			2.5%	2.44	2.33	3.71	3.42
			1%	2.82	2.62	4.21	3.77

Critical value is selected at a 5% significance level

Table 2.7 Results of the bound test

t-Bounds test			*Null hypothesis: No levels relationship*	
Test statistic	*Value*	*Significance level*	*I(0)*	*I(1)*
t-Statistic	-6.0823	10%	-1.62	-3.49
		5%	-1.95	-3.83
		2.5%	-2.24	-4.12
		1%	-2.58	-4.44

Critical value is selected at a 5% significance level

enduring correlation can be observed between growth and government spending, investment or imports in the context of South Africa. This implies that only exports and consumption can sustainably contribute to South Africa's long-term economic growth. Moreover, upon incorporating additional variables into model II, we found a substantial long-term correlation among all of them.

The ARDL bound test method is utilised subsequent to the examination of the cointegration of the long-run relationship between economic growth and its determinants. In the bound test, the null hypothesis posits that no long-term relationship exists between the variables. Conversely, the alternative hypothesis challenges this conclusion. The findings are succinctly presented in Tables 2.6 and 2.7, which demonstrate that the null hypothesis regarding the absence of the long-run relationship is denied in cases where the critical value exceeds both the lower I(0) and upper I(I) limits. The critical values for determining whether a long-run relationship exists in models I and II are 4.9799 and 81.1816, respectively, as shown in Table 2.6. These values exceed the lower and upper limits of 2.14 and 3.34, respectively, at a significance level of 5%. The lower and upper bounds are 2.11 and 3.15. This results in the rejection of the null hypothesis, which posits the absence of a long-run relationship between the variables. Consequently, a comprehensive long-term correlation exists among the variables under investigation.

To confirm this relationship, we have also tested for each variable and the result is consistent with the overall results. For example, in Table 2.7 we also found that the negative critical value selected at a 5% level of significance is also greater than the negative values of the lower bound of (1.95) and the upper bound of (3.83). This shows that there is a long relationship between the variables and economic growth.

2.8 Conclusion

In addition to having an abundance of natural resources, South Africa is a middle-income developing economy with well-developed financial, legal, communications, energy and transport sectors. It also has the biggest stock exchange in Africa and is ranked among the top 20 in the world. Economic growth has slowed in recent years and it is not projected to substantially improve for many years. The problems of high levels of inequality, poverty and unemployment persist. Over 30% of the workforce is officially unemployed, with black youth experiencing much higher rates of unemployment.

South Africa's economic strategy has centred on empowering a larger economic base while containing inflation. However, the country faces structural challenges that also restrict economic growth, such as a lack of skilled workers, a decline in its global competitiveness and frequent work halts brought on by strikes. Urban constituencies are putting increasing pressure on the government to enhance the provision of basic services to low-income regions, to boost employment creation and to offer university-level education at competitive pricing. Economic development is at danger due to political infighting within South Africa's ruling party and the volatility of the country's currency. State-Owned Enterprises (SOEs) have become a drain on the fiscus and they are limiting economic growth due to inefficiencies, which are also widespread in the government as a whole. While pursuing the various structural reforms, it is critical that the structure of the economy is prioritised. In addition, to boost economic growth it is important that interventions to increase exports and investments as well as savings are implemented because, together with government consumption, these factors are important for economic growth.

References

Akalpler, E. (2017). The Role of Net Export on Economic Growth in the USA. *Journal of Applied Economic Sciences, 3*(49), 772–781.

Barilee, B. N., & Benvolio, J. (2021). Government Expenditure on Transportation and Economic Development in Nigeria. World Bulletin of Management and Law (WBML). Retrieved from https://www.scholarexpress.netvolume-5, December-2021 ISSN: 2749-360.

Barilee, B. N., & Christain, M. L. (2021). Government Expenditure and Economic Development: Evidence from Nigeria. *Social Science and Humanities Research, 4*, 40–58.

Barro, R. J. (1990). Government Spending in a Simple Model of Endogeneous Growth. *Journal of Political Economy, 98*(S5), 103–125.

Bewley, R. A. (1979). The Direct Estimation of the Equilibrium Response in a Linear Model. *Economics Letters, 3*, 357–361.

Chindengwike & Tyagi. (2022). The Vector Auto Regressive Analysis Identifying Government Expenditure Policy Impact on Sustainable Economic Development. *Journal of Global Economy, 18*(2), 110–122.

Day, R. H., & Yang, C. (2011). Economic Growth and the Effects of Fiscal Policy. *Metroeconomica, 62*(1), 218–234.

Ezeji, C. E., & Ajudua, E. I. (2015). Determinants of Aggregate Consumption Expenditure in Nigeria. *Journal of Economics and Sustainable Development, 6*(5), 164–168.

Fedderke, J. W., & Mengisteab, D. K. (2017). Estimating South Africa's Output Gap and Potential Growth Rate. *South African Journal of Economics, 85*(2), 161–177.

Freitas, F., & Serrano, F. (2015). Growth Rate and Level Effects, the Stability of the Adjustment of Capacity to Demand, and the Sraffian Supermultiplier. *Review of Political Economy, 273*, 258–281.

Ghani, E., & Din, M. (2006). The Impact of Public Investment on Economic Growth in Pakistan. *The Pakistan Development Review, 45*(1), 87–98.

Girardi, D., & Pariboni, R. (2016). Long-Run Effective Demand in the US Economy: An Empirical Test of the Sraffian Supermultiplier Model. *Review of the Political Economy, 28*(4), 523–544.

Goldsmith, A. H. (2008). Rethinking the Relation between Government Spending and Economic Growth: A Composition Approach to Fiscal Policy Instruction for Principles Students. *The Journal of Economic Education, 39*(2), 153–173.

Gumede, G., & Bila, S. (2022). Applying the National Income Identity Approach in Examining Determinants of Economic Growth in South Africa. *AJER, 10*(2), 166–181.

Hasdinawati & Wahid, E. A. (2021, January-June). The Role of the Village Government in the Economic Development of Fisherman Communities in Pulau Harapan Village. *Journal Administrare: Journal Pemikiran Ilmiah Ddan Pendidikan Administrasi Perkantoran, 8*(1), 27–36. Retrieved from http://ojs.unm.ac.id/index.php/administrare/index

Hassler, U., & Wolters, J. (2005). *Autoregressive Distributed Lag Models and Cointegration*. Diskussionsbeiträge, No. 2005/22, Freie Universität Berlin, Fachbereich Wirtschaftswissenschaft, Berlin.

Hsu, M., Lee, J., & Zhao, M. (2019). Economic Fluctuations, Volatility Changes and the Role of Government Spending in China: A Structural Analysis. *Pacific Economic Review, 25*, 512–538.

ILO. (2018). Unified Budget Results and Accountability Framework (UBRAF) 2016–2021.

Jooste, C., Liu, G. D., & Naraidoo, R. (2013). Analysing the Effects of Fiscal Policy Shocks in the South African Economy. *Economic Modelling, 32*(1), 215–224.

Kavese, K., & Erero, J. L. (2018). Impact of Fiscal Expansion in South Africa—The Case of the Eastern Cape Province. *Journal of Economics and Management, 34*(4), 103–127.

Khambule, I. (2018). The Role of Local Economic Development Agencies in South Africa's Developmental State Ambitions. *Local Economy, 33*(3), 287–306.

Khan, K., Fei, C., Kamal, M. A., & Nadeem, B. (2015). Impact of Government Spending on Private Consumption. *Asian Economic and Financial Review, 5*(2), 239–248.

Kneller, R., & Misch, F. (2014). The Effects of Public Spending Composition on Firm Productivity. *Economic Inquiry, 52*(4), 1525–1542.

Ladaique, M. (2006). *Alternative Measures of Well-Being*. France: OECD. Retrieved from http://ec.europa.eu/eurostat/documents/1001617/4577263/2-3-LADAIQUE-MERGED.pdf. Accessed 20 May 2016.

Mabugu, R., Robichaud, V., Maisonnave, H., & Chitiga, M. (2013). Impact of Fiscal Policy in an Intertemporal CGE Model for South Africa. *Economic Modelling, 31*, 775–782.

Makrelov, K., Arndt, C., Davies, R., & Harris, L. (2018). Fiscal Multipliers in South Africa. The Importance of Financial Sector Dynamics. WIDER Working Paper 2018/6. Helsinki: UNU-WIDER.

Mo, P. H. (2007). Government Expenditure and Economic Growth. The Supply and Demand Sides. *Fiscal Studies, 28*(4), 497–522.

Montenegro, F., & Shenai, V. (2019). Government Expenditure, Economic Development and Economic Growth in Brazil. *International Journal of Business Marketing and Management, 4*(10), 35–58.

Naimzada, A. K., & Nicolo, P. (2017). Dynamics of a Multiplier–Accelerator Model with Nonlinear Investment. *Nonlinear Dynamics, 88*(2), 1–15.

Onwuka, C. E. (2022). Disaggregated Government Expenditure and Economic Development in Nigeria: An Econometric Analysis. (1981–2020), *J Eco Res & Rev, 2*(3), 206–216.

Pegkas, P. (2018). The Effect of Government Debt and Other Determinants on Economic Growth. *Economies, 6*(10), 1–19.

Pesaran, M. H., & Shin, Y. (1998). An Autoregressive Distributed-Lag Modelling Approach to Cointegration Analysis. In S. Strom (Ed.), *Econometrics and Economic Theory in the 20th Century. The Ragnar Frisch Centennial Symposium* (pp. 371–413). Cambridge University Press.

Pusch, T. (2012). Fiscal Spending Multiplier Calculations Based on Input-Output Tables–an Application to EU. *European Journal of Economics and Economic Policies Intervention, 9*(1), 129–144.

Qazizada, W., & Stockhammer, E. (2015). Government Spending Multipliers in Contraction and Expansion. *International Review of Applied Economics, 29*(2), 238–258.

Qin, D., Cagas, M. A., Quising, P., & He, X. H. (2006). How Much Does Investment Drive Economic Growth in China. *Journal of Policy Modeling, 28*, 751–774.

Radulescu, M., Serbanesceu, L., & Sinisi, C. I. (2019). Consumption vs. Investments for Stimulating Economic Growth and Employment in the CEE Countries-Panel Analysis. *Economic Research-Ekonomska Istrazinja, 32*(1), 2329–2353.

Roman, M. D., & Padureanu, A. (2012). Models of Foreign Direct Investments Influence on Economic Growth: Evidence from Romania. *International Journal of Trade, Economics and Finance, 3*(1), 25–29.

Romero de Vila, D., & Strauch, R. (2003). *Public Finances and Long-Term Growth in Europe-Evidence from a Panel Data Analysis.* European Central Bank Working Paper Series, Working Paper No. 246.

Rugeiyamu, R., Kashonda, E., Shayi, A., & Mohamed, B. (2021). Role of Local Government Authorities in Promoting Local Economic Development and Service Delivery to Local Communities in Tanzania. *Local Administration Journal, 14*(2), 123–144.

SARB. (2021). Full Quarterly Bulletin – No 301 – September 2021.

Schaltegger, C. A., & Benno, T. (2006). Growth Effects of Public Expenditure on the State and Local Level: Evidence from a Sample of Rich Governments. *Applied Economics, 38*(10), 1181–1192.

Serrano, F. (1996). *The Sraffian Supermultiplier.* Ph.D diss., University of Cambridge.

Shaldehi, S. K., Noor, H., Roodsari, A. S., Goodarzinezhad, S., & Goodarzinezhad, B. (2020). Foreign Direct Investment, Government Reform, and Their Role in Economic Development and the Rise of the Middle Classes in East and Southeast Asia. *The Indonesian Journal of Southeast Asian Studies, 4*(1), 25–45.

Stiglitz, J. E. (2021). The Proper Role of Government in the Market Economy: The Case of the Post-COVID Recovery. *Journal of Government and Economics, 1*(2021), 100004.

Sulakshna & Singh, S. (2018). Role of Government in Economic Development. *Journal Global Values, IX*(1), 2018.

Tapsin, G., & Hepsag, A. (2014). An Analysis of Household Consumption Expenditures in EA-18. *European Scientific Journal, 10*(16), 2–3.

Tsen, W. H. (2008). Exports, Domestic Demand and Real GDP Per Capita: Empirical Evidence from Malasia. *International Journal of Management Studies, 15*(2), 119–141.

Wang, X., & Wen, Y. (2017). Macroeconomic Effects of Government Spending in China. *Pacific Economic Review, 24*(4), 416–446.

CHAPTER 3

Socio-economic Transformation in South Africa

3.1 Introduction

Socio-economic transformation in South Africa was advancing in a commendable way since the mid-1990s until the late 2000s. The various measures of wellbeing were confirming that human development was improving. The economy had been performing relatively well and jobs were being created, albeit insufficiently. The deterioration in the economy and in inclusive development began to show signs prior to the global economic recession of 2009/10. The South African economy has not recovered from the global economic recession. When the performance of the economy was returning to the levels before the global economic recession, Covid-19 happened. The economy further worsened resulting in further deterioration in socio-economic transformation because of Covid-19's negative effects.

This chapter analyses social and economic development since 1994, starting with looking at various social and economic indicators. There has not been new data as we finalise the book—although there was Census in 2022, the data has not been released. It is in this context that this chapter draws extensively from Gumede (2022). The analysis of socio-economic transformation points to a deterioration in the recent years. The decline in social and economic development can be attributed to inefficiencies in the government which also explains the reversals in the economy. The chapter

V. Gumede et al., *South African Economy*, African Histories and Modernities, https://doi.org/10.1007/978-3-031-54180-3_3

also briefly explains the policies that South Africa has implemented since 1994 aimed at socio-economic transformation. Chapter 2 has laid bare the character and weaknesses in the South African economy.

3.2 Social and Economic Development

3.2.1 *Access to Basic Services*

Much has been achieved regarding the implementation of the government's priority on addressing the lack of access to basic social services. However, as the discussion will show, there is still a long way to go in ensuring a 'Better Life for All' which is the ticket through which the African National Congress (ANC) got into power in 1994. Statistics South Africa (Stats SA) data and government records indicate that impressive progress has been achieved in ensuring that people have access to basic services such as clean water sources despite numerous more people still not receiving piped (tap) water. The service delivery challenges remain unabated. Progress has varied: some areas show improvements while others are deteriorating. For instance, as Table 3.1 illustrates, there has been an increase in access to formal dwellings and a decline in informal and traditional dwelling, although these improvements are not that significant, particularly from 2011.

There remain significant backlogs. For instance, approximately 18% of households do not have access to a flush toilet and about 14% of

Table 3.1 Access to services and type of dwelling in South Africa (1996–2019)

Type of main dwelling	*1996*	*2001*	*2011*	*2018*	*2019*
Formal	65.1	68.5	77.6	81.1	81.9
Informal	16.2	16.4	13.6	13.1	12.7
Traditional	18.3	14.8	7.9	5.0	4.1
Other	0.4	0.3	0.9	0.8	0.3
Household basic services					
Piped water (tap)	80.3	84.5	91.2	89.0	88.2
Electricity (lighting)	58.2	51.4	84.6	84.7	85
Toilet facilities					
Access to a flush toilet	82.9	82.3	90.6	83.0	82.1
Bucket toilet	4.7	4.1	2.1	2.8	2.4
No toilet	12.4	13,6	7.3	14.2	–

Source: Adapted from various Stats SA surveys

households do not have a toilet at all, as is shown in Table 3.1. Table 3.1 provides apt reasons for the public protests that have increased significantly in the recent past. Access to numerous critical services has not improved since 2011 and especially since 2018. The percentage of people with access to piped water and access to flush toilet declined since 2018.

South Africa's social assistance programme, the cash transfer system, has made up for both unemployment and declines in access to basic services. Table 3.2 indicates that South Africa has an extensive social assistance programme that has helped cushion households against extreme hardship. In 2012/13, approximately 16 million people received social grants which constituted 3.1% of gross domestic product (GDP). By 2018/19, there were 17.8 million grant recipients in total. The 12.5 million child support grant recipients constituted 70.2% of the total grant recipients in 2018/19. This grant is provided to children in need until they reach the age of 15. It is expected that children under 18 will, over time, also receive the child support grant as per the means test. The age requirement for the old age pension for men was also reduced to 60.

The challenge with the social assistance programme is its financial sustainability and possible unintended consequences. Although it was stabilising as a share of the GDP, it is still remarkably high (over 3%). As for the unintended consequences, the fundamental issue relates to the kind of society South Africa aspires to be. Ideally, as in Brazil and India, more people should be gainfully employed than on social assistance.

The grants, however, especially in the context of a small informal sector, play an important role in mitigating severe hardship endured by those in need. As some findings on poverty suggest, the grants may have cushioned the poor against the global economic recession. In addition, the grants have helped during Covid-19. Government introduced in addition social assistance grant (i.e. Social Relief of Distress) as a result of Covid-19. This is one area (viz. social grants) in which the South African government has tried to help the majority of citizens amidst hardship. South Africa's social protection, social security and social insurance interventions play a big role in helping those in desperate need. South Africa is reported to have the biggest cash transfer programme in the world.

The absence of a comprehensive social policy, however, is one of the major limitations in South Africa when it comes to socio-economic transformation. The various interventions to help the neediest would be more effective if implemented within a comprehensive social policy and works in tandem with economic policy. A comprehensive social policy is about

Table 3.2 Number of social grants per grant type, 2012/13–2019/20

Grant type	*2013/14*	*2014/15*	*2015/16*	*2016/17*	*2017/18*	*2018/19*	*2019/20*
Old age	2,969,933	3,086,851	3,194,087	3,302,202	3,423,337	3,553,317	3,676,791
War veterans	429	326	245	176	134	92	62
Disability	1,120,419	1,112,663	1,085,541	1,067,176	1,061,866	1,048,255	1,042,025
Grant in aid	83,059	113,087	137,806	164,349	192,091	221,989	273,922
Care dependency	120,632	126,777	131,040	144,952	147,467	150,001	154,735
Foster child	512,055	499,774	470,015	440,295	416,016	386,019	355,609
Child support	11,125,946	11,703,165	11,972,900	12,081,375	12,269,084	12,452,072	12,787,448
Total	**15,932,473**	**16,642,643**	**16,991,634**	**17,200,525**	**17,509,995**	**17,811,745**	**18,290,592**
Annual growth	-1.08%	4.46%	2.10%	1.23%	1.80%	1.72%	2.69%

Source: South African Social Security Agency, Annual Report (2019/2020)

coordinating the various pillars of social protection and social security with the clear intent of improving wellbeing and growing the economy. Chapter 6 will deal with these policy issues in detail, including clarifying the argument that we are making regarding a comprehensive social policy in South Africa. Many people look carelessly surmise that there is a social policy in South Africa when looking at South Africa's various interventions in healthcare, education, social wage and social grants.

3.2.2 The Economy

The gross domestic product (GDP) per capita has been increasing at an impressive rate, particularly since 1996. With all its shortcomings, the GDP per capita is an important indicator of improving standards of living in a society. Whereas the GDP per capita was declining from 1980 to 1994/5, South Africa has seen marked improvements in economic growth. During the 1994–2004 period, the growth averaged at about 3%, which is a considerable improvement on the decade prior to 1994 when the growth averaged at 1% per year.

Since 2004, growth has exceeded 4% per year, reaching about 5% in 2005. Whereas the steady growth of the economy could be interpreted as positive, the pace has not been matched with the requisite elements to support such an economy. In other words, although the improvement in GDP (per capita) cannot be entirely attributed to macroeconomic stabilisation alone, it coincides with key macroeconomic interventions, specifically Growth, Employment and Redistribution (GEAR). For an economy to perform well, macroeconomic stabilisation is a prerequisite.

As Table 3.3 shows, the GDP, and not the per capita income per se, has been performing relatively well in South Africa. Looking at the recent period, following the macroeconomic stabilisation programme of the 1990s, GDP has averaged—barring the recent global economic recession—about 3.5%. However, the expected jobs have not been forthcoming despite the economy creating a relatively good number of jobs in the growth period of 2005–2008.

Although South Africa's GDP performance could be celebrated, it has not performed well enough given the size of its economy within a comparative context. Looking at comparable countries such as Botswana, India, Brazil and Malaysia, South Africa's economic performance has been low. The low GDP growth rate, compared to similar countries, supports the point that it is not only the global economic recession that has lowered

Table 3.3 Gross domestic product: South Africa and other emerging countries (2010–2020)

	South Africa	*Nigeria*	*Brazil*	*Poland*	*Malaysia*
2010	3.04	8.01	7.53	2.93	7.42
2011	3.17	5.31	3.97	5.04	5.29
2012	2.40	4.23	1.92	1.55	5.47
2013	2.49	6.67	3.00	0.86	4.69
2014	1.41	6.31	0.50	3.84	6.01
2015	1.32	2.65	-3.55	4.38	5.09
2016	0.66	-1.62	-3.28	2.95	4.45
2017	1.16	0.81	1.32	5.14	5.81
2018	1.52	1.92	1.78	5.95	4.84
2019	0.30	2.21	1.22	4.45	4.41
2020	-6.34	-1.79	-3.28	-2.02	-5.53
2021	4.91	3.65	4.99	6.85	3.09
2022	2.04	3.25	2.90	4.87	8.69

Source: World Bank data (various issues)

SA's economic performance, but that GDP appears to have begun to decline after its highest point in the post-apartheid dispensation in 2006.

There were no significant economic policy reforms undertaken for effectively ten years (1996–2006). Macroeconomic stabilisation was achieved, through GEAR, in 2000. The obvious next policy or strategy would have been the one focusing on accelerating GDP growth, which had happened in 2002. There was a significant policy reform lag because the AsgiSA began in 2005. And because it takes a while for any policy to gain traction, AsgiSA would have begun to deliver optimally around 2008. However, there was a state of flux and relative instability in the public sector due to the recall of former President Mbeki in 2008, the immediate resignation of former vice president, Phumzile Mlambo-Ngcuka, and others who championed AsgiSA.

There was also an exodus of critical technocrats and policy gurus such as Joel Netshitenzhe, who left government in 2009. The caretaker administration of Kgalema Motlanthe during mid-2008 to mid-2009 maintained relative stability and continuity, but the politics of that specific period made governing a challenge. It was always understood in the ANC that Kgalema Motlanthe was temporarily holding the reigns for Jacob Zuma (who became president of the ANC, replacing Thabo Mbeki, in December 2007). During 2009 and 2010, there were many changes in government, exacerbating the state of flux and relative instability. The new ministries, which had been conceptualised during the Thabo Mbeki administration, were introduced in 2009—the Department of Planning and the Department of Monitoring and Evaluation. These two departments were meant to strengthen the functioning of government to deliver on the mandate of the Reconstruction and Development Programme (RDP). The process of rethinking the organisation and capacity of the state began in 2005 when President Mbeki led the process of how government could be better organised and structured. The period also helped in the identification of requisite capacities necessary to ensure that derived objectives of strengthening the functioning of government delivering on the mandate of the RDP were met. That process of rethinking the organisation and capacity of the state culminated in the revisiting of the notion of South Africa achieving its developmental goals.

The point is GDP growth could have remained higher and perhaps even increased if the correct reforms were implemented on time. The relative instability and sometimes confusion during 2008–2009 further compounded the challenge as, it would seem, insufficient attention was paid to economic policy and policy reforms when they were most needed. Just as AsgiSA was starting to work, it was replaced by the New Growth Path (NGP). There has been an inconsistent medium-term policy direction since 2006, where the GDP growth rate began declining from 2006. Table 3.3 illustrates GDP of the comparative countries from 2010 to 2020.

The South African economy grew rapidly between 2010 and 2011, however, since then, similar to manufacturing value added, GDP growth in South Africa has stagnated, having recorded even a negative growth of about -6.34 in 2020 partly due to Covid-19. Comparing South Africa to comparable emerging market economies (i.e. Nigeria, Brazil, Poland and Malaysia), we find that GDP growth for South Africa has been constantly lagging behind these countries. It is a fact that between 2012 and 2013 it grew better than Poland, but this was only for those two years. Moreso, while South Africa appears to have recorded very low growth rates, other countries such as Nigeria and Malaysia seem to have grown well with average growth rates of about 3.2% and 4.6%, respectively. However, these are also not without a room of improvement. For example, they both recorded some negative growth in 2016 and 2020. The most plausible explanation for this negative growth is the international commodity prices and Covid-19, both for Nigeria and Malaysia.

What could be argued is that a recession in South Africa was inevitable from 2009 because of its own poor economic management, considering the mismanagement of public finances from 2008. Compared to similar economies, the relatively low rate of GDP growth resulted in fewer jobs being created. The situation has worsened. GDP has shrunk in the post-Covid period, the growth in per capita income has been negative, inflation and interest rates have been increased, unemployment has significantly increased and those in poverty have increased.

One of the most critical challenges facing the government of South Africa or society broadly is the creation of employment and the fight against poverty. The Government's goal was to reduce unemployment by at least half between 2004 and 2014 and to a maximum of 14% in 2014. However, the employment performance of the economy has inadequately met the needs of society. The number of jobs created has lagged behind the demand for jobs. Several newly created jobs have been precarious and of poor quality, while many of those jobs are under pressure or have disappeared as a result of the recession and poor economic management.

An unemployment rate of 27.1% in the fourth quarter of 2018 compared to 29.1% in the fourth quarter of 2019 is considerably high by global standards. The 2011 census also revealed an unemployment rate of 28.9% (Stats SA, 2012). Using its expanded definition, unemployment stands at approximately 40%, reflecting the high volumes of discouraged job seekers. Since the low point in 2010, South Africa has gained a total of 447,000 jobs. For the period 2000–2008, the unemployment rate averaged 26.3%, reaching a historical high of 31.25 in March 2003, reaching a relatively low 23% in September 2007 (Stats SA, 2012). Many of the unemployed are low-skilled or poorly educated workers, mostly women and youth in rural areas, for whom demand has been shrinking due to changes in the domestic structure of production in the economy.

South Africa is further faced with the complexities relating to an uneven labour market environment, the changing nature of work, lack of labour market measurement instruments and serving multi-class service beneficiaries such as vulnerable workers and unemployed job seekers. The fragmented nature of the labour market, increasing informality, casualisation and externalisation have exacerbated the job crisis and economic status of the ordinary working class. Millions of workers are trapped in informal, temporary, involuntary part-time or casual work that offers minimal benefits and limited prospects for advancement. This is the case particularly for youth, women and immigrants, who constitute the biggest proportion of South Africa's workforce.

3.2.3 Access to Education

Bloch (2006) is of the view that although many challenges remain, there were significant achievements in turning apartheid education around in the first decade of democracy. This has, according to Kraak (2008), been evident in increased access to education, headcount enrolment in schools, investment by government and the private sector in education, and institutional rationalisation processes and regulation.

The changes pursued in the education sector have resulted in great strides. The government has made progress in the expansion of education access, particularly improving access for disadvantaged groups. Progress is also visible in the different sectors, as presented in the 2008 Review of National Policies for Education in South Africa by the OECD. For instance, the OECD notes that what government was able to achieve in the space of 14 years is commendable and that it is understandable that some policy goals were as yet unrealised.

In this instance, data from the Towards a Fifteen Year Review (2008) indicates that education participation has increased since 1994, especially in the case of primary schooling. This is attributed to those interventions geared towards increased access. In terms of the growth in enrolments for the age group 7–15 between 2002 and 2007, the enrolment of five-year-olds improved from 40% to 60%, for six-year-olds the improvement was from 70% to 88% and for 15-year-olds the improvement was from 96% to 98%.

Data from the Department of Basic Education's 2010 Education Statistics in South Africa report, according to Table 3.4, shows relatively high gross enrolment rates: 94% for the foundation phase (Grades 1 to 7), 86% for the senior phase (Grades 8 to 12) and an overall 91% for Grades 1 to 12. South Africa has been successful in facilitating access to primary and tertiary education, particularly for the girl child. Based on the

Table 3.4 Gross enrolment ratios by gender and level of education, 2016

Gender	*Primary phase (Grades 1–7) (%)*	*Secondary phase (Grades 8–12) (%)*	*Total (Grades 1–12) (%)*
Female	97	97	97
Male	101	91	96
Total	99	94	97

Source: Department of Basic Education (2018)

Millennium Development Goals (MDGs) target for 2015 of universal primary education, the country has achieved its goal.

Indeed, South Africa is close to achieving universal basic education. The enrolment for the age group 7–15 years confirms that almost all children of school-going age entering school are at school and the majority reaching the end of Grade 9.

Table 3.4 shows improved access to education between 2001 and 2011. Although the numbers of those not attending school are still high, the percentage of those attending has increased from 71.5% in 2001 to 73.4% in 2011, while the percentage of those not attending school has decreased to 26.6% in 2011 from 28.5% in 2001. There are also increases in percentage shares, in terms of attendance, for all types of educational institutions except pre-school, as Table 3.5 shows. In the ten-year period 2001–2011, there has been an increase of about 100,000 for universities. This

Table 3.5 Access to education in South Africa (2011–2016)

Education	*2011*		*2016*		*2018*
	Number	*Percentage*	*Number*	*Percentage*	*Number*
School attendance					
Yes	13,837,961	73.4			10,400,000 (7–17 Years)
No	5,023,110	26.6			
Type of educational institution					
Pre-school	128,719	0.9	2,438,552	12.6	2,123,000 (5–6 years)
School	12,862,961	92.9	14,520,809	74.9	11,332,000 (7–17 years)
FET college/ College	359,228	2.6	735,392	3.8	657,133
University/ Technikon	410,063	3.0	1,065,256	5.5	1,283,466
ABET	22,730	0.2	187,698	0.9	100,286
Other	57,883	0.4	433,267	3.0	
Public or Private					
Public	11,924,285	92.7	17,124,357	88.6	
Private	934,480	7.3	2,211,380	11.4	

Source: Gumede (2022)

reiterates the point that the number of those seeking higher education increases over time in any society and, as such, more universities are needed.

What is of concern, however, as the Department of Higher Education and Training (DHET) states, is the number of students who registered, wrote and completed examinations for the General Education and Training Certificate (GETC): Adult Basic Education and Training (ABET) Level 4 has been on the decline since 2015.

In terms of enrolments, it can be noted that the extent to which the higher education system can actually produce highly skilled graduates is predicated on three important factors: the number of school 'graduates' that qualify for entry into higher education institutions; the number that elects to enter higher education institutions and the number that complete their qualifications (Breier & Mabizela, 2008). However, the quality of Grade 12 school-leaving throughput is said to be questionable.

Other important areas are literacy and numeracy. Various datasets and publications show a steady increase in the literacy rate in South Africa. In 2012, indicators by the Presidency indicated that, according to General Household Surveys, the literacy rate has increased from 70.7% in 2002 to approximately 80% in 2009. Although there are improvements, much progress still needs to be done to ensure that the 20% that is classified as illiterate becomes literate. Bloch (2009) shows that even though South Africa has higher levels of educational spending than most countries, it is among the worst performing countries internationally on literacy and numeracy.

Despite improved literacy rates and access to education, it remains evident that key historical factors have continued to constrain and limit the successful transformation of the education sector. Over the past year and a half, it has become increasingly evident that South Africa's education institutions remain untransformed. There is emerging consensus that the quality of education is poor, and the curriculum, as part of the legacy of the Bantu education system, is not well structured.

Recent data from the latest census highlights the reality that access to education, not to mention the quality of the education system, remains a challenge. For instance, the number (at above 5 million) and the share of those not attending school remain remarkably high. Also of importance is that there is slow progress with rolling out early learning. Lastly, although the enrolment of Africans in higher education institutions has increased, detailed analysis of data reveals historical disparity in participation rates among population groups. The total gross participation rate remains the same at approximately 15.7% in early to mid-2000 and increased marginally to 16.18% in 2007. The numbers of those enrolled in higher education have been increasing. However, participation rates for the African student population do not seem to be increasing at any significant rate.

The unification of the education system and standards also remains an issue. The two-tier education system is accentuated by an increasing share of those attending a private education system. Also, it remains to be seen whether the approach adopted in restructuring the higher education landscape was appropriate. The Higher Education Monitor of the Council on Higher Education (CHE, 2007) reflects on several pertinent issues pertaining to the challenges confronting the South African higher education landscape. Overall, the picture looks bleak but there is some progress, especially in the context of proposals contained in the 2012 Green Paper for Post-School Education and Training.

In 2014, the Department of Higher Education and Training (DHET) published the White Paper for Post-School Education and Training, which represented "government's vision for an integrated system of post-school education and training, with all its institutions playing their role as parts of a coherent but differentiated whole" (DHET, 2014).

The White Paper's main policy objectives are:

- a post-school system that can assist in building a fair, equitable, non-racial, non-sexist and democratic South Africa
- a single, coordinated post-school education and training system
- expanded access, improved quality and increased diversity of provision
- a stronger and more cooperative relationship between education and training institutions and the workplace
- a post-school education and training system that is responsive to the needs of individual citizens, employers in both public and private sectors and broader societal and developmental objectives.

Government's drive to integrate the post-school education and training is laudable, as it will assist in rectifying the fragmentation besetting the sector. Such fragmentation has resulted in inefficiencies in the administration and provision of post-school education.

Further, acknowledging the dire impact of apartheid on special needs education, a policy to transform the education sector was effected in 2001 through the publication of the Education White Paper 6: Special Needs Education (National Department of Education, 2001). As indicated earlier, during apartheid, the segregation of learners based on race was extended to incorporate segregation on the basis of disability, therefore special schools were organised according to two segregating criteria: race and disability. Schools that accommodated white disabled learners were well resourced, while the few schools for African disabled learners were systematically under-resourced, resulting in only 20% of learners with disabilities being accommodated in special schools (National Department of Education, 2001). For this reason, the National Department of Education, now the National Department of Basic Education, drives the policy on special needs education by outlining how the education and training system must transform to accommodate the full range of learning needs and the mechanisms that should be put in place.

The fourth notable education sub-sector is Further Education and Training (FET), which has been renamed Technical and Vocational Education and Training (TVET), whose transformation was well articulated as the desire for a "coordinated, comprehensive, interlocking sector that provides meaningful experiences to learners at the post-compulsory phase" (Department of Education, 1997, p. 10). A clear role was identified for the 'new' FET sector within the new economy, and this was soon followed by the introduction of the FET Act (No. 98 of 1998).

Looking at recent estimates, Table 3.6 on the gross enrolment ratio (GER) at primary school and Table 3.7 on GER at secondary school reflect that there has been minimal change since the publication of the OECD report. In fact, it demonstrates that even though the number of those attending school has increased, many still do not attend school. Data from these tables shows a relatively high gross enrolment ratio in the year 2015: 90.75% for primary school (Grades 1 to 7), and a relatively low gross enrolment ratio for secondary school (Grades 8 to 12) of 79.55% and an overall 85.15% for Grades 1 to 12. A GER of above 90% suggests that South Africa is closer to achieving universal access for the official age group. In contrast, the GER of above 100% reflects enrolment of under- and over-aged persons as per the official age yardstick.

Tables 3.6 and 3.7 indicate that the South African government is doing well in ensuring access to basic education. However, it is also important to note that access to education has not improved for all four races. Race has significant bearing in the equitable distribution of education. For instance, if we compare the GER of primary schools for all four races during the period 2014 to 2015, it is evident that for some racial groups, the GER

Table 3.6 Gross enrolments (by race) at primary school

Year	*Black African*	*Coloured*	*Indian/Asian*	*White*
2002	90.3	79.4	74.2	76.3
2003	89.3	79.6	77.6	78.7
2004	91.4	80.1	78.9	81.6
2005	88.4	78.2	80.5	74
2006	89.9	82.1	87.8	82.2
2007	91.7	83.3	76.8	81.6
2008	92.6	86.3	86.6	76.7
2009	99.1	92.9	85.8	85.5
2010	99	92	89.6	88.4
2011	99	93.2	84.8	89.9
2012	97.6	91.7	87.4	92
2013	96.2	90.2	89.7	86.1
2014	95	92	88.4	87.7
2015	96.2	92.5	85.8	88.5

Source: Calculations based on Statistics South Africa data (various issues)

Table 3.7 Gross enrolments (by race) at secondary school

Year	*Black African*	*Coloured*	*Indian/Asian*	*White*
2002	93.1	80.8	115.4	118.9
2003	94.7	79	110.2	119.7
2004	95.4	77.1	114.9	114.3
2005	97.2	85.9	110	120.5
2006	97.7	80.1	93.3	116.9
2007	99.2	86.7	105.5	116.9
2008	96.4	86.8	105.6	112.8
2009	84.1	64.3	72.7	81.8
2010	83.2	63.9	82.9	77.3
2011	90.2	67.8	81.6	79.4
2012	89.2	73	85.3	77.7
2013	92	70.6	77.9	82.4
2014	92	73.1	71.8	75.9
2015	95.5	68.8	72.3	81.6

Source: Calculations based on Statistics South Africa data (various issues)

has not only decreased, but that it is also below 90%. The GER at primary school for the Indian/Asian group has decreased from a low 88.4% in 2014 to an even lower 85.8% in 2015. This is contrary to the increase in GER at primary school level for Black Africans, Coloureds and Whites.

Similarly, the GER at secondary schools for certain racial groups has not only decreased from 2014 to 2015, but it has remained below 90%. In this instance, the GER at secondary schools for Indians/Asians increased from 71.8% to 72.3% in 2015 and has decreased for Coloureds from 73.1% to 68.8%. In fact, of concern in this instance is the fact that GER for Whites, Indians/Asians and Coloureds remains below 90%.

These figures reflect that South Africa has done enough to facilitate access to primary and secondary education. However, it is not close to achieving the universal target for access to education. In fact, GERs are expected to be over 100% due to the introduction of Adult Basic Education and Training (ABET), and the propensity to repeat classes, although it is expected that there will be variation by province and population group.

Based on the most recent literacy estimates, one can conclude that the challenge of illiteracy remains. Literacy refers to the ability to read and write, while the GER is calculated as total enrolment in a specific level of education, regardless of age, expressed as a percentage of the eligible official school age (7–18) population. As Table 3.8 reflects, approximately 12.6% of South Africans were unable to read and write in 2015. Increasing the literacy rate to an overall 87.4% was a fairly good accomplishment for the post-apartheid government, especially in light of the fact that the post-apartheid government targeted 83% by 2015 from 67% in 1996 for people aged over 15 years old, and increased the functional literacy rate of 15 to 24 year-olds from the 1996 levels of 83% to 92% by 2015 (Gumede, 2022, p. 10).

As a measure of increasing the literacy rate, the government committed to expanding lifelong learning and adult education and training opportunities. The government then implemented several programmes, such as

Table 3.8 Number and percentage of persons in the population aged 20 years and older who have not completed Grade 7 and above by gender, 2009 and 2019

Gender	*2009*			*2019*		
	Number	*% Share*	*Illiteracy rate %*	*Number*	*% Share*	*Illiteracy rate %*
Male	2,480,923	43.2	17.4	2,046,127	46.3	11.6
Female	3,265,779	56.8	20.9	2,375,457	53.7	12.5
Total	**5,746,702**	**100.0**	**19.2**	**4,421,584**	**100.0**	**12.1**

Source: Gumede (2022)

ABET and a mass literacy campaign. These programmes were primarily geared towards eradicating illiteracy and have been made available to adults seeking to finish their basic education by offering learning tools, knowledge and skills under nationally recognised qualifications.

South Africa is still on track in its goal to achieve the literacy target. However, even though it has achieved and exceeded its goal of increasing the literacy rate to 83%, as Table 3.8 demonstrates, the percentage rate of literate people in 2011 has fallen from 95.1% and 93.6% to 94.6% and 92.8% for males and females, respectively.

An examination of gender-disaggregated data reveals that female literacy rates remain consistently lower than male literacy rates, often by a margin of about 1.8%. As can be seen from Table 3.8, the gender differentiation between unschooled illiterate adults suggests that men are more literate than women. Male literacy rates range from a low of 93.7% to a high of 95.1%, and by contrast, female literacy rates range from 91.9% to a high of 93.6%. Although this might suggest a growth in gender-based discrimination in access to schooling, it contradicts what is known about there being currently more girls than boys in schools.

In addition, because of South Africa's apartheid history, race, location, parent education and economic status have a significant influence on literacy and numeracy rates. Table 3.9 shows that Black Africans have had consistently low numbers for literacy in comparison to other races. In fact, between 2009 and 2011, the literacy rate among Black Africans remained relatively unchanged. In 2015, the literacy rate among Black Africans was

Table 3.9 Number and percentage of persons in the population aged 20 years and above who have not completed Grade 7 and above, by population group, in 2009 and 2019, and the illiteracy rate

Population group	*2009*			*2019*		
	Number	*% Share*	*Illiteracy rate %*	*Number*	*% Share*	*Illiteracy rate %*
Black African	5,289,177	92.0	23.4	4,037,328	91.3	14.0
Coloured	399,305	6.9	14.3	336,637	7.6	10.3
Indian	46,704	0.8	5.3	35,502	0.8	3.3
White	11,516	0.2	0.3	12,117	0.3	0.3
Total	**5,746,702**	**100.0**	**19.2**	**4,421,585**	**100.0**	**12.1**

Source: Gumede (2022)

recorded at a low 93.3%, while the literacy rate among Coloureds was 96.5%, 99% among Indians/Asians and 99.6% among Whites. Even though the literacy rate among Black Africans is higher than the national target, one can immediately conclude that there are more illiterate black females.

In addition to race, location has offered insightful provincial contributions. Table 3.10 reflects that the literacy rate has been consistently low in five provinces: Northern Cape, North-West, Limpopo, the Eastern Cape and Mpumalanga. In the five-year period from 2009 to 2015, the Northern Cape remains the province with the lowest literacy rate of 88.7% in 2009, rising to 89.2% in 2015, while Gauteng and the Western Cape consistently indicate the highest literacy rates, both with a literacy rate of 97.8% in the year 2015. A considerable explanation for the differences between the provinces is explained, to some extent, by the differences between apartheid designated 'race' groups. As would be expected, African adults had the lowest literacy rates at 93.3% in 2015, which was the case in 2009 with 91.3%. Therefore, one can conclude that since there are far more Black Africans living in South Africa, this is to be expected.

Turning to curriculum reforms, Outcomes-Based Education (OBE) was implemented as a competency-based learning and teaching methodology aimed at facilitating the strategic and technical skills of learners until

Table 3.10 Literacy rates by province, for individuals ten years or older

Province	*2009*			*2019*		
	Number	*% Share*	*Illiteracy rate %*	*Number*	*% Share*	*Illiteracy rate %*
Western Cape	420,468	7.3	11.7	339,714	7.7	7.4
Eastern Cape	933,882	16.3	26.7	679,400	15.4	18.2
Northern Cape	184,852	3.2	28.1	123,974	2.8	16.0
Free State	346,782	6.0	21.0	271,106	6.1	14.9
KwaZulu-Natal	1,262,453	22.0	22.4	979,592	22.2	14.5
North West	552,925	9.6	27.0	437,751	9.9	17.8
Gauteng	772,837	13.4	9.8	579,664	13.1	5.6
Mpumalanga	514,700	9.0	23.7	428,023	9.7	15.5
Limpopo	757,802	13.2	27.8	582,361	13.2	17.6
Total	**5,746,701**	**100.0**	**19.2**	**4,421,584**	**100.0**	**12.1**

Source: Gumede (2022)

2010. Some of the identified outcomes of such a system included ensuring that learners identify and solve problems; make decisions using critical and creative thinking; work effectively with others as members of a team, group, organisation and community; organise and manage themselves and their activities responsibly and effectively; collect, analyse, organise and critically evaluate information; and communicate effectively using visual, symbolic and/or language skills in various modes.

The rationale for such a curriculum within a new democracy made both political and economic sense with the country's aspirations to establish itself as a strong, globally competitive knowledge economy. Where it has worked, OBE performed relatively well but generally there have been many challenges with the curriculum owing to insufficient teacher training, unsatisfactory teacher-learner ratios, lack of availability of learning materials and other resources, as well as language barriers.

Based on race, Table 3.11 shows that the completion or graduation rate for white students was on average 32.8% higher than Black African students. Indian/Asian students have the second highest completion with an average of 19.38%, while Black African and Coloured students have the lowest graduation rate, Black African being the lowest.

In order to achieve South Africa's developmental goals, in particular in regard to building an effective and capable state, the education system has

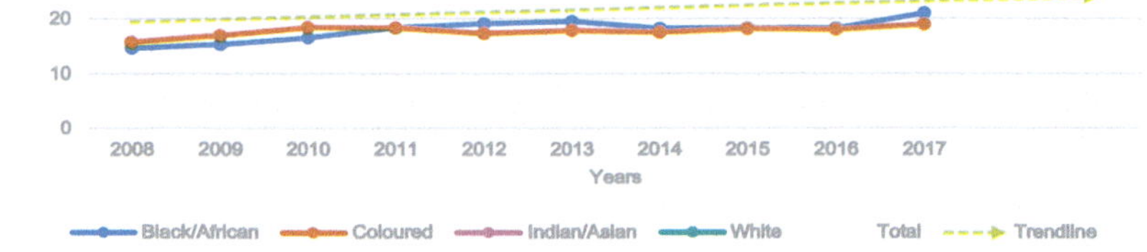

Source: Department of Higher Education, HEMIS

Fig. 3.1 Gross enrolment ratio by population group for females in public higher institutions

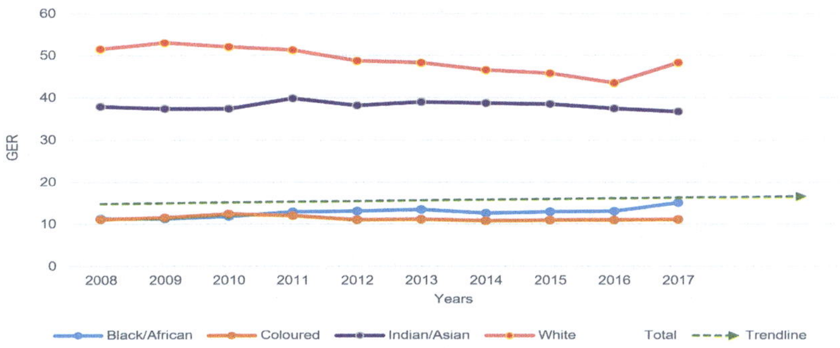

Source: Department of Higher Education, HEMIS

Fig. 3.2 Gross enrolment ratio by population group for males in public higher institutions

to address a number of philosophical and practical questions. The post-apartheid government may have done well in addressing the philosophical questions, but the practical question remains. In fact, the government has overrated its performance to increasing access to education.

Another critical observation is the racial inequality in number of students enrolled in public higher education institutions and the number of students completing. The data shows that there are more females enrolled in public higher education institutions, and there are more white students completing from public higher education institutions. This can only imply that graduating students that are absorbed into the labour market are white female students. This affirms the finding that South Africa's unemployment rate is made up of black females (see Gumede, 2016).

The low completion rates among black students are largely attributed to the difficulty of subjects, depending on the preparedness of individual students by the schooling system. Importantly, however, it has been noted that higher education faces the serious challenge of student attrition. It was reported in 2000 that 30% of first-time entrants into the system dropped out within the first year while 20% dropped out after two or three years of study. Of the group, 50% was out of the system before attaining their qualification (Breier & Mabizela, 2008). This is obviously worrisome in light of the country's unemployment challenge. Also of concern is that even qualified graduates are struggling to find employment. For instance, Moleke (2006) found that most of the unemployed fall under the categories of Africans, females, those who studied humanities and arts and those who studied at so-called historically black universities.

Table 3.11 Rate of completion at tertiary

Rate of completion at tertiary														
	2002	*2003*	*2004*	*2005*	*2006*	*2007*	*2008*	*2009*	*2010*	*2011*	*2012*	*2013*	*2014*	*2015*
Black African	5.6	5.6	6	6.8	6.1	6.2	7.5	6.9	7.3	7.5	8.4	8.7	9.2	10
Coloured	5.7	5.9	5.2	7.5	5.4	7.6	9.4	8.1	8.4	8.8	8.4	8.9	9.9	9.7
Indian/Asian	13.9	14.1	17.3	15.8	14.8	17.5	22.4	21.1	20.6	23.3	20.5	22.7	23	24.4
White	31.6	32.4	32.4	30.7	30	33.4	35.3	35.1	34.8	35.6	36.1	36.9	37.6	39.7
National average	14.2	14.5	15.2	15.2	14.1	16.2	18.6	17.8	17.8	18.8	18.3	19.3	19.9	20.9

Source: Calculations based on Stats SA data (various issues)

3.2.4 Healthcare Access

The challenge of the provision of social services is similar in many cases, and it is largely a legacy of the apartheid system. Undoing the legacy of the apartheid system is enduring. In addition, however, as this book demonstrates, the challenge relates to policy and policy reform. Redressing the legacy of apartheid with regard to social provisioning requires robust and appropriate policies. As in education and other areas, there are policy constraints that have limited the extent to which South Africa can address the impact of apartheid on the healthcare system.

Concisely, healthcare administration was fragmented during the apartheid dispensation. For instance, there were 14 separate healthcare departments for the different racial groups, the homelands and self-governing territories. The healthcare transformation was guided by the Constitution, which requires the state to take "reasonable legislative and other measures within its available resources, to achieve the progressive realization of each of these rights". As indicated, section 271 of the Constitution states that "everyone has the right to have access to healthcare services, including reproductive health" (Cullinan, 2006, p. 131).

Numerous policies have been pursued to redress the legacy of apartheid with regard to healthcare. Of note are the policies that ensured access to healthcare by children, pregnant women, the aged and by those with disabilities and the poor in general. The other set of policies focused on improving the public healthcare system, which was in dire straits on the eve of democracy. This challenge remains one of the main severe ones, implying an inability of policy and policy reforms to reconfigure the public healthcare system. This is not to say that other challenges such as poor implementation have not limited progress. Weaknesses of policy and policy reform are more pressing than other challenges that may have slowed socio-economic transformation. While there has been commendable progress in healthcare, as in other areas of socio-economic development, the progress would have been better if policies worked well or if policy reforms were sequenced accordingly. The institutional reforms that have taken place since 1994, which were necessary, could have delivered better results if they had been informed by appropriate policies and policy reforms.

Increasing access to healthcare, as in education, was a starting point. It was obvious that access needed to be expanded because of the discriminatory and exclusionary apartheid system. Other policies and programmes, such as those that target specific diseases such as HIV/AIDS and Tuberculosis (TB), appear to have ameliorated the healthcare challenge that relates to the 'burden of disease'. However, major policy issues that relate to equity were insufficiently addressed. As such, almost 20 years since the dawn of democracy, the two-tier healthcare system remains. The National Health Insurance (NHI) policy addresses this important challenge. As indicated, it is primarily aimed at making significant changes and improvements in the healthcare system. It aims at promoting equity, fairness and social solidarity in the healthcare system. The main objective of the policy is to ensure that all South Africans have full access to appropriate, efficient and quality healthcare services.

This important and overdue policy can significantly improve the health profile of the country. There are, however, some critical risks with any health insurance policy. In many instances countries implement Social Health Insurance (SHI), often with the plan of graduating it to the NHI. SHI could be a good start, particularly when a country needs to first improve the public healthcare system and pool and equalise risks. As discussed, the South African healthcare system remains a two-tier system: an efficient and well-funded private healthcare system and an inefficient and poorly funded healthcare system. The well-funded and efficient healthcare system remains largely for the minority. Conceptually, it is difficult to mention equity. Another major policy issue regarding any health insurance is that income through gainful employment is critical. It is difficult to imagine a successful implementation of an NHI without some form of wage subsidisation in a context of a very high unemployment rate. It is in this context that an argument is made that an SHI, coupled with wage subsidy, would have been a better policy option. The starting point, and perhaps policy emphasis, should have been on fixing the ailing public health sector, which could have been done with a better focus on risk equalisation for a relatively significant period of time in order to avoid running into financial constraints that can compromise a noble policy.

The healthcare challenge is even more pronounced in rural areas. For instance, although 43.6% of the population in South Africa lives in rural areas, they are served by only 12% of the doctors and 19% of nurses. Also, it is reported that of the 1200 medical students graduating annually, about 35 of them end up working in rural areas in the longer term. Further, about 21.3% of households in metropolitan areas belong to a medical aid in comparison with an estimated 5% of households in rural districts. In comparison, the infant mortality rate is 32.6 per 1000 live births in urban areas compared to 52.6 on average in rural areas (Human Resources for Health SA, 2012, pp. 34–35).

Shisana (2011) states that the two-tiered financing healthcare system has led to a situation whereby more state resources are used to cater for a minority who can access private healthcare systems, while the public health sector is under-resourced and caters for the majority of the country's population. According to Shisana (2011), South Africa spends 8.3% of its GDP on health, yet 4.1% of this GDP is spent on the private health sector which caters for only 16.2% of the total population of which 4.2% is allocated to public health that caters to 84% of the population.

South Africa is dealing with a severe 'burden of disease'. For instance, Tuberculosis (TB) infections are very high. Also, and equally challenging, the HIV prevalence levels remain very high. Although it is reported that prevalence of HIV has stabilised since 2009, at a national antenatal prevalence of about 30% it is still very high. With regard to infections, despite the treatment given to HIV-infected individuals, the number of infections seems to be increasing. Table 3.12 shows that the infection rates increased from an estimated 4 million in 2002 to over 5 million in 2012.

The trend for HIV incidence has been declining since 2002. In terms of HIV prevalence for women and adults aged 15–49, in general, there are marginal increases over time. With regard to youth (15–24) the trend is that HIV prevalence has declined from 6.39% in 2002 to 5.34% in 2020.

Although mortality rates are improving, the challenge remains severe. The United Nations (UN) estimates suggest that under-5 mortality rates have declined between the period 2002–2020 from 75 per 1000 live births to 34 per 1000 live births (which is indeed a significant improvement). This is probably linked to a decline in HIV/AIDS infections and ameliorated sanitation systems. There is a noteworthy decline in the transmission of mother-to-child HIV infections.

Table 3.13 also demonstrates that the trend for life expectancy has been marginally increasing, incidentally from 2006—this is the year when HIV prevalence and infection rates started to stabilise. The death rate also began to decline from 2006. As indicated, the challenge of mortality

Table 3.12 HIV prevalence estimates and the number of people living with HIV (2002–2020)

	Prevalence %				*Incidencerate %*	*HIVpopulation(in millions)*
	Women15–49	*Adults 15–49*	*Youth 15–24*	*Total population*	*15–49*	
2002	15.39	13.31	6.39	8.22	1.95	3.81
2003	16.12	13.90	6.39	8.70	1.86	4.08
2004	16.69	14.33	6.35	9.09	1.78	4.31
2005	17.12	14.66	6.28	9.40	1.71	4.50
2006	17.50	14.91	6.19	9.65	1.66	4.68
2007	17.84	15.15	6.10	9.87	1.62	4.85
2008	18.18	15.39	6.04	10.09	1.59	5.02
2009	18.71	15.76	6.04	10.37	1.59	5.23
2010	19.25	16.11	6.03	10.65	1.52	5.45
2011	19.83	16.50	6.00	10.96	1.52	5.70
2012	20.43	16.92	6.01	11.27	1.50	5.95
2013	20.94	17.27	5.96	11.54	1.40	6.19
2014	21.41	17.60	5.87	11.80	1.34	6.43
2015	21.83	17.90	5.80	12.05	1.31	6.67
2016	22.12	18.10	5.65	12.24	1.18	6.88
2017	22.40	18.30	5.55	12.44	1.17	7.10
2018	22.64	18.48	5.47	12.64	1.14	7.32
2019	22.83	18.61	5.40	12.83	1.14	7.54
2020	22.95	18.70	5.34	13.01	1.13	7.76

Source: Statistics South Africa (2020)

remains significant and under-5 mortality is still extremely high despite a steady decline over time.

With regard to TB, the incidence reached a peak in 2009 and has since been declining. Concerted efforts by the National Department of Health (NDoH) to test, treat and ensure people infected with TB are cured have yielded results, as shown by the data in Table 3.14.

Experience from dealing with TB has proved invaluable to the South African populace in the face of the Covid-19 pandemic. The NDoH activated protocols akin to those used for TB in dealing with the coronavirus, with the main one being contact tracing. Community Health Workers (CHWs) and Ward-Based Outreach Teams (WBOTs) are used for tracking and tracing people who could have been in contact with others with TB. CHWs and WBOTs also assist in ensuring adherence to treatment by

Table 3.13 Fertility and mortality levels, 2002–2020

Year	*Crude birth rate*	*Life expectancy*			*Infant mortalityrate*	*Under-5 mortalityrate*	*Crude deathrate*	*Rate of natural increase(%)*
		Male	*Female*	*Total*				
2002	21.2	53.5	57.9	55.8	55.5	75.3	12.9	0.8
2003	21.1	52.9	57.6	55.4	57.2	76.8	13.2	0.8
2004	22.3	52.6	56.7	54.7	55.7	76.5	13.7	0.9
2005	23.0	52.4	56.0	54.2	55.6	75.1	14.1	0.9
2006	23.5	52.3	55.7	54.1	53.8	72.4	14.3	0.9
2007	23.9	52.8	56.2	54.6	49.5	68.0	14.1	1.0
2008	24.1	53.4	57.0	55.2	47.4	64.0	13.8	1.0
2009	23.9	54.5	59.3	57.0	44.0	57.1	12.8	1.1
2010	23.5	55.8	60.9	58.4	38.2	53.5	11.8	1.2
2011	22.9	57.4	62.8	60.2	36.9	48.8	10.8	1.2
2012	22.4	58.4	63.9	61.2	34.0	44.1	10.3	1.2
2013	22.0	59.0	64.6	61.9	31.7	41.0	10.0	1.2
2014	21.6	59.8	65.7	62.8	30.3	39.8	9.6	1.2
2015	21.4	60.2	66.0	63.2	29.0	39.2	9.5	1.2
2016	21.1	60.9	66.5	63.8	27.9	38.7	9.2	1.2
2017	20.8	61.5	66.8	64.2	26.9	38.2	9.1	1.2
2018	20.4	61.8	67.3	64.6	26.0	37.9	8.9	1.2
2019	20.0	62.2	67.8	65.0	24.7	36.5	8.8	1.1
2020	19.7	62.5	68.5	65.6	23.6	34.1	8.7	1.1

Source: Statistics South Africa (2020)

facilitating the formation and running of TB treatment clubs, where patients walk the treatment journey with others to provide support for each other.

The high HIV/AIDS and TB prevalence places the country at risk of experiencing a high mortality rate due to compromised immune systems. Despite South Africa having approximately 324,000 people who had tested positive by mid-July 2020, the death rate was 1.4%—which is below the global average of 4.3%.

There are other challenges regarding healthcare in South Africa, for instance, the major challenge pertaining to the shortage of healthcare workers. The World Health Organisation (WHO) estimates that close to 60% of posts in the health sector in South Africa are vacant, including over 4000 vacancies for general practitioners and 32,000 vacancies for nurses in all provinces. It is argued that besides the international migration of healthcare workers, there is a misdistribution of healthcare workers

Table 3.14 Incidence of TB (all types) by province and nationally, 2007–2015 (cases per 100,000 population)

	2007	*2008*	*2009*	*2010*	*2011*	*2012*	*2013*	*2014*	*2015*
EC	806.6	962.7	953.4	922.3	913.7	862.7	823.1	785.0	691.7
FS	844.1	889.5	859.7	837.2	841.5	760.6	720.9	631.7	574.8
GP	174.1	489.5	517.1	113.6	454.1	418.2	403.3	378.2	329.9
KZN	880.7	928.1	1215.5	1161.8	1185.2	1060.4	952.5	813.7	685.2
LP	329.1	397.2	433.5	419.8	410.6	371.8	383.3	334.1	300.7
MP	227.3	637.1	745.0	715.5	613.6	512.7	477.1	461.5	401.6
NC	859.2	935.5	932.5	892.2	893.8	758.1	798.0	764.3	644.6
NW	766.5	815.0	903.8	894.4	816.6	705.0	658.1	630.7	528.4
WC	938.3	948.1	930.1	909.5	827.4	776.5	742.9	709.9	681.4
SA	**608.2**	**752.8**	**831.8**	**718.4**	**762.3**	**689.3**	**648.9**	**592.7**	**519.8**

favouring the private healthcare sector. Many of the well-trained medical practitioners are employed in private hospitals, which as stated earlier serves a minority group of the country's total population. Thus, development and functioning of public healthcare is further undermined by this uneven distribution of healthcare workers. Furthermore, the quality of the healthcare provided is also undermined by this shortage. Government is aware of this challenge, like many others, and there are efforts to address it.

3.2.5 *Poverty and Inequality*

Two important development issues that continue to haunt post-apartheid South Africa are poverty and inequality. Our calculation shows that the share of those living below the poverty line of R515 per person per month has declined, although marginally, from 46% in 2008 to 45% in 2010. The latest data might show that the number of those classified as poor might have increased because of the economic hardship that South Africa is increasingly navigating. South Africa is reported to have a Gini Coefficient of 0.69 (Bhorat & Van Der Westhuizen, 2010).

These two issues (i.e. poverty and inequality) are linked to the structure of the economy. On the one hand, the economy or the labour market is not creating jobs that could dent structural poverty, which is largely a legacy of apartheid. On the other hand, the structure of the economy reproduces inequality through benefiting those with certain skills or political connections while keeping the rest of society, within the African community, at lower levels of economic or financial wellbeing. The challenge with income inequality is that it remains predominantly a racial phenomenon.

3.3 Explaining Socio-economic Transformation

South Africa has fallen short significantly. The necessary reforms in the economy have been weak because of poor policy development and a lack of vision for the economy. In social development, it is argued that the lack of a social policy has constrained the advancement of wellbeing. Broadly, South Africa has effectively been stagnant following the robust reforms of the 1990s. Granted implementation is a challenge, but this is worsened particularly when policies are inappropriate or weak.

The answer to South Africa's woes is policy and policy reforms in the economy. The strategies and programmes introduced since the mid-2000s have not addressed the constraints that compel the need for policy reforms. Therefore, more policy thinking should be exercised for both social and economic transformation. And most importantly, policy should be in pursuit of the vision for the economy that should be agreed upon through national consensus. Robust and clear policies should still advance the wellbeing of South Africans, even in the context of twisted state-market relations and the lopsided global order. Government, at least through moral persuasion, should be able to navigate the currently inappropriately configured state-market relations to make some gains in economic and social development for most of the population.

3.3.1 The Policies

In 1996, about two years after the dawn of democracy in South Africa, an economic policy framework followed the introduction of the Reconstruction and Development Programme (RDP) that was unveiled in 1994 as a blueprint for socio-economic transformation in South Africa. We say more about the RDP further down and we problematise it in Chap. 6 when we critique the various policies for social and economic development in South Africa since 1994. There is still a debate about the RDP as there are many who believe that it was a sound policy framework for South Africa. The Growth, Employment and Redistribution (GEAR) Macroeconomic Framework unveiled in 1996 took precedence and the RDP was effectively forgotten about. GEAR was intended, as an economic policy framework, to rescue and stabilise a weakening economy (Hirsch, 2005). Others disagree with this perspective as we will demonstrate in Chap. 6.

GEAR was meant to deal with economic fundamentals, so to speak or so South Africans were told. It was inaugurated in an environment of double-digit inflation and interest rates, a run-away budget deficit, negative growth rates and a huge government debt prevalent in the late 1980s and early 1990s. For instance, the International Monetary Fund (IMF) states that the budget deficit in South Africa widened from 2.4% of GDP in 1990 to 7.5% in 1992. According to Calitz, du Plessis and Siebrits (2011), by the year 1994 government debt was just shy of 50% of GDP—a dramatic increase from 31.5% in 1990.

The economy was effectively in a recession when the ANC came into office in 1994; the last period that South Africa had experienced uninterrupted economic growth was the 1960s.

In 2005, government opted for another broader economic policy reform agenda through the Accelerated and Shared Growth Initiative for South Africa (AsgiSA). The intention was to accelerate the growth of the economy and accelerate wealth redistribution. AsgiSA, however, was short lived. The highlight of AsgiSA, in the main, is that it aimed for equitable distribution of growth and skills development.

In 2010, AsgiSA was replaced by the New Growth Path (NGP), which places emphasis on job creation and the need to create decent work; more specifically, it can be conceived of as a new policy orientation towards labour-intensive approaches. The NGP aspired to increase employment by 5 million by 2020 and reduce narrow unemployment by 10%, largely through a public infrastructure programme.

The Reconstruction and Development Programme

The ANC understood that as a party in government, the success of the liberation struggle would be judged on its ability to address issues of poverty, unemployment, underdevelopment and inequality. As the democratic government's development strategy, the RDP sought to attain socio-economic development while at the same time addressing the legacy of apartheid colonialism. As stated in the RDP discussion document, the ANC aimed "to mobilise all people and country's resources towards the final eradication of apartheid … building of a democratic, non-racial and non-sexist future" (African National Congress, 1994, p. 8). The RDP set out various socio-economic commitments for delivery related to employment creation, housing, electricity, water, sanitation, health, education, infrastructure and public enterprises. Chikulo (2003) indicates that during the 1994–1996 period, the RDP was viewed as the cornerstone of government's development policy—a yardstick against which the success of the government's development policy could be assessed.

The RDP remains the most critical policy framework intended to guide government in policy making and implementation. The RDP focuses on addressing the basic needs of the majority. It can be viewed as a renaissance in which economic development, popular participation and respect for human rights are seen as integral components of the transformative process.

Five primary goals were identified as essential to the socio-economic transformation of the South African society (African National Congress, 1994). These were to:

- create a strong, dynamic and balanced economy to eliminate poverty and meet the basic needs of every South African
- develop the human resource capacity of all South Africans
- ensure that no one suffers racial or gender discrimination in hiring, promotion or training situations
- develop a prosperous, balanced regional economy in Southern Africa
- democratise the state and society.

The primary vision of the RDP lies in the values it espouses and the strategic approach through which it proposes to achieve the National Democratic Revolution (NDR) towards the creation of a National Democratic Society (NDS). The NDS can be described in simple terms as a society that is free of poverty, racism, gender and other forms of discrimination; a society that is prosperous where its people exercise free will, free choice and, in the economic philosophy of Sen (1999, p. 18), where "people lead the kind of lives they value and have reason to value". As mentioned, a debate on the NDR and its related philosophies is due.

Like some, Chikulo (2003) argues that as a development policy framework, the RDP has several shortcomings. Evidently, most societies in a similar position to South Africa in 1994 could have pursued these overarching objectives. However, the RDP was, and still is, criticised for being too broad and all-encompassing—something the likes of Chikulo (2003) consider as a 'wish list' instead of a strategy document focusing on opportunities and constraints. It has, in some quarters, been pointed out that the misplaced criticisms of the RDP are merely grandstanding at best and lack knowledge of policy development at worst. Second, the RDP made no attempt to set priorities or assign responsibility for the implementation of each programme component. Third, it lacked mechanisms for inter-departmental coordination. Finally, local government, which had been assigned the constitutional responsibility for promoting socio-economic development, had inadequate planning and implementation capacity. The possible downside of the RDP, perhaps in hindsight, is the setting of targets. This appears to be a particular weakness of the successive post-apartheid administrations—almost all set targets have not been achieved.

Target setting is a challenge confronting governments the world over. However, the margin by which South Africa misses its set targets appears worse when compared to other countries. What is baffling is that a wild target such as halving unemployment by 2014 was set against poor conditions for job creation without the existence or development of a concurrent policy. Moreover, a target of creating 5 million jobs by 2020 is inexplicable in a time of recession and with no job creation policy. An important aspect of a job creation policy—the youth wage subsidy, designed in 2007—could not be immediately implemented even after the pilot phase. In defence of the RDP, it never presented itself as the policy or strategy. In its core, it is explicitly a policy framework. In other words, the RDP presents aspirations on what policies and programmes should entail and pursue.

As with other policies and programmes, and other frameworks and strategies, the RDP set itself up for failure by specifying several unattainable targets. In 1994, the priority should have been to create a proper foundation for socio-economic development. Of course, several socio-economic development initiatives had to start, given the deeply entrenched legacy of apartheid colonialism. Apartheid colonialism is a shorthand for over 350 years of discrimination and exploitation of blacks in South Africa by the minority whites.

The RDP set targets such as:

- the creation of 2.5 million jobs over a ten-year period
- the building of one million houses by the year 2000
- the connection to the national electricity grid of 2.5 million homes by 2000
- the provision of running water and sewerage to 1 million households
- the distribution of 30% of agricultural land to emerging 'black' farmers
- the development of a new focus on primary health care
- the provision of ten years of compulsory free education for all children

- the encouragement of massive infrastructural improvements through public works
- the restructuring of state institutions by 1997 to reflect the broader race, class and gender composition of society.

A difficulty with setting targets is particularly the dates by which the targets must be met. These targets are often achieved many years after the predetermined date. An elementary issue is having the right foundation and an enabling environment for targets to be achieved. A critical issue is policy clarity that is commensurate with the intended objectives, making it feasible to achieve set targets.

Despite its shortcomings, however, the RDP played a critical role in inspiring hope for a better tomorrow among many South Africans, particularly the poor. As Munslow and Fitzgerald (1997, p. 57) aptly put it, "there is no doubt that the RDP played a pivotal role in ensuring the successful transition from separate development towards a more sustainable development future". Furthermore, the RDP's projects on basic needs provision would count among its successes. As discussed in later sections of this chapter, much has been achieved with specific regard to the implementation of the government's priority in addressing the lack of access to basic social services as well as other important areas such as economic development.

The Growth, Employment and Redistribution Strategy

The Growth, Employment and Redistribution (GEAR) strategy came into effect in 1996. The debate remains unresolved as to whether GEAR was an appropriate policy for South Africa's context at the time. The debate has remained ideological: GEAR was a Structural Adjustment Programme (SAP) akin to the Bretton Woods Washington Consensus neoliberal agenda. A useful debate should centre on the type of economic stabilisation programme South Africa should have pursued if GEAR was unsuitable. Many have argued that South Africa, or the government, succumbed to international pressure to replace the RDP with GEAR. The proponents of this argument contend that the 'socialist' RDP was not viewed amicably by international investors, leading government to shift to the 'neoliberal' GEAR.

GEAR, in simple terms, was aimed at strengthening economic development, broadening employment and encouraging the redistribution of wealth while increasing socio-economic opportunities through structural reforms in the economy. Some of the major targets of GEAR were:

- an economic growth rate of 6% per annum by 2000
- up to 400,000 jobs per annum
- an increase of exports by up to 8% per annum
- reduction of the budget deficit to below 4% of GDP.

However, there have been real differences over the question of macroeconomic policy and its potential effects. According to Chikulo (2003), GEAR assumed that the expansion of the private sector would have a substantial impact on the economy while the role of the state would largely be a facilitative one. There are quite a number of similar views that serve largely as a critique of GEAR. The gist of the critical views is that it is a self-imposed Structural Adjustment Programme (SAP). SAPs are associated with the International Monetary Fund (IMF) and the World Bank (WB), and the neoliberal agenda. SAPs have a notorious history in sub-Saharan Africa as they resulted in low investments in human capital because of tighter fiscal and monetary policies.

COSATU has been one of the prominent critics of GEAR. Knight (2001, p. 4) refers to a COSATU policy document that argues that GEAR brought about deep cuts in government spending between 1996 and 1999. As a result, efforts to improve services to the poor suffered despite the continued reprioritisation of spending on the rich to the poor. GEAR failed to effectively attain many of its goals. Although changes in corporate tax levels, foreign exchange controls and interest rates have yielded some degree of increased investment, many of the strategy's long-term targets were unmet. Notwithstanding its weaknesses or failures, the most important objective of GEAR, that of macroeconomic stabilisation, was achieved.

Mathekga (2013) in Ndletyana and Maimela (2013) argues that GEAR brought ANC legitimacy to the international community. Hirsch (2005) concludes that GEAR was not only a good policy but that it achieved most of its targets. I concur that a macroeconomic stabilisation policy or programme was necessary in the mid-1990s, but GEAR appears to have further entrenched inappropriate state-market relations that were prevalent during the apartheid era. In hindsight, although it was important to stabilise the economy, government should have ensured that the stabilisation programme took place under differently configured state-market relations.

Like the RDP, however, and other policy frameworks of the post-apartheid government, as indicated, GEAR set unrealistic targets such as achieving an economic growth rate of 6% per annum by 2000 and creating 400,000 jobs per annum. Given the potential capacity of the South African economy in 1996 (and its global ranking), in hindsight, the focus could have been on macroeconomic stabilisation. In other words, the priority should have been to reverse the downward spiral of the economy first instead of aiming for far-fetched targets. The democratic government or the ANC, although it had accurately diagnosed the challenges confronting South Africa, always fell short in policy options.

GEAR was succeeded by AsgiSA, which was short lived as it was replaced by the NGP within three years of its implementation. The AsgiSA was not just a government programme but a national initiative supported by key groups in the economy. Launched in 2005, it prioritised government's commitment to halve unemployment and poverty by 2014 and to accelerate economic growth and ensure wealth redistribution. One of its main components was the Joint Initiative on Priority Skills Acquisition (JIPSA), a partnership programme to address scarce and critical skills to meet the AsgiSA's economic growth objectives.

AsgiSA identified six 'binding constraints' preventing South Africa from achieving the desired growth rate:

- The relative volatility of the currency
- The cost, efficiency and capacity of the national infrastructure system
- Shortages of suitably skilled labour and the spatial distortions of apartheid affecting low-skilled labour costs
- Barriers to entry, limits to competition and limited new investment opportunities
- The regulatory environment and the burden on small and medium enterprises
- Deficiencies in state organisation, capacity and leadership.

Given the time it takes to effectively implement any policy, it is hard to assess the efficacy of AsgiSA or the effectiveness of the NGP which succeeded AsgiSA in 2010. The NGP was launched in 2010 as an ambitious and imaginative government developmental framework, broadly set to pursue economic growth and employment creation through an infrastructural development programme. Primarily, it was aimed at creating 5 million jobs by 2015 and a 10% reduction in unemployment by 2020. Like

GEAR, the NGP has not reached its targets. Indeed, target setting appears to be problematic. Often the diagnosis of the policy challenge is conclusive, but targets are usually unsubstantiated. Targets are set without clear policy choices to inform targets.

Lastly, the National Development Plan (NDP) cannot be thought of as a policy document. It is a sort of consensus-building mechanism towards some envisaged end state where issues such as poverty, inequality and unemployment would be drastically reduced. Worth noting is that there is value in a vision such as the one presented by the NDP for South Africa. What it offers is a relatively robust diagnosis of society and the economy but the proposed solutions, as in the NGP, do not address the identified policy challenges.

Probably, it is in the nature of governments to focus on specific policy questions instead of attempting to address all challenges at once. The NDP does not address the practicalities of how its goals would be achieved; for instance, how would 'sustainable communities' come about? As indicated in Chap. 3, the vision for society should be clear and succinct. The NDP is rather longwinded and voluminous.

Some have concluded that the NDP will not work (see, for instance, Terreblanche, 2012), while others remain optimistic, for example, Habib (2013). Perhaps Habib sees the NDP as a step towards a new 'political settlement' or 'social pact' emanating from new 'political management' brought about by 'astute leadership'. Terreblanche (2012, p. 118), on the other hand, argues that the 'hyper-optimism' characterising the NDP is because "the NDP has not considered the historical trends of the past 130 years". The National Planning Commission should have, according to Terreblanche, "concentrated on the unequal power relations, the unequal property relations and the unequal opportunities that are making the new South African society a very unjust society—just as similar inequalities made apartheid South Africa a very unjust place".

It is also of importance to note that all major stakeholders were involved, or at least represented, in the drafting of the NDP. Taken together with the 2014–2019 Medium-Term Strategic Framework, the NDP provides a good basis for crafting a development programme or agenda for South Africa. The fundamental challenge regarding the NDP has been the inability of government to rally the whole of society behind the proposed vision for South Africa and that government has been unable to get all the stakeholders to work together in achieving the goals indicated in the NDP.

3.3.2 State, Property Relations and Social Transformation

In 1998, the ANC—or the broader National Liberation Movement (NLM)—undertook what must be one of the most incisive probes of the economy and society in the State, Property Relations and Social Transformation discussion document. This document made an important attempt at clarifying the NLM paradigm on the economy and society.

The following paragraph captures the essence of what was (to be) pursued in post-apartheid South Africa: pursuing the kind of state whose character is developmental. Development is about improving the quality of life; it is about equity and justice. As the RDP document asserts, development entails a growing economy in which redistribution is a critical element. It includes modernisation of the productive forces and a redefinition of production relations, the preservation and development of human resources in the form of skills training, job creation and the provision of education, health services, infrastructure, an adequate social security system and so on. It is also about democracy and popular participation (African National Congress, 1998).

The discussion document also, for the first time, explained in detail the type of state pursued by the NLM. The discussion document contends that the state:

- should use the resources that it commands to ensure redistribution of wealth in the interest of the poor and disadvantaged
- should put in place regulatory and other mechanisms that not only seek to obviate market failure, but also afford the state the capacity to intervene in a pro-active way to facilitate growth and redistribution
- should be able to strike the correct balance between state ownership of productive forces and private ownership, guided, inter alia, by the prerogatives of strategic interest, efficiency, technology transfer, affordability of services and narrow cost-benefit considerations
- must define and regulate its interaction with private capital in such a way that mutual benefit can be derived. This includes an industrial policy that helps to direct private capital into critical sectors and a labour market policy that prevents super-exploitation and encourages skills development and workplace democracy. It includes offering aspirant black capitalists' opportunities that encourage the expansion of this class.

The recent policies have largely been about responding to economic crises and Covid-19. Chapter 6 deals with all the policies comprehensively, focusing on what modification or additions as well as subtractions that can bring about policies that can ensure that the economy grows sustainably and it is inclusive.

3.4 Conclusion

The chapter has reviewed social and economic indicators as an effort to examine socio-economic transformation in post-apartheid South Africa. Data confirms that social and economic development has not been improving of late, largely because the poor performance of the economy in South Africa. Indeed, there are other factors that account for weakening social and economic development outcomes. Implementation and policy are among key factors that have resulted to poor socio-economic transformation. Government has not been functioning optimally as a result of inefficiencies. Of critical importance is that the policies discussed may have remained out of context and necessary reforms not pursued.

Chapter 2 confirms that policies (lack thereof or their inappropriateness) and the structure of the South African economy have been the main obstacles to economic growth. The same issues and inefficiencies in government have negatively affected socio-economic transformation.

References

African National Congress. (1994). *Reconstruction and Development Programme: A Policy Framework*. Umanyano Publications.

African National Congress. (1998). The State, Property Relations and Social Transformation. Umrabulo 5. 3rd Quarter. Available from http://amadlandawonye.wikispaces.com/1998,+ANC,+State,+Property+Relations,+Social+Transformation. Accessed on November 29, 2022.

Bhorat, H., & Van Der Westhuizen, C. (2010). *Poverty, Inequality and the Nature of Economic Growth in South Africa. Testing Democracy: Which Way Is South Africa going*, 46, 70.

Bloch, G. (2006). *Building Education Beyond Crisis*. Development Bank of Southern Africa.

Bloch, G. (2009). *The Toxic Mix: What's Wrong with South Africa's Schools and How to Fix It*. Tafelberg.

Breier, M., & Mabizela, M. (2008). Higher Education. In A. Kraak & K. Press (Eds.), *Human Resources Development Review 2008: Education, Employment and Skills in South Africa* (pp. 278–299). HSRC Press.

Calitz, E., Du Plessis, S., & Siebrits, K. (2011). An Alternative Perspective on South Africa's Public Debt, 1962–1994. *South African Journal of Economics, 79*(2), 161–172.

Chikulo, B. (2003). Development Policy in South Africa: A Review. *DPMN Bulletin, X*(2). Retrieved March 20, 2009, from http://www.dpmf.org/pub-bulletin.html

Council on Higher Education (CHE). (2007). *Higher Education Monitor: A Case for Improving Teaching and Learning in South African Higher Education*. Council on Higher Education.

Cullinan, K. (2006). Health Services in South Africa: A Basic Introduction. *Health-e News Service, 1*(1–38).

Department of Basic Education. (2018). *Education Statistics in South Africa*. Department of Basic Education.

Department of Education. (1997). *Education White Paper. A Programme for the Transformation of Higher Education*. Department of Education.

Department of Higher Education and Training. (2014). *White Paper for the Post-School System*. DHET.

Gumede, V. (2016). *Poverty and Inequality in Africa: Towards the Post-2015 Development Agenda for Sub-Saharan Africa*. Retrieved June 10, 2018. https://www.vusigumede.com/content/2014/DEC%202014/Poverty%20&%20Inequality%20in%20SSA%20(draft%20paper).pdf

Gumede, V. (2022). *South Africa: State and Development*. SAPAM & UNISA.

Habib, A. (2013). *South Africa's Suspended Revolution: Hopes and prospects*. Wits University Press.

Hirsch, A. (2005). *Season of Hope: Economic Reform under Mandela and Mbeki*. UKZN Press.

Human Resources for Health South Africa. (2012). *HRH Strategy for the Health Sector*. University of Witwatersrand.

Knight, R. (2001). *South Africa: Economic Policy and Development*. http://homestead.juno.com/rknight1/files/sisaecompolicy.htm, version 11.28.2001.

Kraak, A. (2008). The Education-Economy Relationship in South Africa, 2001–2005. *Human Resources Development Review, 28*, 1–25.

Mathekga, R. (2013). State Evolution and Sovereignty; The Case of South Africa. In M. Ndletyana & D. Maimela (Eds.), *Essays on the Evolution of the Post-Apartheid State: Legacies, Reforms and Prospects*. Real African Publishers.

Moleke, P. (2006). *Finding Work: Employment Experiences of South African Graduates*. HSRC Press.

Munslow, B., & Fitzgerald, P. (1997). Search for a Development Strategy: The RDP and Beyond. In P. Fitzerald, A. McLennan, & B. Munslow (Eds.), *Managing Sustainable Development in South Africa*. Oxford University Press.

National Department of Education. (2001). *Education White Paper 5 on Early Childhood Education: Meeting the Challenge of Early Childhood Development in South Africa*. Government Printers.

Ndletyana, M., & Maimela, D. (2013). *Essays on the Evolution of the Post-Apartheid State: Legacies, Reforms and Prospects*. MISTRA.

Sen, A. 1999. *Development as Freedom*. Anchor.

Shisana, O. (2011). The South African Healthcare System: A Goal of Quality Healthcare for All. *Medical Solutions*. September, 91–95.

Statistics South Africa. (2012). *Census 2011*. Statistics South Africa.

Statistics South Africa. (2020). *General Household Survey*. Statistics South Africa.

Terreblanche, S. (2012). *Lost in Transformation: South Africa's Search for a New Future Since 1986*. KMM Review Publishing.

CHAPTER 4

Macroeconomic Resilience: South Africa and Selected Emerging Market Economies

4.1 Introduction

Emerging economies play a very important role in the global economic stage. Countries like Brazil, South Africa, Nigeria, Malaysia and Poland or Hungary have significantly contributed to poverty reduction, decreased unemployment and increased global economic opportunities. Nonetheless, with the mushrooming visibility and prominence of emerging economies emanates amplified exposure to local and international shocks. Thus, assessing the resilience of these economies to shocks appears to be an important matter with far-reaching economic implications of these economies. We attempt to shed some light on whether these economies can absorb the shock or bounce back after facing negative economic shocks. It seeks out to untangle the elaborate factors that enable these economies to absorb shocks and adapt to shifting economic conditions. Given the mushrooming influence of these economies to the world's economic order, it goes stands to reason that their resilience has become a necessary area of study. By unpacking the economic challenges (i.e. economic shocks), including economic opportunities that are faced by these economies, the chapter intends to provide valuable insights for policy makers.

To this end this chapter delves into the nuanced parts of resilience in the context of emerging economies. Using annual data, and empirical evidence, we intend to shed light on the diverse facets of macroeconomic

V. Gumede et al., *South African Economy*, African Histories and Modernities, https://doi.org/10.1007/978-3-031-54180-3_4

resilience, contributing to a deeper analysis of the economic intricacies that define emerging economies, equipping policy makers to face the economic challenges of the future with greater wisdom and foresight.

4.2 Literature Review

This section looks at the literature regarding the degree to which economies are able to bounce back after facing negative economic shocks (such as the global financial crisis that hit many economies in 2008/2009). After a negative economic shock some economies show some resilience—self-regulate and go back to a position they were before the shock took place. Various metric measures can be used to understand the degree to which economies respond to economic shock. One of the metrics captures the effect of the Crisis. Specifically, it measures how well an economy absorbs a shock. A related but different metric captures the recovery from the shock—assesses how well an economy rebounds and stabilises after being hit by the shock. Some metrics like Medium-Run Performance look at how an economy adapts and adjusts to the shock over time. A growing body of literature have attempted to measure the impact of the shocks on the economy. For example, Mendoza (1995): Mendoza's research, using a real business cycle (RBC) model, reveals that trade shocks explain nearly 50% of the changes in economic activity and exchange rates for Latin American economies. The study by Kose (2002), using a dynamic stochastic general equilibrium (DSGE) model, found that shocks related to global price contribute substantially to economic cycle changes in developing economies as well as in Latin America. Reaching a similar conclusion, Brada et al. (2021) observed that Baltic states suffered a rapid decrease in economic growth. A study carried out by Al-Hassan and associates in 2010 called attention to the sizable effects of global financial shock/crisis on Kuwait and other Middle East and North Africa (MENA) countries. Researching oil-dependent economies (focusing on Kuwait) Mirzaei and Al-Khouri (2016) find evidence to confirm their vulnerability to the economic shocks. Within the Middle East and North Africa (MENA) region, a study by Awartani, Maghyereh and Ayton explored the effects of oil price fluctuations on economic growth across six countries, revealing disparities in their impacts.

Contrastingly, another group of studies point to a limited influence of external shocks. For instance, Ahmed and Murthy (1994) take the view that external shocks do not play an important role in explaining economic cycles in Latin American economies. Similarly, Hausmann et al. (1995) and Hoffmaister and Roldós (1997) affirm economic activity fluctuation in developing nations cannot be largely attributed to external factors. Poland, among others, notably succeeded in preventing a recessionary contraction in output. Taiwan effectively navigated the challenges posed by the 2008–2009 global financial crisis, partly attributed to an improved regional landscape fostered by enhanced collaboration among Asian economies. This transformation was influenced by a growing awareness and responsiveness among East Asian policy makers (Yun-Han).

Abdul et al. (2015) observed that Emerging Market and Developing Economies (EMDEs) were quite resilient to global financial crisis, experiencing a relatively insignificant decrease in median output per capita during economic downturns between 2000 and 2006. Impressively these economies did not even take that long (roughly two years) to return to their pre-shock. In addition, the authors argued that even during the Great Recession, which is regarded as the most significant external shocks in the past several decades, Emerging Market and Low-Income Country put on a display a rather strong performance. In agreement with Abdul et al. (2015), Ammer et al. (2011) found some evidence to suggest Emerging Markets (EM) might be less predisposed to economic crisis, thus aligning with the view that there have been enhancements in the fundamental economic aspects of Emerging Market economies in the decade forgoing these shocks, reflecting increased resilience.

What makes some economies absorb the shock and bounce back from it more swiftly than others? According to Martin (2012), economies with stable economic growth patterns appeared to be more resilience to economic crises and displayed instantaneous recovery compared to those with unstable economic activity. Additionally, some scholars, such as, Lagravinese (2015), investigated the manner in which some economies gravitated back to their original state in the aftermath of the crises and found evidence to suggest that there are many factors at work that influence the ability of an economy to bounce back. They observed that these factors are interconnected, making the course of recovery quite complex.

4.2.1 Data Collection, Sources and Variables

To investigate the extent to which South African economy is resilient to shock and how this compares to its counterparts Brazil, Nigeria, Malaysia and Poland, the chapter collected an extensive data on different macroeconomic variables. Moreso, the data spanned from 1980 to 2022, the rationale behind the choice of the period was to ensure that we cover two main periods, pre- and post-apartheid. To measure the degree of shock, the chapter uses the negative growth. Understanding that different factors can lead to a shock, the chapter also tried analysing shocks transmission mechanisms and this was captured through factors such as consumption expenditure, government spending, investment as well as exports, all the above variables sourced from the World Development Indicators (WDI). Along the same lines, diversification has also been put forward as shock buffer; therefore, it was important to see how diversified those countries are; to do so, we collected the export diversification index from the Harvard growth lab. Other factors such as interest rate, debt stock and debt service were also sourced from the WDI.

4.2.2 *Emerging Countries' Macroeconomic Performance*

Macroeconomic crises have caused severe social and economic repercussions in economies that have high levels of poverty and inequality such as South Africa and Nigeria (Chitiga et al., 2014). The impact of such crises triggers attention to the roles that fiscal, monetary and social policies can play in promoting economic recovery and resilience to future crises. This section delves into presenting the macroeconomic outlook of the selected pear countries, South Africa, Brazil, Malaysia, Nigeria and Poland; these countries were selected due to their similar economic structure and for being developing countries. For the purpose to this book, shock is defined as a negative growth (see, e.g. Athukorala, 2010); further, the chapter gives an attempt to outline different shocks that hit these countries and resulted in a negative growth.

As can be depicted from Fig. 4.1, all five countries, although low, seemed to have experienced relatively stable growth. More specifically, when comparing South Africa to its counterparts, it is noticed that over the covered period, it grew relatively less than Malaysia, Poland and Nigeria, while on the other hand, it grew in a similar growth rate as Brazil. However, something that worth noting is that while some countries exhibited high growth rates for the last years, historically South Africa recorded better growth rates compared to those countries, such as Brazil and Nigeria.

Generally, all the countries seem to have recorded low growth in response to global shocks. For example, with the exception of Malaysia, all

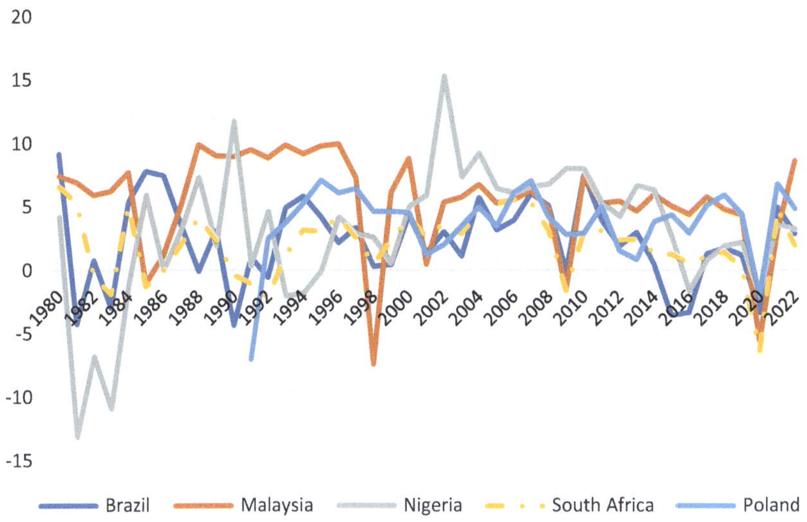

Fig. 4.1 GDP growth. (Source: Authors' own calculations based on the WDI data)

the countries seem to have grown negatively between 1980 and 1984, this might have been due to the international increase in the oil price. Moreso, 2009 was characterised by a low and in some cases negative growth for all the countries, expect Nigeria. Another notable negative decline was also observed in 2020–2021 due to the Covid-19 pandemic.

On the other hand, the chapter also sheds light on how South Africa compares to its counterparts in terms of the per capita gross domestic product (GDP), see Fig. 4.2. Something interesting is that although Nigeria, for example, has grown relatively higher compared to South Africa, the former's GDP per capita is quite below that of South Africa. This is explained by the high population growth rate in Nigeria, where this is a home of about 200 million people while South Africa accommodates about 60 million. This is sustained by Solow (1956) when arguing that an increase in population leads to a decrease in economic growth thus increasing the vulnerability to shocks. Different from Nigeria, other countries have a greater per capita GDP compared to South Africa and this exhibits an increasing trend with Poland showing the highest GDP per capita compared to its counterparts. This is also explained by its high economic growth in the observed period.

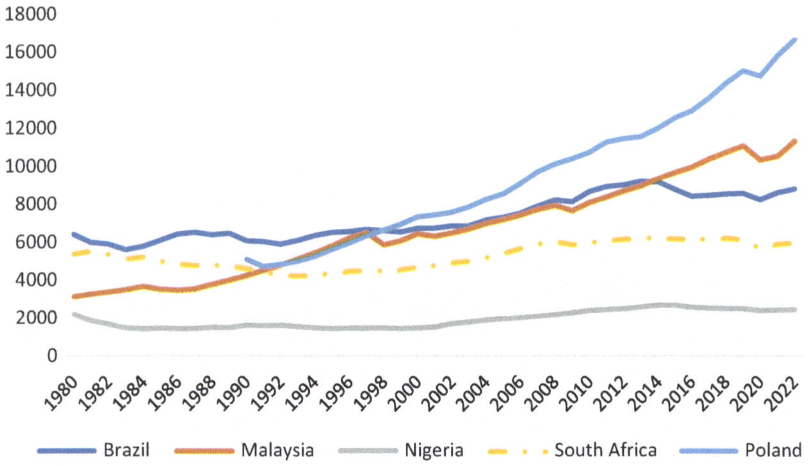

Fig. 4.2 GDP per capita. (Source: Authors' own calculations based on the WDI data)

4.2.3 Country Case Studies

After presenting an overall countries economic outlook, the study further examines country's economic growth and outlines different shocks that have driven the economies into a deep recession.

The Case of South Africa

South Africa has widespread socio-economic exclusion. The country faces economic challenges such as high unemployment, poverty and inequality (Bila & Biyase, 2023). Apartheid's systematic exclusion of black people from respectable or skilled labour possibilities contributed to several economic issues.[1] Unfortunately, the post-apartheid government did not adequately protect or promoted new work prospects. Although economic growth was constant in the 2000s, it has been continuously low in the last decade, especially compared to their counterparts Poland and Malaysia. According to (Stiftung, 2022c and Statistics SA 2017), the poverty rate for the most common UBPL declined from 66.6% in 2006 to 53.2% in 2011. Despite a modest decrease in the number of people living below the

[1] Input obtained from the Industrial Development Corporation (2013). "The South African Economy: An overview of key trends since 1994."

UBPL, the poverty rate rose to 55.5% in 2015. In South Africa, poverty is still prevalent and racially and gender based. White South Africans, who benefited most from apartheid, have low poverty rates, while black South Africans have higher rates. Although the above doesn't directly lead to a vulnerability, indirectly it does. As per Fig. 4.3, South Africa, on its turn as shown above, registered about five shocks, most of them global/exogenous. For instance, like Brazil, Malaysia and Nigeria, the country was also hit by the increase in the international oil price between 1980 and 1982. After giving a sign of bouncing back, it again suffered another shock around 1985–1986. The transition from the apartheid regime into a democratic regime also had its consequences; as can be noted from Fig. 4.3, the country recorded negative growth of about -2%. Something interesting is that in comparison of the two regimes, the data show that economic growth was much more stable in the post-apartheid regime, and this is depicted by a small growth fluctuation between the two periods.

As can be noted, the country went over 12 years without going through a negative growth until the global financial crisis which also seemed to have low impact. Finally, the country was also hit by the Covid-19 global pandemic with severe impacts, decreasing GDP growth to about -6%.

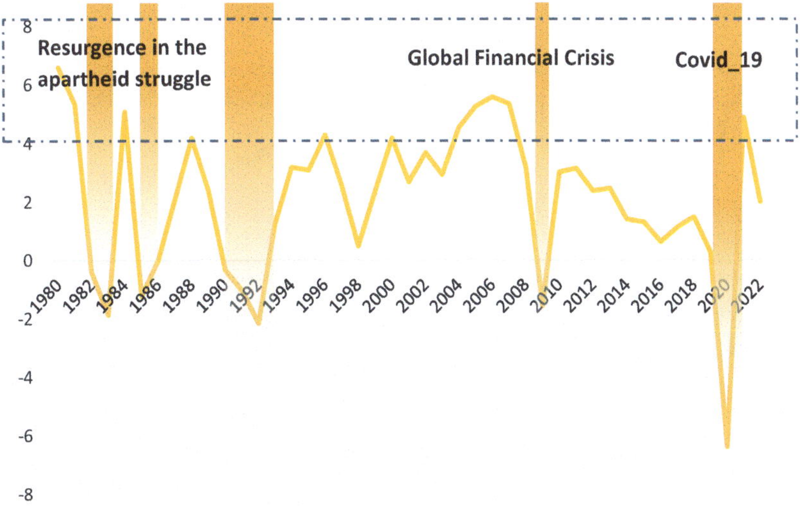

Fig. 4.3 South Africa GDP growth. (Source: Authors' own calculations based on the WDI data)

Transmission Mechanisms

As Figs. 4.4 and 4.5 depict the years that the country witnessed negative growth, was also possible to note that both consumption and private investment registered a huge decline, suggesting that the entire economy was harshly hit by the shock which culminated with low consumption as well as low investment thus a decline in the overall income level. Along the same lines, as the country's growth shrank, the production of export goods followed the same trend (see Fig. 4.6). Although this can appear to be one of the transmission mechanisms, the study also acknowledges that this can also occur as a result of a decrease in investment; therefore, consumption and investment continue to be considered the major transmission mechanisms, while government spending served as a shock absorber throughout the period.

Economic Diversification

Like Brazil and Malaysia, South Africa is also a diversified economy ahead of Nigeria. As indicated in Fig. 4.7, its export diversification basket includes the Platinum (18.02%), Gold (9.76%), Iron ores and concentrates (7.07%), Coal (3.41%), Cars (3.41%) and ICT (3.02%). The wide diversification is in part responsible for the country's resilience to shocks.

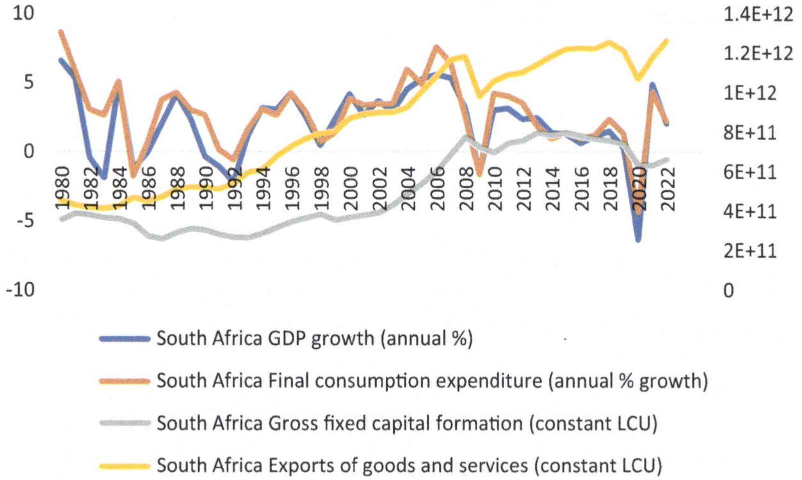

Fig. 4.4 South Africa GDP components. (Source: Authors' own calculations based on the WDI data)

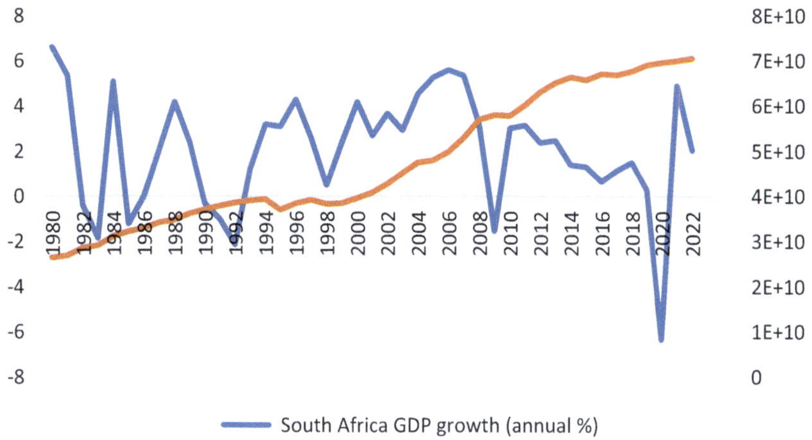

Fig. 4.5 South Africa GDP components. (Source: Authors' own calculations based on the WDI data)

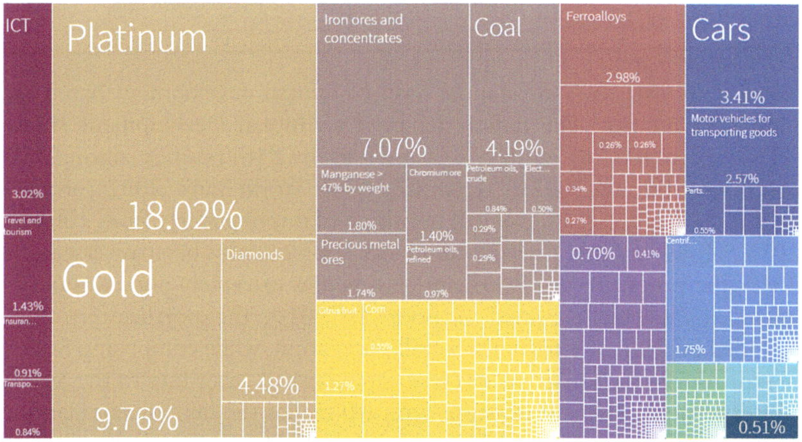

Fig. 4.6 Brazil GDP components. (Source: Authors' own calculations based on the WDI data)

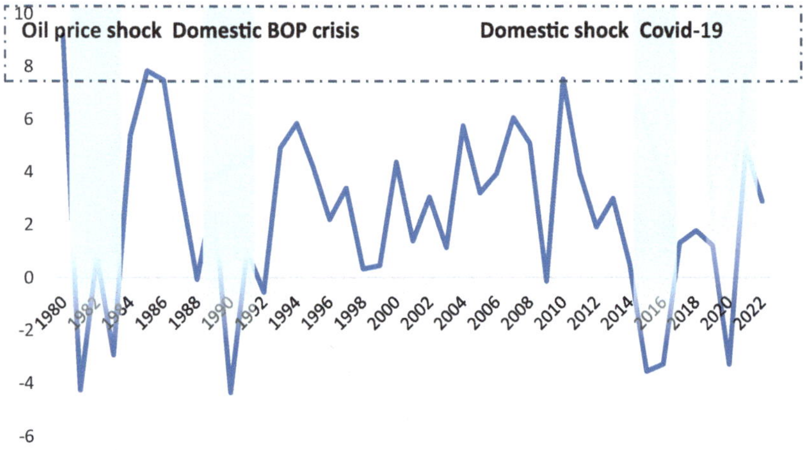

Fig. 4.7 South Africa export diversification as % of the total export. (Source: Authors' own calculations based on the Harvard Growth lab data)

The Case of Brazil

Brazil demonstrates a substantial level of human development based on significant metrics. The nation achieved a Human Development Index (HDI) score of 0.765 in 2019, placing it at the 84th position among 189 countries (Stiftung, 2022b). According to the World Bank (2022), around 24.2 million individuals in Brazil transitioned out of poverty from 2004 to 2015. However, this positive trend has subsequently been reversed. In 2019, the proportion of Brazilians classified as extremely poor was 6.5%, while 24.7% were classified as poor. In 2019, the northeastern area included 27.2% of the nation's overall population, while comprising 56.8% of individuals categorised as severely impoverished according to the $1.90 PPP threshold. The southeastern area, which has the highest population, comprised between 20% and 27% of the impoverished population, depending on the poverty definition employed.

The brief country overview gives a sense of what can be expected when analysing the country's resilience to shocks. Figure 4.8 shows that Brazil recorded negative growth between 1980 and 1984. This is due to a global shock of an increase in the international oil price (Brinca & Costa-Filho, 2021). An increase in the oil price increased production costs of goods and services which in turn reduced the private consumption and thus

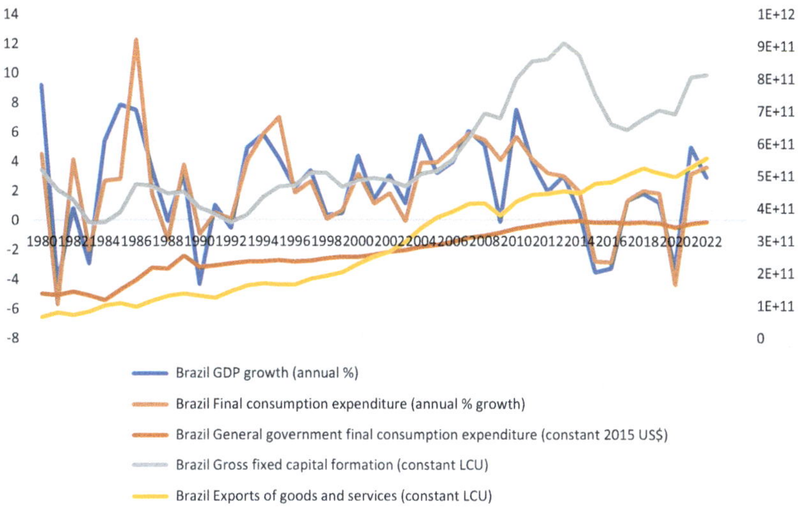

Fig. 4.8 Brazilian GDP growth. (Source: Authors' own calculations based on the WDI data)

aggregate demand. Moreso, the country also recorded a negative growth in 1991 triggered by the domestic Balance of Payment (BOP) shock (Brinca & Costa-Filho, 2021), 2016–2018 domestic shock (Azzoni & Castro, 2023) and 2020–2021, and this is due to the global Covid-19 pandemic. This indicates that, despite the country's low growth rates, it is resilient to shocks compared to other countries. However, this resilience is not sustainable as it has been fluctuating over time.

Transmission Mechanisms

To understand how different shocks in Brazil were transmitted into the overall economic growth, the study analyses GDP growth along with its key determinants, such as consumption, government spending, investment and exports, these indicators are selected based on the national identity account (see Blanchard et al., 2015). Figure 4.9 shows that while other GDP determinants (consumption, government spending, investment and exports) were increasing, consumption seemed to follow the GDP growth, this may be due to the fact that on average private consumption in Brazil accounts for 62.7% in the overall GDP (CEIC, 2023).

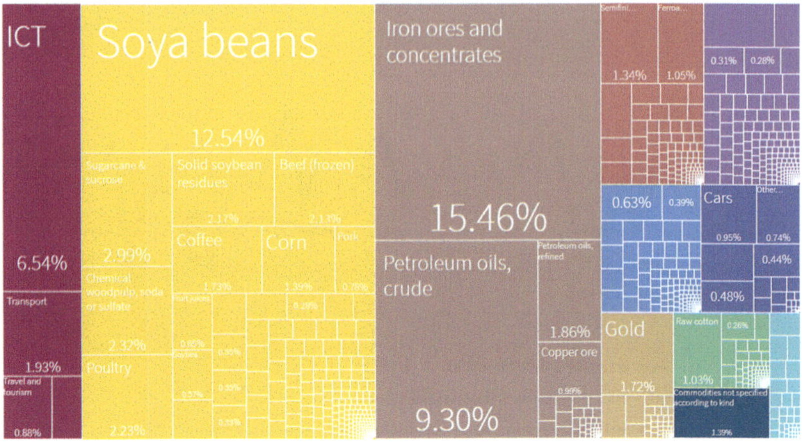

Fig. 4.9 Brazilian export diversification. (Source: Authors' own calculations based on the Harvard Growth lab data)

For example, from Fig. 4.9, it is noticeable that when the international oil price shock hit in 1980, as a production factor, it led to an increase in production cost causing a disruption in the supply hence triggering an increase in the goods prices which later culminated with a decrease in demand of goods. In addition, due to the fiscal constraints, government spending also shrunk a bit around the same period which could also have transmitted the impact of the shocks into the overall economy. Along the same lines, similar trends occurred around 1990–1991 with the surge of the domestic BOP shock. Something interesting is that in this period, apart from consumption and government spending, the export of goods and services also witnessed its trend decreasing a little bit as a response to the shock which in turn resulted in low aggregate demand in Brazil. Furthermore, investment also played a significant role in transmitting the impact of the shock in 2015–2016. For instance, although private consumption underperformed as usual, private investment also recorded a steep drop since the beginning of the decade, this definitely exacerbated the impact of the shock while export might have served as an absorber. Finally, the data also show that there is no clear indication of the transmission component in response to the Covid-19 shock because all the indicators had their portion in the transmission mechanisms. This can heavily be attributed to the lockdown measures adopted by different countries (including Brazil) that constrained different economic agents from doing their economic activities.

Overall, although all other GDP components play a role in transmitting the shocks, the big chunk can be attributed to private consumption due to this accounting for more than half in the GDP components, following the government spending and investment, while export in most of the cases served as a shock absorber.

Economic Diversification

To further access the transmission mechanism, it is believed that the lack of diversification makes the country vulnerable to shocks (World Bank, 2017). Therefore, below we try analysing the extent to which Brazilian economy is diversified to tackle or pledge itself against commodity price volatility. Figure 4.9 from the Harvard Growth lab shows that Brazil is a diversified economy, with commodities such as iron ores and concentrates, soya beans, petroleum oil crude and ICT accounting for 15.46%, 12.54%, 9.30% and 6.54% of the total country exports, respectively. This may justify why Brazil is resilient to shocks as it relies on different commodities, hence less vulnerable to oil price fluctuation.

The Case of Malaysia

The 2018 data update of Human Development Indices and Indicators from the UNDP reveals that key indicators indicate a significantly elevated level of human development. The nation's ranking in the UNDP's 2020 Human Development Index was 0.810, indicating progress in comparison to prior years (Stiftung, 2022a). Malaysia's score falls below the mean of 0.898 for countries in the highly developed category but surpasses the mean of 0.747 for the East Asia and Pacific area. Malaysia was ranked 62nd in the overall ranking. From 1990 to 2019, Malaysia experienced a 26% growth in its HDI score, rising from 0.643 to 0.810 (Stiftung, 2022a). According to the UNDP, the average Malaysian today has a life expectancy that is 5.5 years longer than in 1990, with a current life expectancy at birth of 76.2 years.

Based on World Bank data from 2015, the proportion of the population in Malaysia living on less than $3.20 per day, adjusted for purchasing power parity (PPP) at 2011 international prices, is 0.2%. Based on statistics from 2015, Malaysia experienced a substantial reduction in inequality during the past ten years, with a value of 41.0. When analysing that hit Malaysia, it is noted that this also followed a similar trend as that of Brazil, the difference is that apart from the 1980 global commodity shock (Athukorala, 2010), Malaysia also registered one in the period between 1998 and 2000, associated with the Asian Financial Crisis, the 2008–2009 Global Financial Crisis (Athukorala, 2010), and lastly in the period between 2020 and 2021, explained by the Covid-19 shock (see Fig. 4.10). Different from Brazil, Malaysia is pretty much resilient although having similar shocks, this presents low fluctuations compared to Brazil.

Transmission Mechanisms

Likewise Brazil, we also analysed the most transmission mechanisms of the shocks into the overall economy and the results are shown in Fig. 4.11. As can be noted, as a transmission mechanism consumption also plays a big role in channelling the impact of the shock into the overall economy while on the other hand exports are absorb the shock or at mitigate it. In more details, private consumptions fell right before GDP growth reaching negative rates in 1985 and 1998/9, respectively (see also Nabir, 2009), this might be due to the fact that private consumption accounts on average 48% in the total GDP (CEIC, 2023). While export and government spending in both crises served as absorbers, investment seemed to have transmitted the 1998/9 shock into the overall economy. Furthermore, different from the previous two shocks, during the global financial crisis

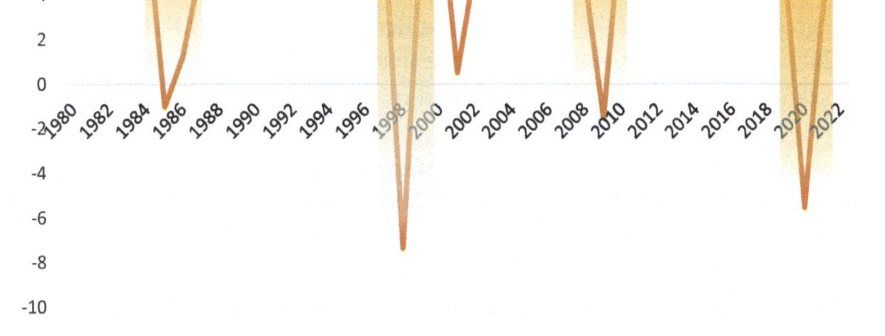

Fig. 4.10 Malaysia growth rate. (Source: Authors' own calculations based on the WDI data)

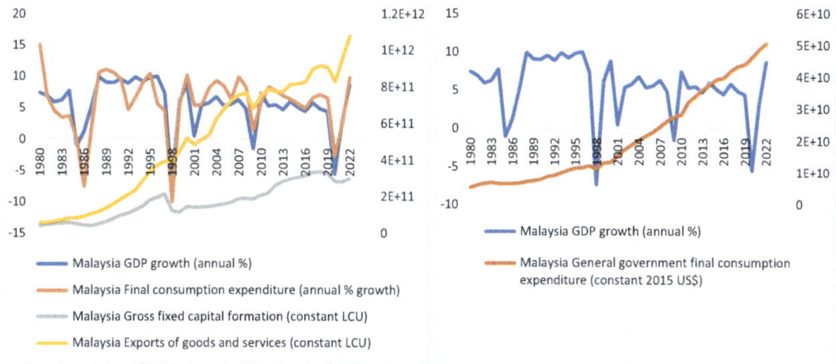

Fig. 4.11 Malaysia's GDP components. (Source: Authors' own calculations based on the WDI data)

shock, all the GDP components seem not to have resisted to the crisis to the extent that they transmitted it into the overall economy while increasing government spending was used to contain the shock. Moreso, similar trends occurred during the Covid-19 pandemic.

Economic Diversification

Malaysian exports are well and much more diversified when compared to those of Brazil. While Brazil has about three commodities (iron ores and concentrates, soya beans, petroleum oil crude and ICT), Malaysia appears to have a share (although small) in more commodities, for example: electronic integrated circuits (22.03%); petroleum oils, refined (6.79%); ICT (4.19); palm and oil (3.84%); vulcanised rubber article of apparel (3.69%) and petroleum gases (3.02%) (see Fig. 4.12). Compared to Brazil and South Africa, Malaysia maybe resilient to shocks as it is able to pledge itself against price volatilities of a certain commodity, this can also be confirmed from the fact that the country did not register a negative growth in the period between 1980 and 1985 as a result of the hike of the international oil price, in fact, this worked in favour for the country.

The Case of Nigeria

According to the 2018 statistic, key indicators provided by the UNDP indicate a very high degree of human development. Key indicators continue to indicate a poor state of development, which significantly limits

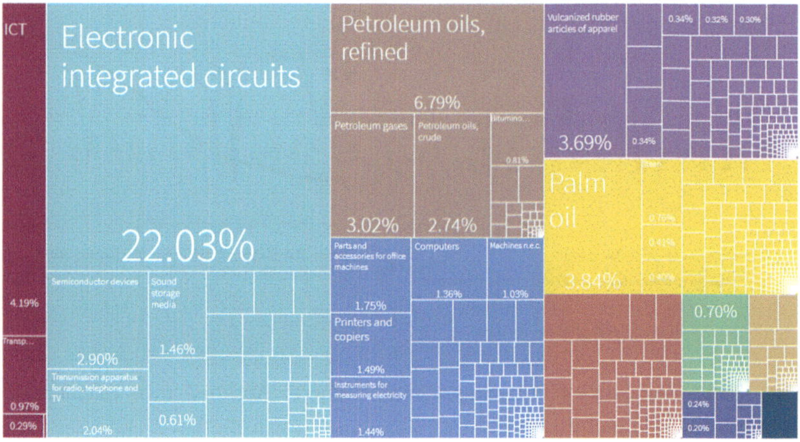

Fig. 4.12 Malaysia export diversification as % of the total export. (Source: Author's own calculations based on the Harvard Growth lab data)

personal freedom. Nigeria is rated 161st out of 189 nations due to its extremely low 2020 HDI score of 0.539. Poverty contributes to broad and pervasive social exclusion (Stiftung, 2022d). Over 200 million Nigerians, or over 60% of the population, make less than $2 per day. In 2018, it was calculated that inequality caused a loss in HDI of 35.4%. In the same year, the poverty rate was 70.1% and the Gini Index was 35.4. Nigeria was not different from the above-described countries, data show that the country also went through periods of great recession when it experienced negative growth (Fig. 4.13).

To give some examples, likewise Brazil and Malaysia, Nigeria also felt the consequences of the international oil price hike in the periods between 1980 and 1982 (Igberaese, 2013). This is due to the fact that commodity price shocks can have significant and enduring effects, causing abrupt fluctuations in fiscal and external positions, which frequently result in diminished and unpredictable growth performance (Al-Sadiq et al., 2021).

Moreso, the country registered once more a negative growth between 1994 and 1996, this negative growth can be attributed mostly to a domestic shock. Although the global financial crisis seems to have wiped out most economy's growth, Nigeria was resilient, in fact it even registered about 8% of growth. Yet, right before the Covid-19 pandemic, it was hit

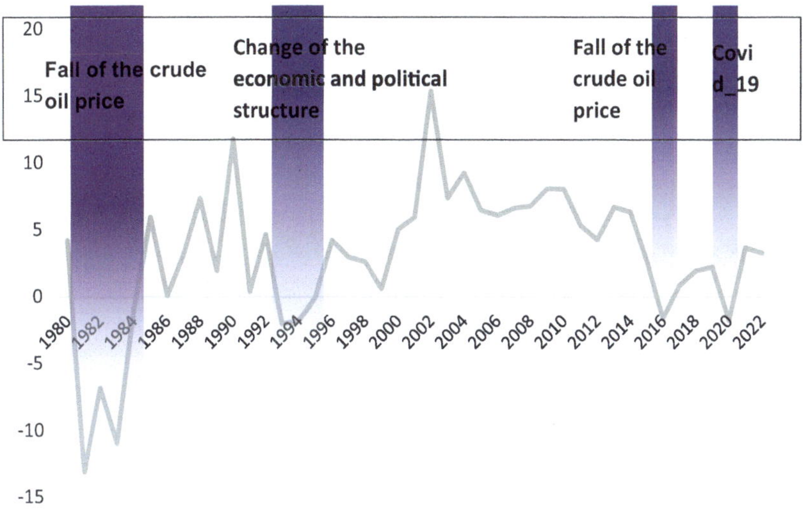

Fig. 4.13 Nigeria's growth rate. (Source: Authors' own calculations based on the WDI data)

by a domestic shock between 2016 and 2017 (Ministry of budget and national planning, 2017) and lastly the pandemic crisis.

Transmission Mechanisms

Nigeria, although its growth was negative only in four periods, over the analysed period looks so unstable. This may suggest a high vulnerability to shocks and almost all the GDP components appear to be transmission channels. As can be seen from Figs. 4.14 and 4.15, GDP components (consumption, investment, government spending and exports) are pretty much volatile and unpredictable but evidence shows that all of them except government spending are transmission channels to the entire economy only for the period of 2016 that government spending also transmitted the shock.

Economic Diversification

Different from Brazil, Malaysia and South Africa, Nigeria is less diversified. Figure 4.16 gives a clear picture of the lack of Nigerian's export diversification. The country heavily relies on petroleum oils, crude and petroleum gases with 69.28% and 12.48%, respectively. The remaining share is concentrated on transport, ICT, special functions vessels and cocoa beans.

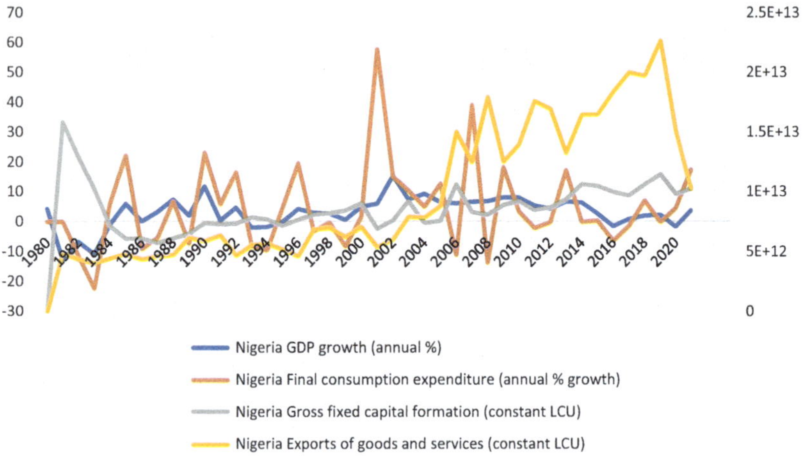

Fig. 4.14 Nigeria GDP components. (Source: Authors' own calculations based on the WDI data)

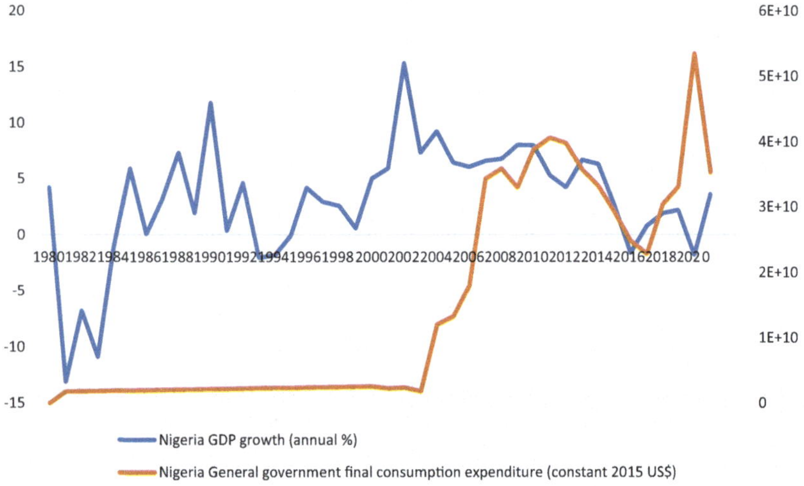

Fig. 4.15 Nigeria GDP components. (Source: Authors' own calculations based on the WDI data)

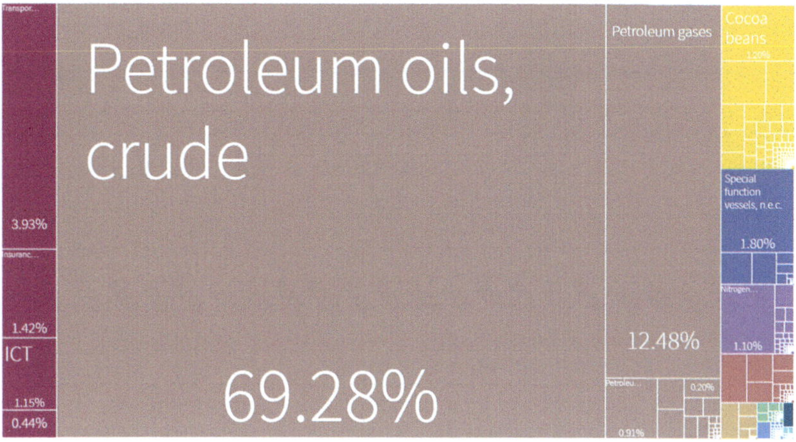

Fig. 4.16 Nigeria's export diversification as % of the total export. (Source: Authors' own calculations based on the Harvard Growth lab data)

The Case of Poland

In Poland, absolute poverty has decreased, but not solely due to the government's welfare policies. Moreover, 14.8% of the population at risk of poverty or social exclusion represents a decrease of 2.5 percentage points from 2016. The 2019 Gini coefficient of 28.5 indicates a high degree of equality. In addition, the HDI index (0.880 in 2019) has improved marginally compared to prior years (Stiftung, 2022e). Unemployed youth, single mothers, and those with special needs continue to be disproportionately vulnerable to poverty. Overall, the macroeconomic outlooks favour the country's ability to resist against shocks, either exogenous or endogenous. This can be attested from Fig. 4.17, where Poland seems to have been a different story compared to its counterparts (Piatkowski, 2018). Contrary to Brazil, Malaysia, Nigeria and South Africa, this appear to be much more resistant. When analysing its growth rate trend, one can see that the country recovered from a deep recession of about -7% in 1992 and was able to bounce back to its original steady state of about 7% in 1995. Although it also recorded some fluctuation, it never went back to negative growth rates, until the global Covid-19 pandemic consequences in 2020 which was at the end able to bounce back, recording a growth rate of about 6.8% in 2021.

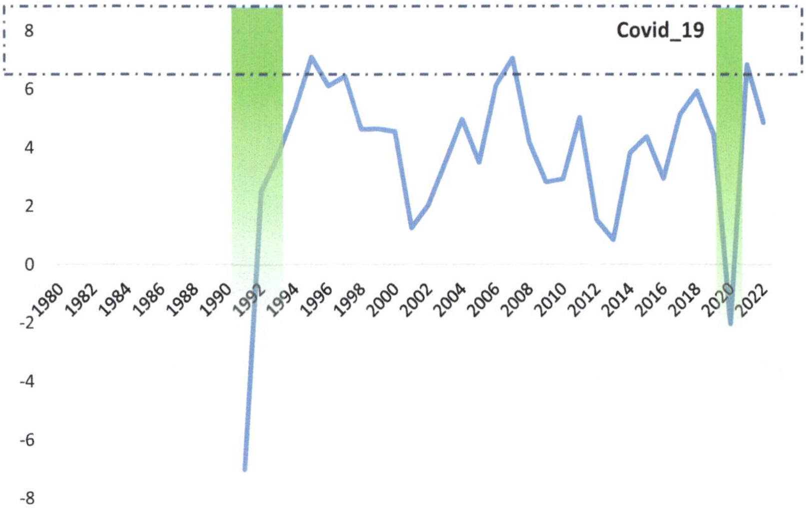

Fig. 4.17 Poland's growth rate. (Source: Authors' own calculations based on the WDI data)

Transmission Mechanisms

Poland is a special case, while in Brazil, Malaysia, Nigeria and South Africa, different GDP components heavenly transmitted the shocks into the overall economy, in Poland they all almost served as shock absorbers. Nevertheless, in 2020, private consumption seems to have hindered growth, transmitting therefore the shock into the overall economy but soon after it was able to bounce back to its normal growth, having grown in about 6% around 2021. In the same period, investment, exports and government spending continued exhibiting positive trend (Figs. 4.18 and 4.19).

Economic Diversification

Something surprising is that different from Brazil and South Africa, Poland is less diversified. For example, from Fig. 4.20 while the former countries have at least four commodities in their export baskets, Poland relies more on the ICT, transport and parts of motor vehicles, counting for 11.48%,

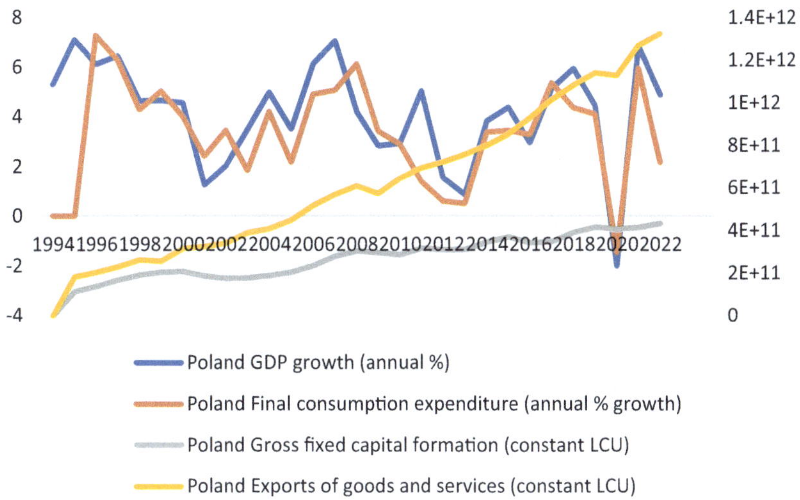

Fig. 4.18 Poland GDP components. (Source: Authors' own calculations based on the WDI data)

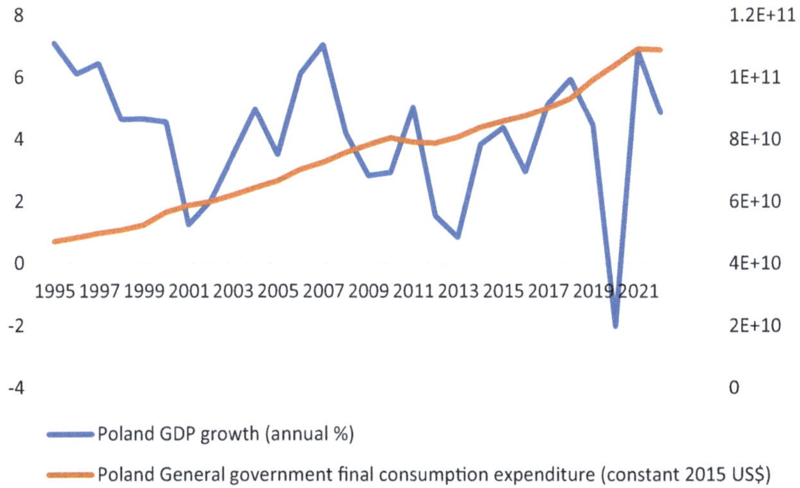

Fig. 4.19 Poland GDP components. (Source: Authors' own calculations based on the WDI data)

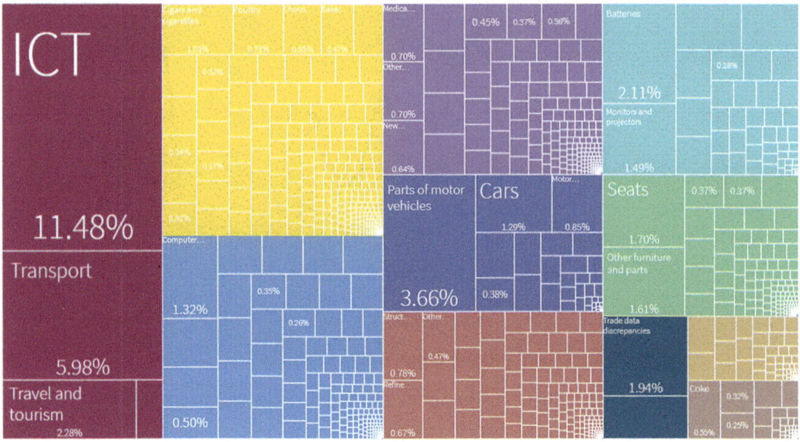

Fig. 4.20 Poland export diversification as % of the total export. (Source: Authors' own calculations based on the Harvard Growth lab data)

5.98% and 3.66%, respectively. Furthermore, when comparing Poland to its counterparts, it is also noticeable that this is not a natural resource-dependent country but service-oriented export country. This may be playing a big role as this is not vulnerable to different commodity price shocks.

Selected Macroeconomic Indicators (Resilience or Vulnerability Indicators)

Assuming that building resilience may also be determinant by the stance of other macroeconomic variables, the chapter goes a step further and compares the performance of different macroeconomic indicators such as debt service, debt stock (short term and external), real interest rate, real effective exchange rate and remittances received.

Debt Service

To start, Fig. 4.21 compares the total debt service across three countries[2] (Brazil, Nigeria and South Africa) and interesting take away allude to the fact that South African debt servicing was quite low compared to Brazil and high to Nigeria until 2012. From then on, there hasn't been a wide difference between Brazil and South Africa, while a wide difference

[2] Poland and Malaysia don't have data for debt service.

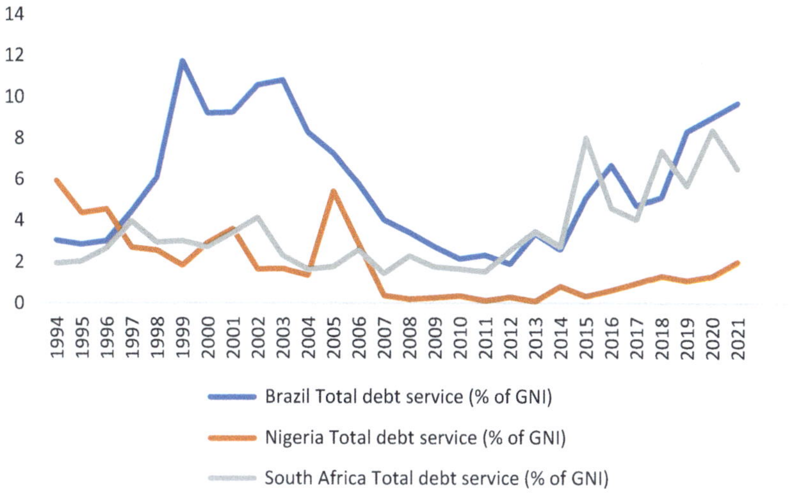

Fig. 4.21 Debt service. (Source: Authors' own calculations based on the WDI data)

continues compared to Nigeria. This contributes positively to building resilience to shocks because debt servicing transmits confidence towards investors and budget support counterparts, thus allowing the country more fiscal space for public expenditure both on goods and services and on investment.

Contrary to South Africa, Nigeria's debt servicing has been quite low, turning the country into a debt distress in the long term and lowering the investors' confidence as well as narrowing its fiscal space. Furthermore, regarding the short-term debts, South Africa appears to champion the trend as shown in Fig. 4.22. Likewise domestic debt, holding short-term debts maybe a leading indicator to vulnerability compared to debts with long-term maturity.

Short-Term Debt

The debt's maturity structure is crucial as it can impact the probability of a rollover problem. Short-term debt, which refers to debt that matures within a year, exposes borrowers to the danger of having to renegotiate the conditions of financing in a way that is disadvantageous to them. This can occur due to self-fulfilling runs, a decline in borrowers' economic

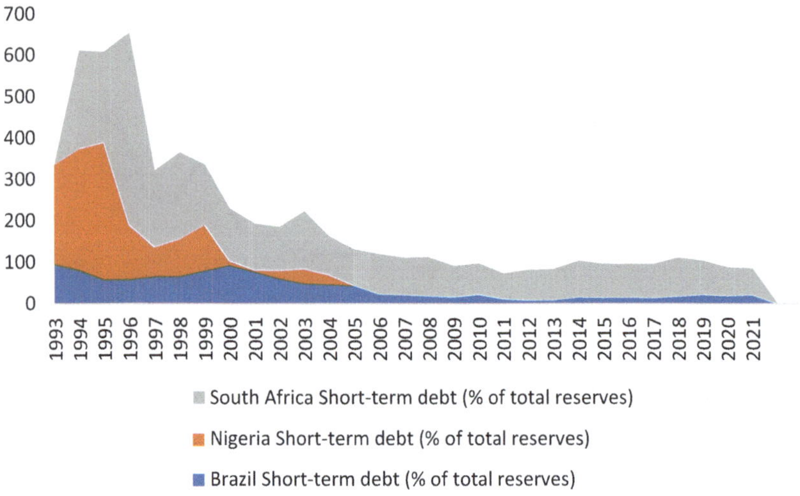

Fig. 4.22 Short-term debt. (Source: Authors' own calculations based on the WDI data)

prospects or global causes. Research has consistently demonstrated that having high levels of short-term debt is linked to a greater likelihood of experiencing crises. This has been supported by numerous studies conducted by scholars such as Brunnermeier (2009), Eichengreen and Hausmann (1999), Gourinchas and Maurice (2012), Lane and Milesi-Ferretti (2012), Raddatz (2010), Rodrik and Velasco (1999), Rose and Spiegel (2011) and Tirole (2003). This makes it important to assess the level of the short-term debt in the covered countries to ensure that they are resilient to shocks. Furthermore, as Fig. 4.22 depicts, South Africa holds more short-term debt compared to their counterparts Nigeria and Brazil. While on the other hand, Brazil seems the one holding less short-term debts. This may be the source of resilience to shocks of this country.

Something interesting is that although South Africa (see Fig. 4.22) holds more short-term debt compared to its counterparts, it is also noticeable that it also holds more of external debt. This is an advantage to the country as normally relying on domestic debt as a financing instrument maybe costly. To make things worse, contracting domestic debt in a context of South Africa that is characterised by low revenue collection and

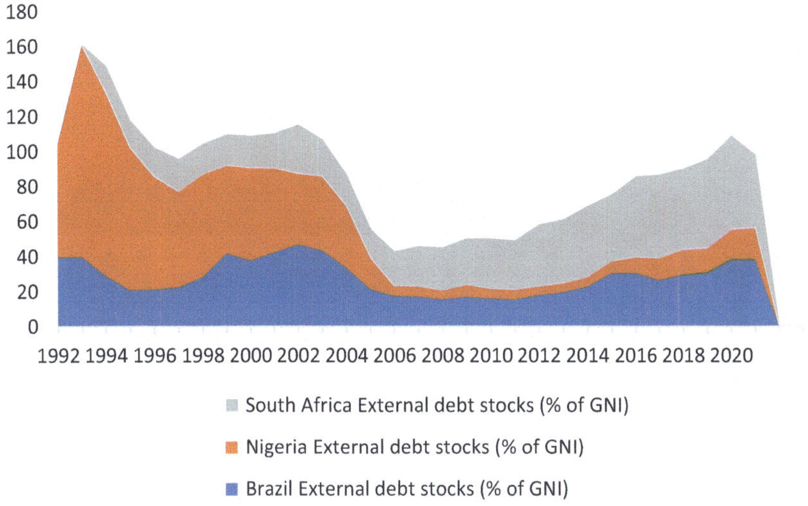

Fig. 4.23 External debt stock. (Source: Authors' own calculations based on the WDI data)

high public spending may trigger severe consequences to the fiscal and increase the likelihood of the rollover of debt distress. Below South Africa there is Nigeria and Brazil (Fig. 4.23).

According to Adrian et al. (2022), to stop inflationary pressures from entrenching, central banks with chronically high inflation tend to tighten monetary policy faster. Additionally, advanced and emerging economies confront increased risks and vulnerabilities across industries and geographies. Furthermore, with rising debt, governments, insurers, pension funds, hedge funds and mutual funds are more vulnerable. Rising rates affect countries with high debt especially domestic. This may respond how some countries are highly vulnerable to shocks, in the countries that are covered by the study, we find that countries such as Malaysia and South Africa have high interest rates compared to Brazil and Nigeria (Fig. 4.24).

4.2.4 *Impulse Response Analysis*

This section employs Impulse Response Functions (IRF), an econometric approach that allows for the possibility to unravel the dynamic response of certain variables to shocks. Specifically the IRF will shed light on the

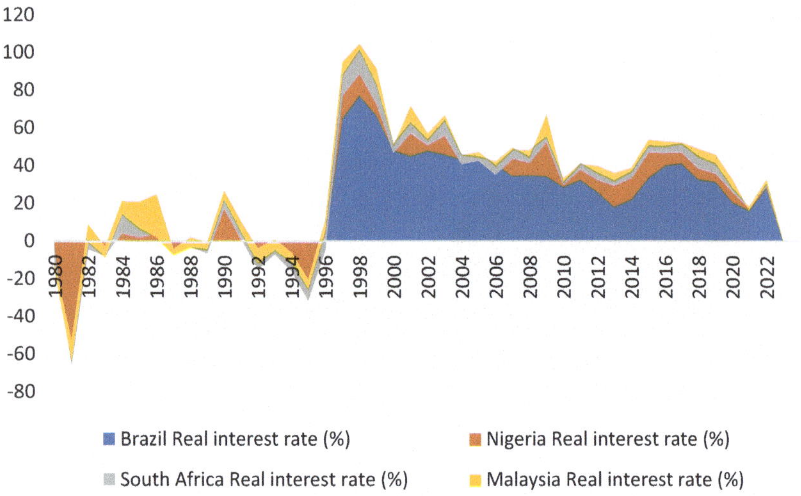

Fig. 4.24 Real interest rate. (Source: Authors' own calculations based on the WDI data)

nuanced response of economic activity and other variables, thus broadening our knowledge concerning the resilience displayed by emerging economies.

A closer look at Fig. 4.25 reveals that GDP growth responds negatively to electricity consumption shocks, signifying that the intensifications of electricity usage bring about a persistent reduction in growth. A plausible explanation of this relationship can be attributed to load shedding or power outages in some of the countries (such as South Africa) in the sample. Figure 4.25 also indicates that when there are sudden and significant changes or shocks in a country's exports, these events have a notable positive effect on the country's economic growth, encompassing the immediate (first to fourth quarters) and the intermediate term (spanning one, two, three and four years into the future). Similarly, the data suggests that economic growth exhibits a parallel response to significant fluctuations in government consumption.

Remittances shows a gradual influence in the first and second period but then progressively becomes more prominent in the succeeding periods, signifying that the effect of remittances on economic growth may build up over time. Economic growth responds positively to the change in

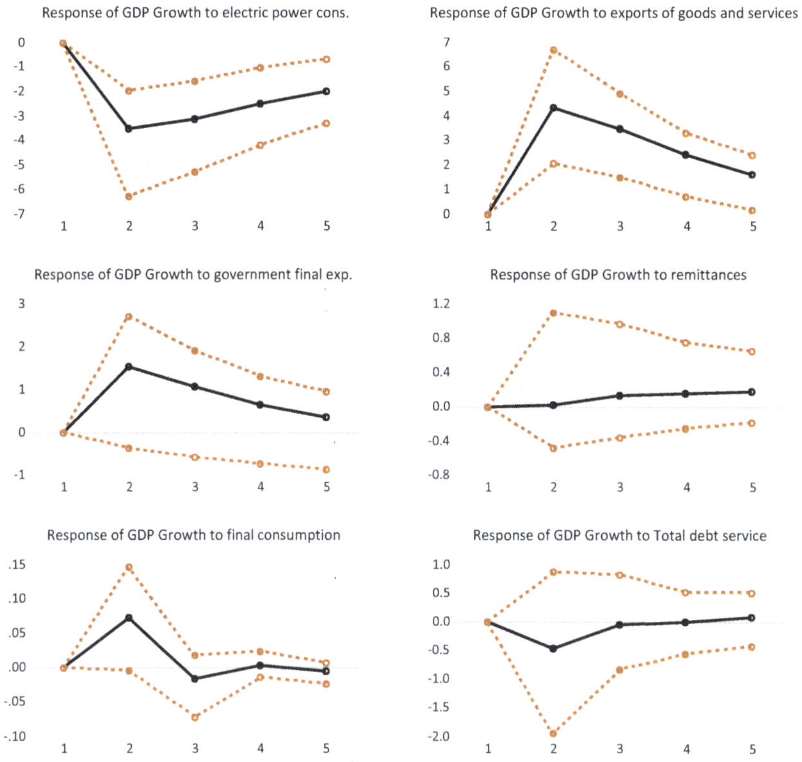

Fig. 4.25 Impulse response functions (IRF) for five periods

final consumption shock. The effect of consumption is quite momentous during the first three periods after the shock. Oppositely, from the fourth period forward, the effect plateaus and economic growth remains at a constant level. Unsurprisingly, total debt presents negative and significant influence on economic growth. The impact of total debt on growth appears to be more substantial during period one to three after the debt shock. Yet, from the fourth period forward, the effect plateaus, demonstrating that the opening negative response of economic growth to increased debt is persistent but not getting worse.

To enhance the validity and the breadth of our results, we extended the analysis to a ten-year period, in addition to the initial five-year assessment (Fig. 4.26).

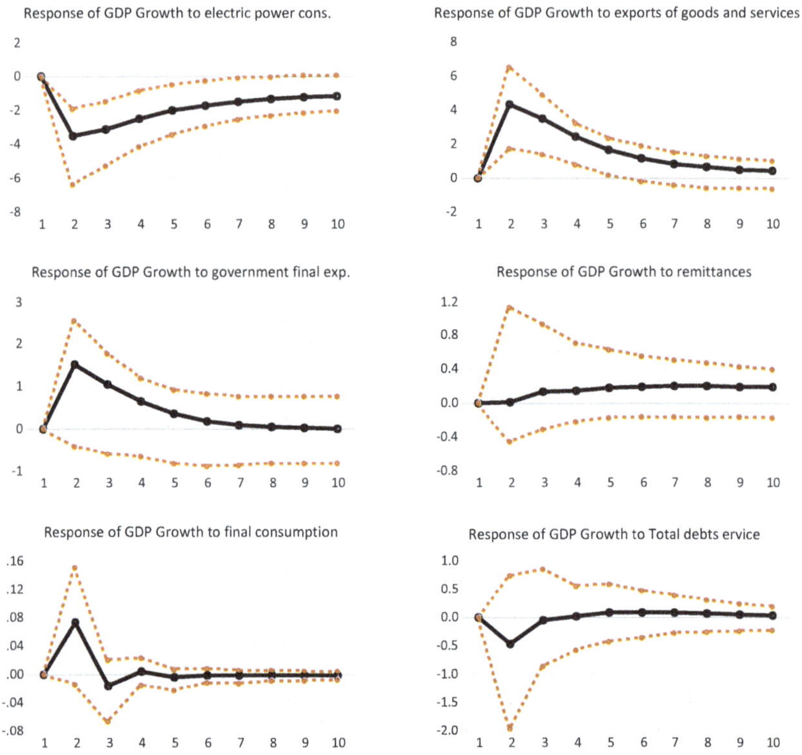

Fig. 4.26 Impulse response functions (IRF) for ten periods

Perhaps reassuringly, the conclusions based on the extended ten-year analysis closely mirror those based on the five-year assessment. For example, electricity consumption shocks continue to display a constant negative effect on growth, conceivably related to power outages. Correspondingly, the positive effect of export shocks on growth continue to hold in this analysis, covering both short-term and medium-term periods. Government consumption fluctuations exhibit a parallel influence on economic growth. Remittances show a consistent early effect, progressively firming over time, demonstrating its increasing influence on economic growth. Increased final consumption maintains its positive effect, maxing out in the first three periods but successively plateauing. Total debt remains negatively related to economic growth during the first three periods, with its impact becoming stable at a lower level from the fourth period forward, implying that the adverse effects of higher debt persist but do not worsen over time.

4.3 Conclusion

The chapter examined the macroeconomic resilience to shocks of South Africa and the selected emerging economies that South Africa can be compared with. The chapter also employed descriptive statistics and Impulse Response Functions (IRFs) for a comprehensive analysis, revealing the evolving impact of economic shocks over time. The analysis shows that South Africa has a somewhat modest resilience, predominantly during the post-apartheid period. In other words, although South Africa confronted various shocks, it was accompanied by reasonably stable growth patterns, demonstrating its ability to cope with difficult economic conditions. Some of spending components such as government expenditure proved to be crucial in absorbing shocks. Perhaps fascinatingly, though Brazil and Nigeria displayed variable resilience, Poland and Malaysia displayed notable resilience than their counterparts. What really stood out about Poland was that it bounced back from a shock and continued on a positive growth trajectory for a lengthy period. Similarly, Malaysia, displayed lower fluctuations in economic growth, thereby demonstrating ability to cope with shocks.

The chapter confirms that there are challenges with the South African economy that require attention. Among the key issues is the structure of the South African economy which should be improved if the South African economy is to respond better to shocks. Similarly, or of equal importance, is that there should be sound policies, at least a clear economic policy, to ensure that the South African economy responds better to shocks.

The degree of transmission mechanisms also varied from one emerging economy to another, with some countries such as South Africa, Brazil and Malaysia displaying consumption and private investment as important channels for transmitting the impact during economic shocks. Other spending components such as government spending seem to have mostly operated as a shock absorber for the emerging market economies in question. Conversely, Malaysia displayed greater resilience with more consistent economic stability. As regards Nigeria, various shocks brought about high instability in GDP components, with many of its components operating as transmission channels, with the exception of government spending. Perhaps uniquely, Poland portrayed a somewhat tenacious resilience marked by all expenditure components operating as shock absorbers. Though private consumption got in the way of growth in 2020, it got back very fast. The other components (i.e. investment, exports and government spending) persisted to show positive trends during this period.

With regard to Impulse Response Functions, the analysis finds that in the case of South Africa electricity consumption shocks have a negative impact on GDP, whereas export and government consumption shocks reveal a positive impact. Total debt has effects on growth, especially early on, stabilising later. As Chap. 2 demonstrated, exports and government consumption are critical for economic growth in the case of South Africa.

The countries that showed higher levels of resilience during the economic shocks, such as Poland and Malaysia, offer valuable lessons for other countries aiming to enhance their macroeconomic resilience. The main takeaways are that both Poland and Malaysia have diversified their markets, diminishing their dependence on a single sector. Needless to say, diversification can alleviate the effect of sector-specific shocks and boost economic stability. In addition, both Poland and Malaysia have established discipline in handling public finances, permitting them to react meticulously to economic shocks. In summary, the recommendations for enhancing macroeconomic resilience encompass diversifying economies and practicing fiscal prudence. As Chap. 3 argues, part of the challenge for South Africa has been the poor management of public finances. Efforts to improve the management of public finances are encouraging because that will also assist in the South African economy responding better to shocks.

References

Abdul, A., & John, B., Jaime, G., & Petia, T. (2015). The Rising Resilience of Emerging Market and Developing Economies. *World Development, Elsevier, 72*(C), 1–26.

Adrian, T., Vitor, G., & Francis, V. (2022). A Medium-Scale DSGE Model for the Integrated Policy Framework. IMF Working Paper WP/22/15, International Monetary Fund, Washington, DC.

Ahmed, S., & Murthy, R. (1994). ìMoney, Output and Real Business Cycles in a Small Open Economyî. *Canadian Journal of Economics, 27*(4), 982–993.

Al-Sadiq, A., Bejar, P., & Otker, I. (2021). *Commodity Shocks and Exchange Rate Regimes: Implications for the Caribbean Commodity Exporters.* IMF Working Paper, WP/21/104.

Ammer, J., Cai, F., & Scotti, C. (2011). Has International financial co-movement changed? Emerging markets in the 2007–2009 financial crisis. In J. A. Batten & P. G. Szilagy (Eds.), The impact of the global financial crisis on emerging financial markets (Contemporary studies in economic and financial analysis, volume 93) (pp. 231–253). Bingley, UK: Emerald Group Publishing Limited. https://doi.org/10.1108/S1569-3759(2011)0000093003

Athukorala, P. (2010). *Malaysian Economy in Three Crises.* Working Paper in Trade and Development No. 2010/12.

Azzoni, C. R., & Castro, G. H. L. (2023). *Economic Crises and Regional Disparities in Brazil in the XXI Century.* NEREUS.

Bila, S., & Biyase, M. (2023). Determinants of Subjective Poverty in Rural and Urban Areas of South Africa. *Journal of Economic Cooperation and Development, 44*(1), 25–55.

Blanchard, O., Cerutti, E., Summers, L. (2015). *Inflation and Activity – Two Explorations and their Monetary Policy Implications.* IMF WP/15/230.

Brada, J. C., Gajewski, P., & Kutan, A. M. (2021). Economic Resiliency and Recovery, Lessons from the Financial Crisis for the COVID-19 Pandemic: A Regional Perspective from Central and Eastern Europe. *International Review of Financial Analysis, 74*(C), 1–12. https://doi.org/10.1016/j.irfa.2021.101658

Brinca, P., & Costa-Filho, J. (2021). *Economic Depression in Brazil: The 2014–2016 Fall.* MPRA Paper No. 107298, Posted 21 April 2021 07:02 UTC.

Brunnermeier, M. K. (2009). Deciphering the Liquidity and Credit Crunch 2007–2008. *Journal of Economic Perspectives, 23*(1), 77–100.

CEIC. (2023). Exclusive Access to Unparalleled Coverage of 200+ Economies Around the Globe.

Eichengreen, B., & Hausmann, R. (1999). Exchange Rates and Financial Fragility. NBER Working Paper No. w7418, Available at SSRN: https://ssrn.com/abstract=196288

Gourinchas, P. O., & Maurice, O. (2012). Stories of the Twentieth Century for the Twenty-First. *American Economic Journal: Macroeconomics, 4*(1), 226–265.

Hausmann, R., Michael, G., & Others. (1995). Overcoming Volatility in Latin America. In Inter-American Development Bank, Report on Economic and Social Progress in Latin America, 1995.

Hoffmaister, A. W., & Roldos, J. E. (1997). *Are Business Cycles Different in Asia and Latin America?* IMF working paper 97/9.

Igberaese, T. (2013). The Effect of Oil Dependency on Nigeria's Economic Growth. Iss, pp. 48.

Kose, M. A. (2002). Explaining Business Cycles in Small Open Economies How Much do World Prices Matter? *Journal of International Economics, 56*, 299–327.

Lagravinese, R. (2015). Economic Crisis and Rising Gaps North–South: Evidence from the Italian Regions. *Cambridge Journal of Regions, Economy and Society, 8*, 331–342. https://doi.org/10.1093/cjres/rsv006

Lane, P. R., Milesi-Ferretti, G. M. (2012). External Adjustment and the Global Crisis. *Journal of International Economics, 88*(2), 252–265.

Martin, R. (2012). Regional Economic Resilience, Hysteresis and Recessionary Shocks. *Journal of Economic Geography*, 1–43.

Mendoza, E. G. (1995). The Terms of Trade, the Real Exchange Rate, and Economic Fluctuations. *International Economic Review, 36*(1).

Ministry of Budget and National Planning. (2017). *Economic Recovery & Growth Plan 2017–2020.* Federal Republic of Nigeria.

Mirzaei, A., & Al-Khouri, R. S. F. (2016). The Resilience of Oil-Rich Economies to the Global Financial Crisis: Evidence from Kuwaiti Financial and Real Sectors. *Economic Systems, Elsevier, 40*(1), 93–108.

Piatkowski, M. (2018). Europe's Growth Champion: Insights from the Economic *Rise of Poland*, 1–364.

Raddatz, C. (2010). Credit Chains and Sectoral Comovement: Does the Use of Trade Credit Amplify Sectoral Shocks? *The Review of Economics and Statistics, MIT Press, 92*(4), 985–1003.

Rodrik, D., & Velasco, A. (1999). Short-term Capital Flows. Annual Bank Conference on Development Economics. World Bank, forthcoming.

Rose, A., Spiegel, M. (2011). Cross-country causes and consequences of the crisis: An update. *European Economic Review, 55*(3), 309–324.

Solow, R. M. (1956). A Contribution to the Theory of Economic Growth. *The Quarterly Journal of Economics, 70*(1), 65–94. https://doi.org/10.2307/1884513

Statistic South Africa. (2017). *Poverty Trends in South Africa an Examination of Absolute Poverty Between 2006 and 2015.*

Stiftung, B. (2022a). *Country Report—Malaysia.* Bertelsmann Stiftung.

Stiftung, B. (2022b). *Country Report—Brazil.* Bertelsmann Stiftung.

Stiftung, B. (2022c). *Country Report—South Africa.* Bertelsmann Stiftung.

Stiftung, B. (2022d). *Country Report—Nigeria.* Bertelsmann Stiftung.

Stiftung, B. (2022e). *Country Report—Poland.* Bertelsmann Stiftung.

Tirole, J. (2003). Inefficient Foreign Borrowing: A Dual- and Common-Agency Perspective. *American Economic Review, 93*(5), 1678–1702.

World Bank. (2017). Economic Diversification, Trade and Competitiveness Global Practice. https://www.google.com/url?sa=t&rct=j&q=&esrc=s&source=web&cd=&ved=2ahUKEwiiuZGO6JSCAxU4WkEAHeIOCf84ChAWegQICBAB&url=https%3A%2F%2Fieg.worldbankgroup.org%2Fsites%2Fdefault%2Ffiles%2FData%2Freports%2FEconomicDiversification.pdf&usg=AOvVaw2UAjk1knT8EdWKhI_JDDpK&opi=89978449

World Bank. (2022). *Brazil Poverty and Equity Assessment Looking ahead of two crises*. World Bank.

CHAPTER 5

Government and the Market: State-Owned Enterprises in South Africa

5.1 Introduction

Several economies have encountered new social and macroeconomic obstacles unique to contemporary economies since the global economic crisis (Baccaro & Pontusson, 2016). Among other things, these difficulties include high unemployment, high income inequality, high public debt, fragile economic growth and a growing reliance on the government for social assistance (Butler, 2017). As a result, more direct economic policy involvement by the government was required to stabilise the economy. It is strongly recommended that intervention levels be increased, particularly in emerging economies (Deeming & Smyth, 2015). According to Refera et al. (2016), while some economies recovered from the global financial crisis rather swiftly, others saw a rise in complicated issues as a result of the shock, and their rates of recovery have been sluggish ever since. South Africa's economy growth trajectory has not been favourable since the end of the Global Financial Crisis.

Given this, during the past few decades, economic policy in East Asian countries has garnered a great deal of attention. Strong and clear economic policies have been a major factor in the early 1960s and 1990s quick and sustained economic expansion of countries such as South Korea, Taiwan, Japan and Singapore (Burger, 2014). The governments in these countries made sure the post-crisis goals were achieved by focusing on

V. Gumede et al., *South African Economy*, African Histories and Modernities, https://doi.org/10.1007/978-3-031-54180-3_5

economic growth consistently, having a competent bureaucracy, enforcing state-led industrial strategy and encouraging growth driven by exports, to mention a few (Pekkanen, 2004; Burger, 2014). The interventionist role that states play in establishing flourishing economic circumstances has garnered significant interest as a result of this phenomena. The term 'developmental state' (Johnson, 1982; Woo-Cummings, 1999) refers to this particular form of intervention and success. This model has been researched and, in some situations, used in economies hoping to attain better growth and development. This specific developmental approach has produced failure in certain situations and success in others.

China is an example of a country where the developmental state was successful and where growth and progress were attained in line with the predetermined economic goals. For instance, the country was a major player in the world economy prior to the nineteenth century. However, it experienced hunger, social turmoil and military losses in the late nineteenth and early twentieth centuries (Maroufkhani, 2016). Due to this, China underwent market reforms that marked the beginnings of the developmental state and the transition from a centrally planned to a market-based economy. A couple of sectors were transformed, including state-owned businesses, the civil service and agriculture. With an annual growth rate of about 10%, this shift sped up social and economic development (Maroufkhani, 2016). On the other hand, a number of problems and circumstances prevented India from achieving the growth and development that was intended under the developmental model. The nation has aimed to rapidly industrialise its way to economic growth and prosperity since 1947 (Sinha, 2003). Affirmative action, corruption and social welfare expenditures are some of the factors contributing to the nation's sluggish development and economic progress, according to Singh and Srinivasan (2006). India's average growth rate since 1947 has been about 6.5%. The nation also has a high amount of public debt, with an estimated 68.91% of gross domestic product (GDP) in 2018 (International Monetary Fund, 2018).

5.2 Background

South Africa's economy has performed poorly over the last 20 years, averaging only 2.77% growth annually (StatsSA, 2018), owing to the country's own set of difficulties and complicated sociopolitical past. Similarly, South Africa is the most unequal country in the world, having seen a widening gap between the haves and have-nots since the end of apartheid in 1994, according to the World Bank (2020) report. This raises concerns about the efficacy of current economic policies and government intervention. Several policy strategies have been implemented since the inception of democracy to tackle the socio-economic issues. Despite the implementation of these economic strategies, the social and economic challenges are still enormous and may require a robust strategy to rescue the economy. At the moment, the main economic policy proposed as a means of enhancing economic development, lowering inequality and raising employment is the National Development Plan (NDP). To attain economic success, the NDP expresses its desire to shift the economy from high consumer spending to higher investment expenditure (National Planning Commission, 2012). Nevertheless, this goal is at odds with the way government spending is now allocated, with less money going into economic development in order to maintain the growing social dependence on the state (National Treasury, 2018).

In the midst of all this economic turmoil, the South African government still maintains its position to directly intervene in the economy as an employer, a producer and a consumer. Government intervention as a producer intensified after the Second World War when the government implemented a protectionist style to grow and develop the economy (Feinstein, 2005). Since the advent of democracy, the goal of State-Owned Enterprises (SOEs) has been enlarged to serve the whole population in the democratic South Africa, regardless of race. This is contrary to their mandate during apartheid dispensation, when SOEs services were racially skewed to service the white minority population (Ibid.). However, SOEs have faced several difficulties, one of them being the lack of a well-defined development mission. These difficulties have been exacerbated and increased by state capture.[1] While the SOEs are crucial in bolstering the capacity of States and play a pivotal role in advancing State-led innovation, their abysmal performance poses the risk of stifling the envisaged sustainable and inclusive economic growth for South Africa. In the recent period, State-Owned Enterprises have been characterised by mismanagement of financial resources, corruption and operational inefficiencies. The main objective of this chapter is to analyse the role of South Africa's government size in the form of SOEs on the economy. Other objectives include appraising the performance of the SOEs over the years.

[1] State capture is a type of systemic political corruption in which private interests significantly influence a state's decision-making processes to their own advantage.

5.3 History and Rationale of State-Owned Enterprises

After the end of the Second World War, the National Party was implementing import substitution policies. The government had a clear goal to directly intervene in the economy as a producer. The government embarked on establishing State-Owned Enterprises to produce and oversee the production of certain goods and services (Feinstein, 2005). In 1923, the government established the Electricity Supply Commission (known as Eskom) to produce electricity. In 1987, the company changed its name by combining the two acronyms, becoming Eskom. Five years after the establishment of ESCOM, the government established the South African Steel and Industrial Corporation (Iscor) which focused on the production of steel products and iron, to boost employment (Feinstein, 2005). At this pace, it was clear that the National Party-led government had a mission to advance Afrikaans empowerment (Gumede, 2015). Iscor closed in 1982 as a result of lower demand for steel products during a widespread recession which started in the late 1970s and lasted until early 1980s. In 1989 Iscor was privatised and it is currently owned by Arcelor-Mittal whose headquarters are in Luxembourg.

In 1934, a state-owned airline was established through the acquisition of Union Airways, a formerly privately owned company and first airline in South Africa. To overcome the overreliance of the economy on primary commodities, the government established the Industrial Development Corporation (IDC) in 1940 with an aim of aiding local businesses with affordable loans and acquisitions. This was to industrialise the economy through supporting the secondary sector. In 1950, the government founded SASOL (Suid-Afrikaanse Steenkool, Olie and Gas Maatskappy in Afrikaans and translates to South African Coal, Oil and Gas Corporation in English) to produce coal-based synthetic oil. In present days, SASOL produces a range of synthetic liquid fuels, chemicals and coal tar. During the 1970s oil shock, South Africa needed additional funds to finance massive new oil-from-coal plants to meet domestic demand (Sparks, 2016). To acquire additional funds, SASOL was privatised in 1979.

In 1968, another prominent SOE was established, the armaments Corporation of South Africa (ARMSCOR) responsible of producing armaments. ARMSCOR was established as a response by the apartheid government to the United Nations embargo against South Africa. In 1992, a subsidiary of ARMSCOR, Denel, was established to separate roles. Denel focused on the production of armaments, while ARMSCOR focused on procurement. In 1991, the Department of Posts and Telecommunications established Telkom, which would be responsible for providing telecommunication services. These SOEs achieved much desired outcomes to industrialise South Africa's economy. However, in recent years, SOEs have been in a dire condition, facing operational challenges, poor governance and financial challenges.

5.4 Performance of State-Owned Enterprises in the Post-1994 Era

The democratic government inherited SOEs that were established prior and in the apartheid era. In the democratic era, the performance of State-Owned Enterprises has been poor and even failing to meet financial obligations and rendering their primary services. With most of the SOEs that are under financial strain, the root cause is corruption and mismanagement of financial resources. Table 5.1 shows the few SOEs that have been surviving through government bailouts since 2008/2009 financial year. The most bailed out SOE is Eskom which accounted for over 50% of the bailouts amounting to R132.7 billion between 2008/2009 and 2019/2020. The power utility has been recording losses and unable to meet its financial obligations. The rolling blackouts have had a negative impact on the economy, particularly the small and medium enterprises that cannot afford alternative power. In addition to mismanagement of funds, another major contributor to the failure of SOEs was not increasing capacity of electricity, while the demand kept on rising.

The second most bailed out SOE is South African Airways (SAA) which recorded the total amount of R22.5 billion between 2008/09 financial year and 2019/2020 financial year. Denel, South African Airways Express and the South African Broadcasting Corporation recorded the total amounts of R2.2, R1.9 and 3.2, respectively. These bailouts have been straining the fiscus, increasing government debt and compromising service delivery. Despite the bailouts, the state of SOEs is still poor.

Privatising these entities will not be an easy way out of the situation. This is due to the political interference in the operations of SOEs. COSATU has been an outspoken critique of SOEs privatisation and restructuring that will result in job losses.

Table 5.1 Summary of recapitalisation and bailouts of SOEs, 2008–2020 (R)

Financial year	*Eskom*	*South African Airways*	*Denel*	*South African Airways Express*	*South African Broadcasting Corporation*	*Total*
2008/09	10.0	–	–	0.4	–	10.4
2009/10	30.0	1.5	–	–	–	31.5
2010/11	20.0	–	–	–	–	20.0
2011/12	–	–	–	–	–	–
2012/13	0.7	–	0.4	–	–	1.1
2013/14	–	–	–	–	–	–
2014/15		–	–	–	–	–
2015/16	23.0	–	–	–	–	23.0
2016/17	–	–	–	–	–	–
2017/18	–	10.0	–	–	–	10.0
2018/19	–	5.0	–	1.2	–	6.2
2019/2020	49.0	5.5	1.8	0.3	3.2	59.8
Total	132.7	22.0	2.2	1.9	3.2	162.0

Source: National Treasury, 2020

5.5 Financial, Governance and Operational Challenges at State-Owned Enterprises

State-Owned Enterprises have been facing major operational and governance challenges. Even when financial position was improving, operational challenges still persisted. An example is Eskom which improved its revenue in 2018, the entity still failed to meet demand and continued to implement rolling blackouts. The financial, operational and governance challenges of selected SOEs are discussed below.

5.5.1 Eskom

Eskom has had chronic operational and governance issues, even bigger than financial problems. During the late presidency of Thabo Mbeki, he admitted that the plans of the Reconstruction and Development Programme (RDP) to intensify electrifying houses would result in supply constraints. In 2008, President Mbeki stated that delaying increasing electricity generation was a wrong move (Lalk, 2012). The start of rolling blackouts in 2007 was going to be a long-lasting challenge. Although there have been an increment in the generating capacity through the construction of Medupi and Kusile power stations, the problem is still not resolved. The operational costs were increased enormously during the construction process of these power stations and were worsened by refurbishment of ageing infrastructure. The challenges were further exacerbated by the *state capture* which saw the migration of skilled workers.

Another operational challenge which weakened Eskom was the purchasing of the primary input required to generate electricity, coal. There have been findings that the contractors appointed to supply coal at Eskom charged exorbitant prices and there were tender irregularities in appointing them. In the midst of these operational challenges that have negatively impacted the financial position of Eskom, there are a number of municipalities that owe Eskom billions of rands. As of 2023, a total of 67 municipalities across the country owed Eskom collectively R56,7 billion rand. This is accompanied by non-paying residents in Soweto and illegal connectors who strain the grid (United Nations Economic Commission for Africa, 2021). Since the beginning of Eskom woes, there have been leadership changes in the hope to turnaround the entity. The recent CEO to resign Mr. Andrew de Ruyter was vocal about many irregularities in the operations of the entity. However, during his tenure as CEO, the country experienced the worst rolling blackouts.

There have been proposals to diversify power generation and branch to renewable energy. During the presidency of Jacob Zuma, there were proposals to move from coal-generated power to nuclear energy. However, that did not receive much support as it would be too costly and was abandoned.

5.5.2 Transnet

The challenges of Transnet started when the freight market was deregulated. This saw the shrinkage of rail transportation as road transport was preferred instead. Prior to the deregulation, it was required that to transport goods longer than 400 kilometres, a rail transport should be used. In present days however, large trucks have become the primary of transport, while even mined products such as coal are transported by tipper trucks. In the post-pandemic period, the passenger services declined significantly, while the infrastructure is constantly vandalised.

Transnet have faced major governance challenges, including irregular awarding of tenders. The Special Investigation Unit (SIU) has found irregularities in tender awarding process, where even officials working in the supply chain unit have been receiving 'kickbacks' to influencing the awarding of tenders. In the State Capture Report, it was found that China South Rail was irregularly appointed, violating the supply chain regulations of the entity.

5.5.3 *South African Airways*

South African Airways, like Transnet, faced more of its challenges with deregulations in the transport system. This saw an increase in competition in the airline industry. SAA was highly plagued by mismanagement of financial resources and corruption. The year 2012 probably was the most challenging for SAA, which saw mass resignation of Board members. In the same year, Ms. Dudu Myeni, who has been arrested on several charges of corruption, was appointed a chairperson of SAA. For the six years of her administration at SAA, the entity recorded losses. The maladministration at SAA led the government into directing SAA to enter into a voluntary business rescue. Entering into a voluntary business rescue, the objective was to restructure the parastatal, which would also saw job losses. To turnaround the entity, the National Treasury allocated R10.5 billion in 2020. The entity's financials were also affected by Covid-19 grounding of air travels. In the post-Covid period, the airline has re-entered the market, expanding its routes to stay competitive.

5.6 Privatisation Versus Nationalisation

The literature on the role of SOEs in the economy lies between those who advocate for privatisation and advocate of nationalisation. Theoretically, these issues would lie between classical economists who advocate for *laissez-faire* and communists who postulate that government should decide on the important economic matters and organisation (Kushari & Chowdhury, 2021). According to the capitalists' view associated with Scottish philosopher, Adam Smith, the economy reaches efficient outcomes when there is less interference by the government and resources are privately owned by profit-maximising agents. According to pure market theory, SOEs would not be recommended to achieve allocative efficiency. However, communists believe that the social woes that exist are due to the class conflict between the capitalists (owners of production resources) and those who do not own production resources (labourers) but yet playing an indispensable role in the production process. These economists envisioned an economy characterised by state-owned conglomerates. After the collapse of communism in the late 1980s and early 1990s, most economies turned towards a mixed approach to reduce the budgetary burden of SOEs and improve their performance (Kikeri, 2022).

Empirical literature on the subject of privatisation and nationalisation entities is mixed. Looking at China's economy as an example, which has a large number of SOEs and managed to achieve consistent growth, the debate on nationalisation versus privatisation has again gained momentum. Zhang (1995) and Szarzec et al. (2021) are of the view that SOEs are inefficient, are a burden to the fiscus and are politically influenced halting economic growth. On the other hand, Qi and Kotz (2020), who look at the role of SOEs on economic growth in China between 1993 and 2012, found that SOEs have had positive impact on growth through the large-scale investments undertaken. Kikeri (2022) argues that for some SOEs, particularly those natural monopolies providing necessities at a lower price may achieve efficiency and correct market failures. According to Kikeri (2022), government intervention does not have to be through to have full control such as SOEs, but can be through Public-Private Partnerships, which would require some level of administrative capacity.

Looking at the health of SOEs, the issue of privatisation may be a consideration to ease the pressure on fiscus and to achieve efficiency. However, it is a social, economic and political question if nationalisation will not achieve far worse outcome considering the high levels of poverty, unemployment and inequality. The rationale of government to directly intervene in the economy is to correct market failures. During the Thabo Mbeki tenure as president, privatisation became popular as he believed that the apartheid government operated as a soviet. During his presidency several SOEs were privatised, and these include ISCOR in 2002, SASOL in 2000 and Telkom in 2002.

These acquisitions of SOEs by the private owners did not sit well with COSATU and SACP as they advocated for nationalisation citing concerns with equity. However, it is a dilemma facing the government as SOEs have proved to be inefficient. Perhaps in case such as South Africa's, a consideration may be to look into SOEs that supply merit goods such as electricity, water, etc.

5.7 Theories on the Role of Government in the Economy

There are two schools of thought concerning the role of government on the economy. The first school of thought contends that the private sector and the natural allocation of resources are disrupted by the expansion of government and its engagement in the economy (Altunc & Aydin, 2013). Consequently, it is maintained that a larger government causes lower productivity, which in turn causes slower economic growth. However, the second school of thought contends that in order to distribute physical and human capital and enable economic growth and development, the government should have a significant role in the economy.

5.7.1 Classical Economic Liberalism

The economic philosophy of classical economic liberalism upholds a market economy that is centred on individualism and private property in the means of production (Adams, 2001). This theory by Adam Smith (1776) advocated for economic liberalism, and his writing is generally regarded as representing the economic expression of nineteenth-century liberalism up until the Great Depression and rise of Keynesianism in the twentieth century. Advocates of this theory argue that government should play a limited role in the economy and only provide essential services such as education, infrastructure and justice as a means to encourage a free market and benefit the whole society. Therefore, intervention should benefit all of society and not only a small portion, as Smith (1776) argues it would be unjust for the expense/burden to be carried by all, whilst revenue spent is confined to a small portion of society. However, in modern society, the government performs functions beyond those identified by Smith, with the increased need for wealth redistribution as a means to stabilise economic growth and socio-economic conditions (Siami-Namini, 2017).

The invisible hand theory served as the cornerstone of laissez-faire economics. The French term 'laissez-faire', which means 'let do', promotes a system in which the government refrains from controlling the market through laws like tariffs and subsidies (Robbins, 1978). The laissez-faire policy is thought to provide the maximum degree of economic success. Because people are free to act in a way that results in a stable and orderly market, the concept of self-interest was therefore believed to be the driving force underlying all economic production (Kishtainy et al., 2012).

5.7.2 Market Failure and the Need for Government Intervention

Following the Great Depression, the role of government in the economy was theorised by Keynes (1936). The theory argues that market failures can be corrected through government intervention, such as new laws or taxes, tariffs, subsidies and trade restrictions. The proponents of this theory argue that government should increase spending to increase the overall demand, hence encouraging the private sector to demand for more labour, which would increase prices and return the economy to full employment. As a result, the contemporary Keynesian viewpoint maintains that the government can stabilise the economy by implementing countercyclical fiscal policy and raising investment spending. When a government employs countercyclical fiscal policy, it means that it has two options for responding to an economic boom or recession. The government would alter its tax and spending policies to create demand in the event of a recession. The government would raise taxes and cut spending in order to stabilise the economy in the event of an economic upturn because inflation and debt are likely to rise significantly (Alesina et al., 2018).

Another prominent theory which advocates for government intervention was formulated by Robert Barro (1990). Barro is an endogenous growth theorist who incorporated government spending and taxation into the endogenous growth model with increasing returns to scale. Barro (1990) made a rigorous analysis on how governments can influence economic growth. Contrary to Keynes who lump together government expenditure, Barro (1990) suggested that expenditure be separated in two categories: productive and non-productive. Similarly, taxation is divided into distortionary and non-distortionary taxes. Barro also warned against enormous government debt and crowding out the private sector. According to Barro (1990), direct taxes have detrimental effects on GDP, while indirect taxes have neutral effects on GDP. In terms of government expenditure, capital expenditure positively impacts economic growth. Government consumption expenditure is postulated to have a neutral impact in South Africa.

5.8 Economic Impact of State-Owned Enterprises on the Economy

This section provides a brief discussion on the burden of SOEs on the fiscus, giving focus to public debt as a share of GDP. As indicated in Table 5.1, government bailouts on SOEs have detrimental impact on the fiscus. Figure 5.1 shows the growth of public debt since the advent of democracy. In the early 1990s, government debt as a share of GDP was high ranging at over 40%.

In 2008/2009 financial year, the public debt as a share of GDP was 24%, which is the lowest since 1994. This followed the robust Growth, Employment and Redistribution (GEAR) policy to reduce public debt as a share of GDP. Since the period the government started injecting funds to bail out SOEs, the budget deficit has been widening, while public debt has also increased significantly. After 2008 public debt has taken an upward trend, reaching 40% as a share of GDP in 2013. In 2019 (prior to Covid-19), government debt reached a high of 56% as a share of GDP. Turnaround strategies may have to be adopted to change the financial position of SOEs to be self-sufficient and not strain the fiscus.

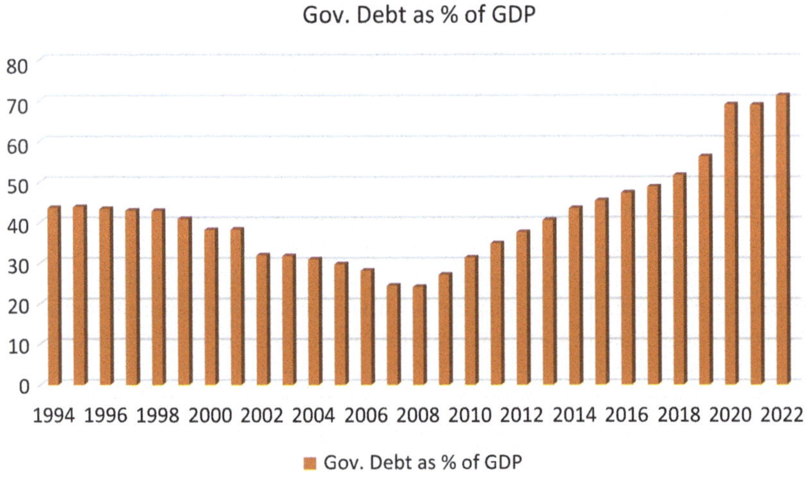

Fig. 5.1 National government debt as a percentage of GDP. (Source: South African Reserve Bank)

In the post-pandemic period, national government debt as a share of GDP increased significantly to Covid-19 relief funds received from the International Monetary Fund. Government debt as a share of GDP reached 68.9% in 2020, over 10% hike compared to 2019. In 2020, national government debt as a share of GDP reached 71.1%, a rate which requires robust strategy.

5.9 The Impact of SOEs on Growth

The impact of SOEs on economic growth cannot be easily explained without quantifying using statistical tools. This is because, even though the SOEs are constantly bailed out, whether it is worth bailing them out or not needs quantitative techniques. In this section, a Bayesian VAR (BVAR) is employed to quantify the impact of domestic debt of SOEs on economic growth in South Africa.

This model is theoretically underpinned by the AK model and log-log linearised function of the model is estimated using the Bayesian Estimation of Structural Vector Autoregressive Models (BSVAR) with a Normal inverted Wishart prior (De Menezes Barboza & Vasconcelos, 2019; Inoue & Kilian, 2020) to mitigate the short time dimension (1994–2022) of the available data on the variables of the study.

This study considered a reduced-form VAR(5.2) model described below:

$$y_t = c + \sum_{l=1}^{2} B_l y_{t-l} + u_t \tag{5.1}$$

The Normal inverted Wishart prior is described as shown below:

$$vec(B) \mid \Sigma \sim N(vec(B_0), \Sigma \otimes \Omega_0 \tag{5.2}$$

$$\Sigma \sim hW\left(S_0, \alpha_0\right) \tag{5.3}$$

where the hyper-parameters B_0, Ω_0 and S_0 are selected in a manner that the moments in B meet the moments in Eq. (5.3) and the expected value of Σ equates to the fixed residual covariance matrix of Minnesota prior.

The variables included in the model are as follows:

- GDP per capita as proxy for economic growth

- SOEs domestic debt—a proxy for measuring their financial position, because whenever SOEs fail to meet their debt obligations, they receive bailouts from the government
- Direct taxes—include all taxes on income, profits and capital gains tax
- Indirect taxes—include all taxes on levied goods and services
- Private investment
- Government consumption expenditure and government investment expenditure

All the data was obtained from the South African Reserve Bank and is annual in frequency and expressed in millions of rands.

5.10 Descriptive Statistics

Table 5.2 and Fig. 5.2 show descriptive statistics at their level form (millions of rands). There are 29 observations, from 1994 to 2022. The average per capita GDP is R72,444.86, reaching a maximum of R80,191 and a minimum of R61,965. Looking at the main determinants of economic growth, private investment and government investment expenditure, it is evident that the private sector is doing much in terms of investment than the government. However, looking as government consumption expenditure, the component is relatively high and almost comparable to the private sector. The SOEs domestic debt averages at R135,155.10 and reached a minimum of R57,209 and a maximum of R269,250, respectively.

Table 5.2 Description statistics

Variables	*Number of observations*	*Mean*	*Standard deviation*	*Min*	*Max*
Per capita GDP	29	72,444.86	6809.991	61,965	80,191
Indirect taxes	29	236,373.8	165,048.6	42,666	567,437
Consumption expenditure	29	691,910.4	156,457.3	472,456	900,045
Direct taxes	29	383,597	272,131.6	57,979	968,703
Private investment	29	402,708.7	113,285.8	206,286	530,467
Government investment	29	86,563.24	54,647.52	16,169	165,015
SOEs domestic debt	29	135,155.1	86,070.61	57,209	269,250

Source: Authors' computation

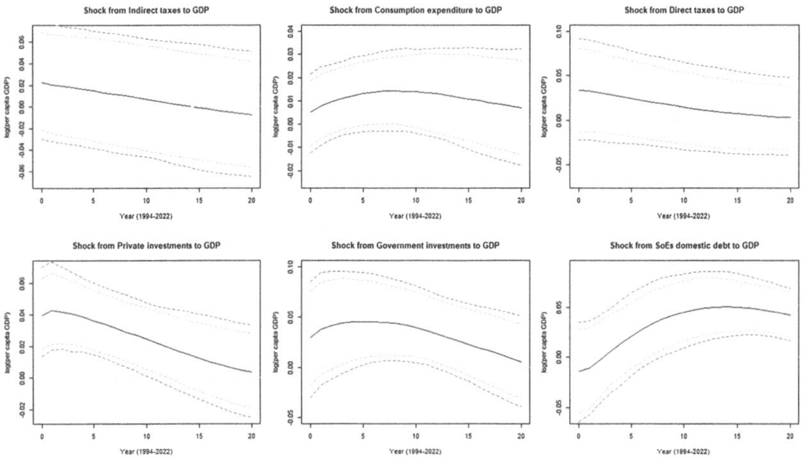

Fig. 5.2 BVAR impulse response functions. (Notes: The impulse responses were generated using the Ibvar package in R. The dashed lines represent the 95% and 99% confidence bands of the Bayesian credible sets obtained through Gibbs sampling with 1000 draws of Σ)

Figure 5.2 shows descriptive statistics of each variable from 1994 to 2022. Between 1994 and 1999, per capita GDP took off on an upward trend, which slightly decreased between 2000 and 2004. After 2004, per capita GDP grew at a sustained positive trend, which was sustained by the commodity boom until 2009. This moderate growth rate was halted by the Global Financial Crisis in 2008/2009. Since the end of the Crisis, per capita GDP has been on a downward trend, reaching a sharp trough in 2019. Indirect taxes, consumption expenditure and government taxes have been resembling a positive and consistent trend during the period of observation. Private investment and government investment have been fluctuating since 1994. Since 1994, private investment sloped positively, reaching a peak in 2010. The major investments during 2004 and 2010 were preparations for 2010 FIFA World Cup. Since the end of 2010, private investment has been fluctuating at a lower rate. Comparing the trends for government investment and private investment, it is evident that the years when private investment was low, investment was compensated by through increasing public investment.

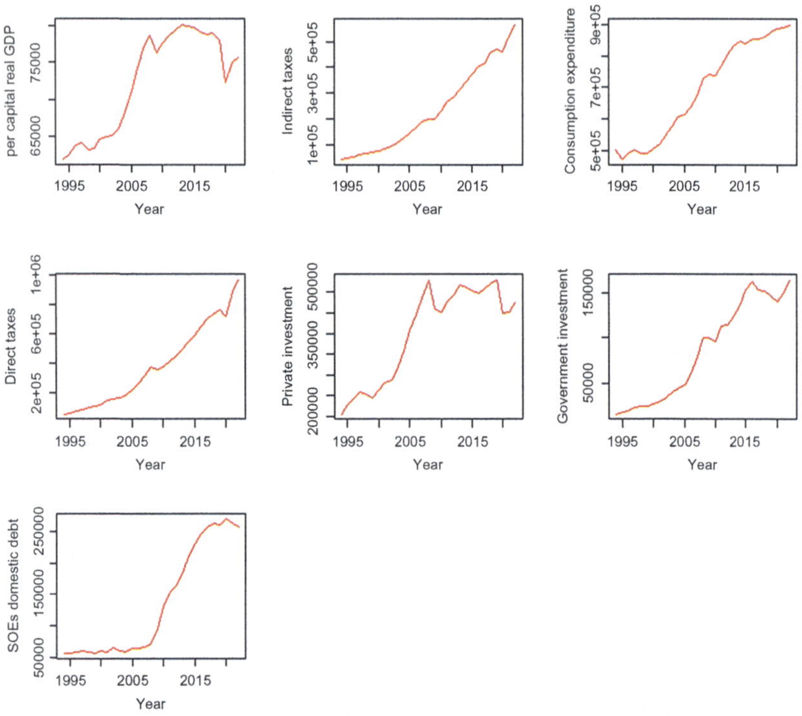

The findings show that the impact of SOEs domestic debt on GDP shifted from negative to positive in the first year of the shock, but remained statistically insignificant until eight years later, when it became statistically significant. This implies that the growth benefits of SOEs' domestic debt can be realised only in the long run, specifically after eight years. The impact of private investment on GDP is positive over the study period, but statistically significant only for the first ten years after the shock. The impact of government investment is also positive, but only statistically significant between the fifth and tenth years. The impact of direct and indirect taxes on GDP is statistically insignificant in both the short and long run. However, while direct taxes had a long-term positive impact on growth, indirect taxes turned negative in the 14th year. Finally, the impact of consumption expenditure on GDP is positive in both the short and long run, albeit statistically insignificant.

5.11 Conclusion

This chapter showed the role of government in the market economy through SOEs. The rationale of government direct intervention is to correct market failure. However, if the size of government is too big, that may crowd out the private sector. Theoretical literature is divided into those who advocate for free market economy and those who believe that the government can intervene in the economy during recession. Chapter 6 attempts to identify the 'right' level of government size on the economy.

In South Africa, the size of the government is relatively significant as government intervenes in the economy as an employer, a producer and a consumer. The direct intervention in the market economy that is evident is the government intervention in the economy as a producer through SOEs. However, these SOEs have been facing financial challenges and even failing to render their services. This is due to corruption and mismanagement of resources. Since 2008/2009 financial year, the government has increased the bailouts to SOEs by significant amounts. These bailouts have been shown to have a negative impact on the fiscus. The impact on growth however is only seen in the short run and fades in the long run.

Government is working on various corrective measures, particularly to deal with problematic governance issues in SOEs. The numerous SOEs are being restructured as part of attempts to improve efficiency. It is indeed critical that government tackles the challenge of corruption through promoting good governance and transparency. Although the impact of SOEs on growth is not detrimental to growth in the long run, the impact may transmit through dire fiscus stance. It is in this context that SOEs should be self-sufficient.

References

Adams, I. (2001). *Political Ideology Today.* Manchester University Press. ISBN 978-0719060205.

Alesina, A., Favero, C. A., & Giavazzi, F. (2018). *Climbing Out of Debt*, from https://www.imf.org/en/Publications/fandd/issues/2018/03/alesina

Altunc, O. F., & Aydin, C. (2013). The Relationship between Optimal Size of Government and Economic Growth: Empirical Evidence from Turkey, Romania and Bulgaria. *Procedia-Social and Behavioral Sciences, 92*, 66–75.

Baccaro, L., & Pontusson, J. (2016). Rethinking Comparative Political Economy: The Growth Model Perspective. *Politics and Society, 44*(2), 175–207.

Barro, R. J. (1990). Government Spending in a Simple Model of Endogenous Growth. *The Journal of Political Economy, 98*(5), S103–S125.

Burger, P. (2014). Facing the Conundrum: How Useful Is the "Developmental State" Concept in South Africa. *South African Journal of Economics, 52*(2), 159–180.

Butler, A. (2017). *Contemporary South Africa* (3rd ed.). Macmillan International Higher Education.

De Menezes Barboza, R., & Vasconcelos, G. F. R. (2019). Measuring the Aggregate Effects of the Brazilian Development Bank on Investment. *The North American Journal of Economics and Finance, Elsevier, 47*(C), 223–236.

Deeming, C., & Smyth, P. (2015). Social Investment After Neoliberalism: Policy Paradigms and Political Platforms. *Journal of Social Policy, 44*(2), 297–318.

Feinstein, C. (2005). *An Economic History of South Africa: Conquest, Discrimination, and Development.* Cambridge University Press.

Gumede, V. (2015). *Political Economy of Post-apartheid South Africa.* CODESRIA.

Inoue, T., & Kilian, L. (2020), The Uniform Validity of Impulse Response Inference in Autoregressions. *Journal of Econometrics, 215*, (2), 450–472.

International Monetary Fund (IMF). (2018). World Economic Outlook Base—General Government Gross Debt. Retrieved February 28, 2019, from https://www.imf.org/external/datamapper/GGXWDG_NGDP@WEO/OEMDC/ADVEC/WEOWORLD

Johnson, C. (1982). *MITI and the Japanese Miracle.* Stanford University Press.

Keynes, J. M. (1936). *The General Theory of Employment, Interest and Money.* Macmillan.

Kikeri, S. (2022). Privatization of State-Owned Enterprises. *The Governance Brief, (Brief 47). Privatization of State-Owned Enterprises: A Summary of Experience (Governance Brief 47) (adb.org).*

Kishtainy, N., Abbot, G., Farndon, J., Kennedy, F., Meadway, J., Wallace, C., & Weeks, M. (2012). *The Economics Book.* DK Publishing.

Kushari, U., & Chowdhury, S. (2021). Communism vs Capitalism: A Comparative Study in the Light of I-O Psychology. *International Journal of Advance Research and Innovative Ideas In Education, 7*(5), 16–28.

Lalk, J. (2012). *South Africa's Energy Future: An Analysis of Government Policies and Strategies.* INCOSE South Africa.

Maroufkhani, P. (2016). *The Developmental State: Theoretical Understandings of the State and Economic Development in East Asia.* Kuala Lumpur: University of Malaya. (Thesis—Masters).

National Planning Commission. (2012). *Diagnostic Overview.* National Planning Commission, Republic of South Africa.

Pekkanen, R. (2004). After the Developmental State: Civil Society in Japan. *Journal of East Asian Studies, 4*(1), 363–388.

Qi, H., & Kotz, D. M. (2020). The Impact of State-Owned Enterprises on China's Economic Growth. *Review of Radical Political Economics, 52*(1), 96–114.
Refera, M. K., Dhaliwal, N. K., & Kaur, J. (2016). Financial Literacy for Developing Countries in Africa: A Review of Concept, Significance and Research Opportunities. *Journal of African Studies and Development, 8*(1), 1–12.
Robbins, L. (1978). *The Theory of Economic Policy in English Classical Political Economy* (2nd ed.). Macmillan.
Siami-Namini, S. (2017). Reverse Privatization and New Government Reforms: A Review of Theory and Evidence. *International Journal of Current Advanced Research, 6*(10), 6846–6856.
Singh, N., & Srinivasan, T. N. (2006). *Indian Federalism, Economic Reform.* University of California.
Sinha, A. (2003). Rethinking the Developmental State: Divided Leviathan and Subnational Comparisons in India. *Comparative Politics, 35*, 459–476.
Smith, A. (1776). *An Inquiry into the Nature and Causes of the Wealth of Nations.* History of Economic Thought Books, McMaster University Archive for the History of Economic Thought.
Sparks, S. (2016). Between 'Artificial Economics' and the 'Discipline of the Market': Sasol from Parastatal to Privatisation. *Journal of Southern African Studies, 42*(4), 711–724.
StatsSA. (2018). Economic Growth Statistics. Retrieved February 3, 2019, from http://www.statssa.gov.za/?cat=30
Szarzec, K., Dombi, Á., & Matuszak, P. (2021). State-Owned Enterprises and Economic Growth: Evidence from the Post-Lehman Period. *Economic Modelling, 99*(C).
National Treasury. (2018). Budget 2018. Retrieved February 5, 2019, from Http://www.treasury.gov.za/documents/national%20budget/2018/sare/Budget%202018%highlights.pdf.
National Treasury. (2020). Budget Review 2020.
United Nations Economic Commission for Africa. (2021). *Governance of State-Owned Enterprises in South Africa.* United Nations Economic Commission for Africa.
Woo-Cummings, M. (1999). *The Developmental State.* Cornell University.
World Bank. (2020). *Poverty and Equity Brief: Sub-Saharan Africa.* Global_POVEQ_ZAF.pdf (worldbank.org).
Zhang, W. (1995). China's SOE Reform: A View of Modern Theory of the Firm. *Journal of Reform (gaige zazi)*, 1.

CHAPTER 6

Searching for an Equilibrium: Balancing Economic Development and Market Efficiency

6.1 Introduction

South Africa has a history of apartheid that led to economic disparities as captured in Chap. 1. After the end of apartheid, the government aimed to address these disparities and promote economic development through various policies and strategies. This has come in the form of government spending. The spending by the government in South Africa has traditionally been substantial, with a significant portion going to social services, infrastructure development and public administration. However, the effectiveness and efficiency of this spending have come under scrutiny due to issues of corruption and mismanagement, hindering the desired economic outcomes.

Despite efforts to address historical economic disparities, fiscal sustainability has been a challenge as rising debt levels and fiscal deficits have raised concerns about crowding out private investment. Nevertheless, government spending remains critical in addressing poverty, improving human capital through social programmes and advancing infrastructure projects, which are essential components of South Africa's long-term economic development strategy. This chapter assesses the impact of the South African government size on macroeconomic outcomes, in a comparative context, with a view of determining the optimal size of government intervention in the economy.

V. Gumede et al., *South African Economy*, African Histories and Modernities, https://doi.org/10.1007/978-3-031-54180-3_6

6.2 Theoretical Foundations of Government Intervention

6.2.1 *Market Failures Theory*

Economists have long entertained the view that markets should be left alone or operate with negligible intervention. A forceful proponent of this view is Adam Smith believed that markets are efficient. Arrow and Debreu's theoretical work demonstrates that in an ideal environment such as perfect competition, no externalities, and a competitive, markets ought to attain an efficient equilibrium where resources are optimally allocated. Other advocates of this view maintain that free markets can help in the way of armouring consumers from the government authorities and induce markets to provide goods and services that are relatively competitive (Tirole, 2015).

Under these circumstances, government does not need to get involved in the markets. However, such idyllic environment hardly ever occur in the real world, which allows for the possibility of market failure. The theory of market failures is a well-known theory in the study of public sector policy. It states that in an environment where economic units pursue their personal interest and markets are permitted to operate competitively (i.e. not kept in check or without any sort of intervention), the distribution and production of goods and services will most likely be socially inefficient (Le grand, 1991).

Part of the reason why markets do not always produce efficient resource allocation can be attributed to various factors like Natural Monopoly, information asymmetry and externalities.

(ii). Natural Monopoly is when a single produce dominates the entire market because of high fixed costs and other related economic conditions. Such dominance can result in market failure for the reason that the producer has no rivals to outperform which can help to reduce prices of goods or increase the quality of service.

(iii). Externalities take place if let's say the actions of a firm positively or negatively impacts on others without any compensation (Baumol & Oates, 1988). With negative externalities, you find that a firm would typically allocate more resources to activities that harm people than activities that add value to people. Many empirical studies have been undertaken on different types of externalities such as on energy externalities in developed countries (see Pearce, 2002) and not so many in developing countries such as South Africa (Van Horen, 1996). Many of these studies have produced external cost results ranging from very large to nearly trivial (Sundqvist, 2004).

(iv). Information Asymmetry: this can occur if let us say a car dealer in a process of selling a car has some information about the quality or potential risks of the car and chooses not to share that information with the person buying the car. In this case the buyer may unfortunately end up making a decision (buying the car in this case) that is not in his/her best interest. This one-sidedness of information is what usually causes inefficiencies and difficulties in the market—transactions do not lead to best results. There are many examples of industries that experience the problem of information asymmetry, including car dealers, financial markets and many more. There is a view that such market failures can be easily rectified by the government to restore efficient resource allocation.

6.2.2 Government Failures Theory

The above section pointed out that markets run into all sorts of difficulties and that if left on its own, may fail to allocate resources optimally. Therefore under these circumstances government involvement turns out to be essential so as to address such market failures. Nonetheless, it is never guaranteed that such government involvement can succeed in attaining its objectives. Government failure theory recognises that when the government gets involved in the economy, it can lead to inefficient outcomes. Inefficiencies related to government involvement in the economy are well documented (De Soto, 1989).

Government engagements in the economy typically result in an unintended consequences. Policy makers may formulate a policy to deal with a certain sector (or any aspect) of the economy but unintentionally hurt another. Moreover, political dynamic forces may influence the actions of the government. For example, policy makers may prioritise short-term political benefits (enticing voters to vote for them in the next election) at the expense of long-term welfare, leading to government failure. Last but not least, government involvement can be persuaded by organised interest groups. These groups may advocate for policies that primarily serve their own interests, potentially undermining the broader public good. The idea of searching for equilibrium in the context of market and government deficiencies is all about finding a balanced position where the challenges encountered by market and government are addressed so as to accomplish the best outcomes. This requires a methodical search for strengths of both the market and government.

6.3 Empirical Studies on Government Intervention and Economic Development

Governments have moral and legal obligations to intervene in society in order to direct, regulate, facilitate and act as catalyst for economic prosperity, social justice and ecological sustainability. The nature and scale of such interventions depend on various factors, which include the ideological reasoning of policy makers, the availability of natural resources, demographical and geographical realities as well as trajectories for economic growth. On a global scale, governments have to address serious challenges such as climate change, ecological dysfunction and the depletion of natural resources.

The literature is replete with unremitting debate on the nexus between the size of government and economic development outcomes. While studies such as Stiglitz (2021), Lin Oo (2019), Chen (2020), Kimaro et al. (2017) and Ghose and Das (2013) provide empirical support on the positive relationship between government size and macroeconomic outcomes, these studies support the Keynesian perspective that government should support the economy through provision of public goods, maintenance of law and order, increased productive investment and research and development and increased human capital development to stimulate short-term and long-term economic growth.

Stiglitz (2021) examined the proper role of government in the market economy post-Covid recovery. The study highlights that Covid-19 pandemic has imposed a huge challenge on public health as well as economic recovery, and government must take an active role in designing and enforcing economic policies to address various problems that pure market forces cannot, such as externalities and the absence of risk markets. Similarly, Chen (2020) examined the relationship between government size and local economic growth in China. Using a panel data of 29 provinces, municipalities and autonomous regions, the study concludes that there is a significant positive relationship between the scale of local government and local economic growth. Ghose and Das (2013), using the methods of panel cointegrations and Dynamic Ordinary Least Square (DOLS), studied the government size and economic growth in 19 emerging markets and suggested that government size affects economic growth positively.

Similarly, Kimaro et al. (2017) analysed the effect of government expenditure and efficiency on economic growth of sub-Saharan African countries. Using the Generalised Methods of Moments (GMM), the study demonstrates that increasing government expenditure accelerates economic growth of low-income countries in sub-Saharan Africa. Likewise, Lin Oo (2019) investigated the impact of fiscal policy on economic growth in Myanmar, using the ordinary least squares (OLS) method with annual data from 1979 to 2016. The empirical outcome revealed a statistically significant relationship between the country's fiscal deficit and economic growth, which confirms Keynesian assumptions.

Other studies discovered that government intervention crowds out domestic investment and discovered a negative relationship between government size and economic growth. These studies also conclude that larger government requires more taxes, which can reduce market incentives and be detrimental to economic growth (see Nourzad and Martin, 2017; Gnangoin et al., 2019; Heitger, 2018; Hauptmeier et al., 2018; Makhoba et al., 2019; Nuru and Gereziher, 2020). These studies support the classical view that an increase in government spending is capable of increasing the demand for me which increases interest rates and crowds out domestic investment.

Another strand of literature supports the non-linear relationship between government size and economic growth. For example, Aznan et al. (2022) examined the asymmetric effects of government size on economic growth in Malaysia. The study utilises a dynamic threshold non-linear approach. Some studies also claim that the relationship between government spending and economic growth is characterised by an inverted U-shape (Zungu et al., 2020) and some posit that the relationship is U-shape (Pelin & Taner, 2017; Phan, 2019).

However, some studies have identified a specific threshold of government size that an economy must maintain to achieve sustainable and inclusive growth. A study by Altunc and Aydın (2013) on Bulgaria, Romania and Turkey using the autoregressive distributed lag (ARDL) model from 1995 to 2011 proposed the optimal government size for these countries to be at 22.45%, 20.44% and 25.21%, respectively. Chen and Lee (2005) performed a study to examine the optimal government size in Taiwan employing the Threshold Autoregressive (TAR) method. The authors found that the Armey curve is present in Taiwan with the use of government investment expenditure, total government expenditure and government consumption as proxies for the government size. Using the data between 1979 Q1 and 2003 Q3, they found the respective optimal point of government size proxied by government investment expenditure, total government expenditure and government consumption expenditure in Taiwan to be 14.96%, 22.83% and 7.20%.

El Husseiny (2011) included quadratic government size variables in the model to examine the optimal government size in Egypt employing data from 1981/1982 to 2014/2015 fiscal year. The researcher noticed that Egypt's optimal government expenditure ranged from 30.50% to 31.20% of its total GDP. Besides, Nouira and Kouni (2021) conducted a study to investigate the optimal government size and its effect on economic growth in selected Middle East and North Africa (MENA) and developing countries over the period of 1988–2016 using the threshold dynamic heterogeneous panel data model with cross-sectionally dependent errors. The results revealed that the threshold effects were significantly greater for MENA countries than for other groups where the threshold was between 10% and 30% for the whole sample, between 20% and 30% for the MENA countries and between 10% and 20% for developing countries.

Zungu and Greyling (2022) test the validity of the BARS theory is derived from the analysis carried out by Barro (1989), Armey and Armey (1995), Rahn and Fox (1996) and Scully (1994, 1995) and determines the threshold level at which excessive government expenditure hampers growth. Using data from ten African emerging economies and the panel smooth transition regression (PSTR) model with one regime, the study revealed evidence of non-linear effects between government expenditure and economic growth, where the size of the government spending was found to be a 27.84% share of GDP, above which government expenditure caused growth to decline in African emerging economies. Lazarus et al. (2017) examined the relationship between government size and economic growth in Africa and the organisation for economic cooperation and development countries. The study established an optimum government size of 36.61% for OECD and 15.61% for African countries. The study confirms an inverted U-shape curve.

In South Africa, a couple of attempts have also been made to understand the nature of the relationship between government size and the economy. For instance, Gadinabokao and Daw (2013) examined the relationship between economic growth and total government expenditure in South Africa over the period 1980 up until 2011. Making use of Ordinary Least Squares (OLS) techniques and the Error Correction Model (ECM), they found a causal relationship between the variables mentioned above and further confirmed a significant long-run positive relationship exists between the variables. Similarly, Chirwa and Odhiambo (2016) made use of the autoregressive distributed lag (ARDL) model to study long-run drivers of economic growth in South Africa and found that total government spending is significantly related to economic growth making it a critical macroeconomic determinant. However, the study found that both in the short run and long run, total government expenditure negatively impacts economic growth.

Kleynhans and Coetzee (2019) analyse the actual and optimal size of the public sector in South Africa. The study uses fully modified OLS (FMOLS) estimation technique and obtained an optimal size of between 18 and 24% of the economy. The study concludes that the South African public sector is significantly larger than optimal.

In conclusion, previous literature review shows the existence of non-linear association between economic growth and government size theoretically and empirically. Such non-linear association between growth rate and government size hence suggests an optimal point where economic growth maximising government size exists as exhibited in the Armey curve.

6.4 Country Case Studies

This section examines the characteristics of the selected countries in terms of development outcomes and the size of government is their economies. Specifically, we looked at Brazil, Malaysia and Poland. We also look at the situation of Venezuela being a high intervention economy and Singapore being a pure capitalist economy.[1]

6.4.1 Brazil

Brazil, along with South Africa, China, India and Russia, was categorised as a rising economy in the past ten years, with the goal of surpassing some developed economies by 2050. Various strands of literature have com...pared and contrasted the Brazilian and South African economies because they are thought to be comparable. Nonetheless, the nation's economy has performed poorly during the past ten years, going into a two-year recession in 2015 and 2016. Concerning economic development, the country has dramatically progressed since the early 1980s. As shown in Fig. 6.1, human development index (HDI) has been on the

[1]We use the economic freedom index to determine countries adopting laissez-faire and countries with high state intervention.

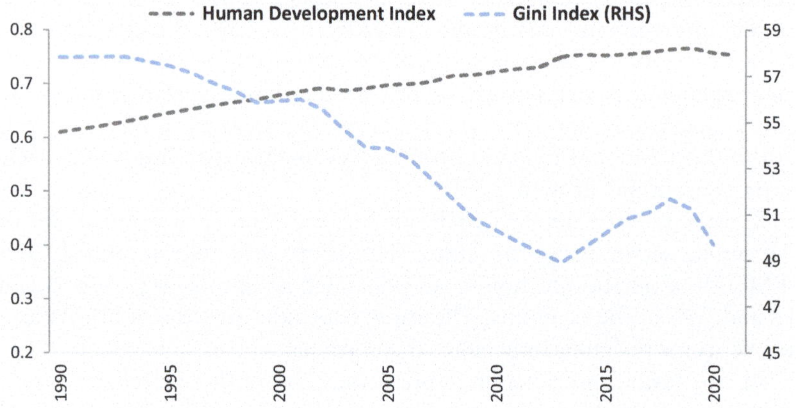

Fig. 6.1 Human development and income inequality in Brazil. (Source: Authors' computation using the UNDP and UNU-WIDER World Income Inequality Database (WIID))

upward trajectory from 0.610 in 1990 to 0.754, a change of 23.6%. Similarly, the country has progressed in terms of income inequality in the last decades, as shown in Fig. 6.1, the Gini index declined from 57.8 in 1990 when it was classified as one of the most unequal societies at that time (World Bank, 2019) to 49.7 in 2020. Thus, during the past three decades, the country's overall living standards and income disparity have significantly improved. Nonetheless, the nation is confronted with the same unemployment issue as South Africa, with a steep fall in the creation of jobs in the private sector (Fendos, 2019).

Fiscal sustainability is one of the most critical challenges facing Brazil in the last couple of years, according to the World Bank (2019). The country has a growing budget imbalance and a comparatively high tax burden (Gobetti & Orair, 2017). Social security receives substantial funding from the Brazilian government, and Higgins and Pereira (2014) report that social spending has increased significantly in recent years. From 1990 to 2022, the government's spending as a percentage of GDP as shown in Fig. 6.2 witnesses a significant improvement. Over the past 30 years, spending as a percentage of GDP has increased, raising concerns about the sustainability of national spending.

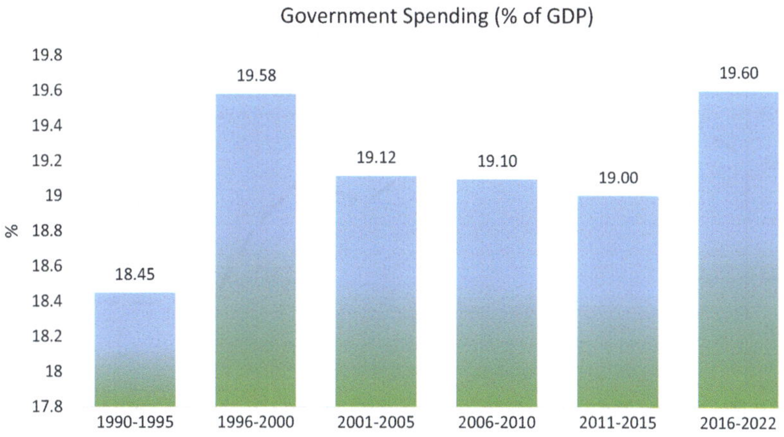

Fig. 6.2 Government spending in Brazil. (Source: Authors' computation from World Bank database)

6.4.2 Malaysia

Malaysia's economy has performed among the strongest in Asia since its creation in 1963. The real gross domestic product (GDP) increased by 6.5% year on average between 1957 and 2005. The economy expanded at a steady pace, averaging over 8% per year, from the early 1980s until the mid-1990s, when performance peaked. The economy's modernisation and diversification were greatly aided by high levels of private investment, both domestically and internationally. Malaysia, which was formerly mostly dependent on primary goods like rubber and tin, is now an upper middle-class nation with a multisector economy centred on manufacturing and services. In terms of economic development outcomes, Malaysian economy has also witnessed a significant improvement in human development and income inequality. As indicated in Fig. 6.3, between 1990 and 2021, Malaysia's HDI value changed from 0.640 to 0.803, a change of 25.5%. Similarly, income inequality, though a persistent issue, has been on a downward trajectory since 1997. These improvements reflect a combination of sound economic policies, investments in social development and stable governance. These factors have contributed to better living standards, increased access to education and healthcare and overall progress in human development indicators.

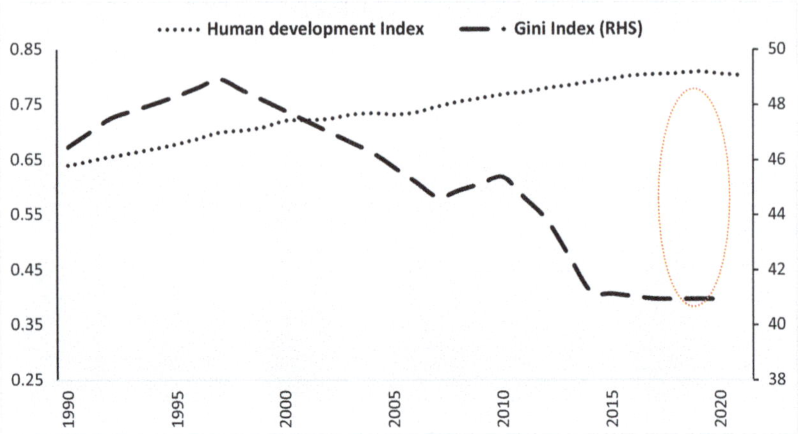

Fig. 6.3 Human development and income inequality in Malaysia. (Source: Authors' computation using the UNDP and UNU-WIDER World Income Inequality Database (WIID))

Malaysian government has over the years played a key role in the economy. In order to contribute more directly and actively to the nation's overall social and economic growth, the government went beyond its conventional roles. This intervention comes in the form of the active involvement of the government in the private sector through the founding of sizable businesses. Faced with this dual deficit issue, the government launched extensive structural programmes to cut spending, realign national goals with the availability of domestic resources, and ensure caution while using foreign borrowing. The goal of the new public policy direction was to further position the private sector as the primary driver of economic growth. The privatisation programme's which diminishes public sector's commercial operations was the most important development. Figure 6.4 also provides the average trend of government spending in Malaysia over the years.

6.4.3 Poland

Poland is the largest country in Central and Eastern Europe and the sixth largest in Europe. The Polish economy has been developing at a steady pace for over 25 years and is the sixth largest economy in the European

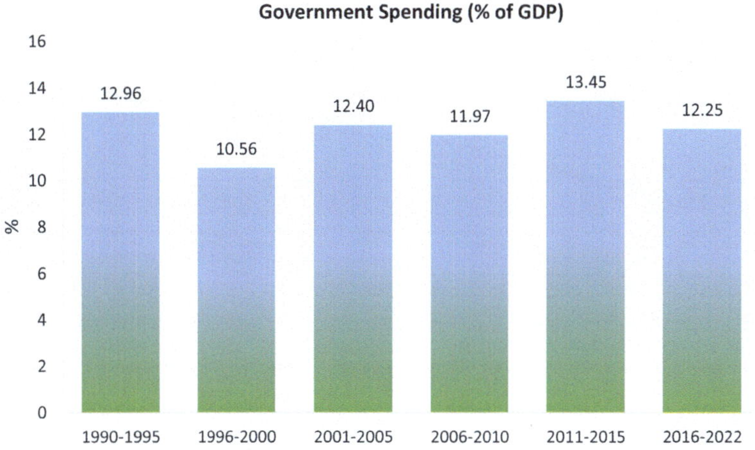

Fig. 6.4 Government spending in Malaysia. (Source: Authors' computation from World Bank)

Union, with GDP per capita being above 70% of the EU average (in terms of purchasing power parity). The fact that Poland, as the only country in Europe, was not affected by the 2008–2010 recession testifies to its exceptionally healthy development foundations. Currently, the main drivers of economic growth are exports and domestic consumption. Furthermore, Poland has recorded milestone achievements in human development and income inequality. For instance, between 1990 and 2021, Poland's HDI value changed from 0.716 to 0.876, a change of 22.3%.

Furthermore, according to Rutkowski (1998), income inequality has significantly increased in Poland since the fall of communism. Those who have gained from income changes are outnumbered by those who have lost. Those who have gained the most were well-educated, highly skilled white-collar workers and entrepreneurs. Overall, families are more dependent on state assistance than before the transition, with family allowance and unemployment benefits being most important in reducing inequality. This narrative also algins with the rise in Gini coefficient from 28.85 in 1990, reaching a peak of 35.7 in 1995. However, the index has been on a downward trajectory since then. Additionally, government size of Poland is high, with an average value of 18% in the last three decades (see Figs. 6.5 and 6.6 for more).

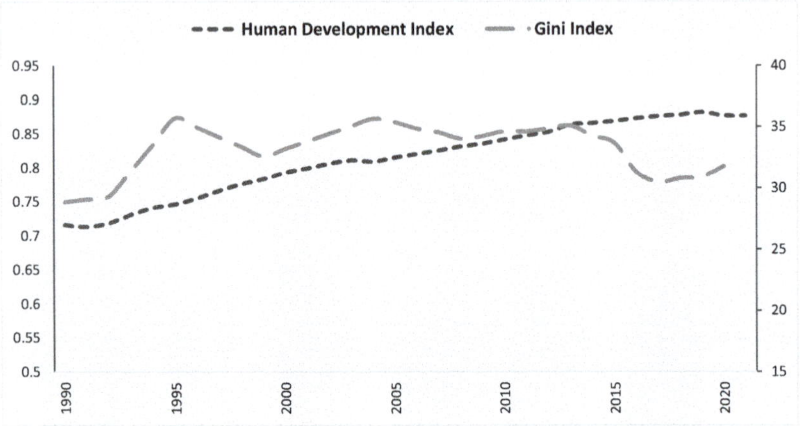

Fig. 6.5 Human development and income inequality in Poland. (Source: Authors' computation using the UNDP and UNU-WIDER World Income Inequality Database (WIID))

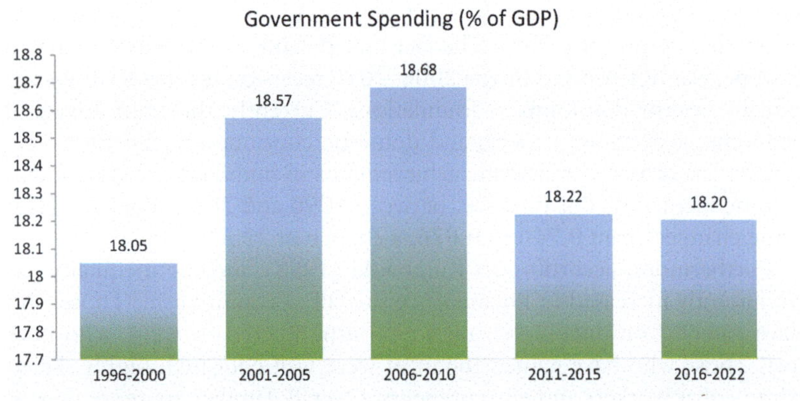

Fig. 6.6 Government spending in Poland. (Source: Authors' computation from using the World Bank database)

6.4.4 *Nigeria*

Nigeria's economy grew broadly and steadily between 2000 and 2014, averaging more than 7% yearly. This is due to favourable global conditions and macroeconomic and first-stage structural reforms. However, from 2015 to 2022, growth rates fell and GDP per capita flattened as a result of distortions in monetary and exchange rate policy, rising fiscal deficits brought on by reduced oil production and a costly fuel subsidy programme. Millions of Nigerians are living in poverty as a result of chronic inflationary pressure due to weak economic fundamentals and slow development. Despite having the largest economy and population in Africa, Nigeria offers limited opportunities to most of its citizens.

With an estimated 84 million Nigerians living below the poverty line, the country is predicted to have the second-highest percentage of poverty in the world, after India, with a 37% poverty rate in 2023. State capacity is inadequate, service delivery is constrained and violence and instability are pervasive across the majority of Nigerian regions. Large gaps in the infrastructure make it difficult to access electricity and impede the integration of the domestic economy, which would enable the nation to take advantage of its sizable market. These persistent development concerns are exacerbated by new issues including the rising intensity and frequency of extreme weather occurrences, particularly in the country's northern regions (Fig. 6.7).

Furthermore, Nigeria's current spending (see Fig. 6.8) needs to improve to promote a sustainable economic development. Despite its vast development needs, Nigeria spends only $220 per Nigerian per year, and lower than 12% of GDP, this is one of the lowest levels of spending in the world. Unfortunately, low public spending translates into poor development outcomes. Compared with similar countries, Nigeria's spending on social sectors—education, health and social protection—is very low.

6.4.5 *South Africa*

South Africa has made significantly progress towards achieving a more equitable society since the end of apartheid, in particular, in the area of rural electrification, access to education and increased equality of opportunities. The trend of poverty reduction was reversed between 2011 and 2015, threatening to undo some of the gains gained since 1994, despite the fact that South Africa has made progress in decreasing poverty since

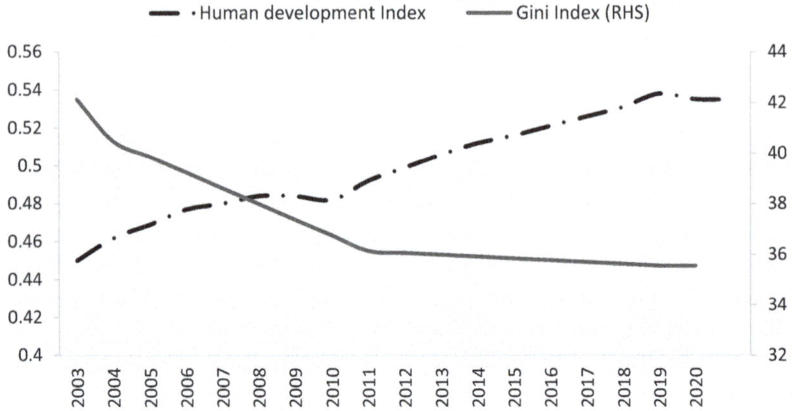

Fig. 6.7 Human development and income inequality in Nigeria. (Source: Authors' computation using the UNDP and UNU-WIDER World Income Inequality Database (WIID))

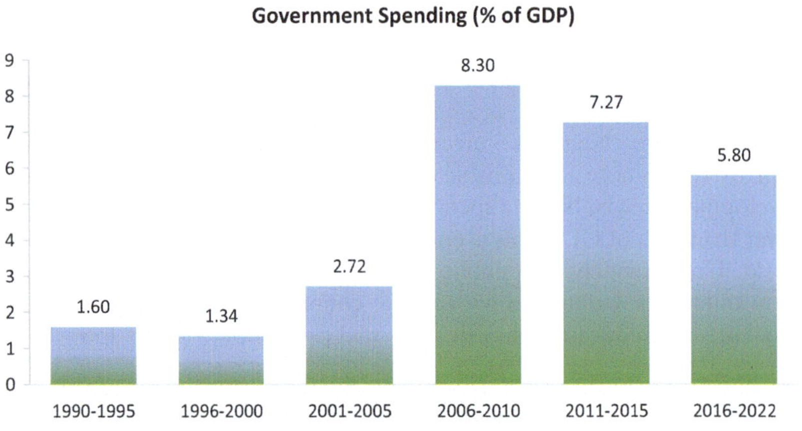

Fig. 6.8 Government spending in Nigeria. (Source: Authors' computation from using the World Bank database)

1994. A total of 13.8 million individuals (or 25% of the population) live in food poverty, whereas around 55.5% (30.3 million people) of the population live below the national upper poverty level (~ZAR 992). Comparably, the estimates of poverty in 2014–15 are 18.9% and 37.6%, respectively, up from 16.6% and 35.9% in 2010–11, assessed at the international poverty standards of $1.90 and $3.20 per person per day (2011 PPP) (World Bank, 2019). However, South Africa has also made much progress in terms of human development. Between 1990 and 2021, South Africa's HDI value changed from 0.632 to 0.713, a change of 12.8% (see Fig. 6.9).

While not as high as developed countries, South Africa's HDI is nevertheless respectably high for a developing nation. Increased funding for public healthcare and high-quality education has been credited as contributing to South Africa's progress (Haile & Nino-Zarazúa, 2017).

Empirical results indicate a threshold of 17.9% of government spending (% of GDP). In reversing the legacy of apartheid and promoting inclusive and sustainable development, South Africa has maintained a high spending pattern. According to Jibao et al. (2012), since 1994, the economy has undergone three broad phases of fiscal reform. Fiscal policy is influenced significantly by national economic policy; objectives to reduce poverty and inequality would usually see an increase in expenditure on sectors such as healthcare and education, which are classified as poverty reducing (World Bank, 2019). Figure 6.10 also buttressed this argument, has government spending as a percentage of GDP has remained high as it amounts to 19.7% between 2015 and 2021. However, our empirical results from

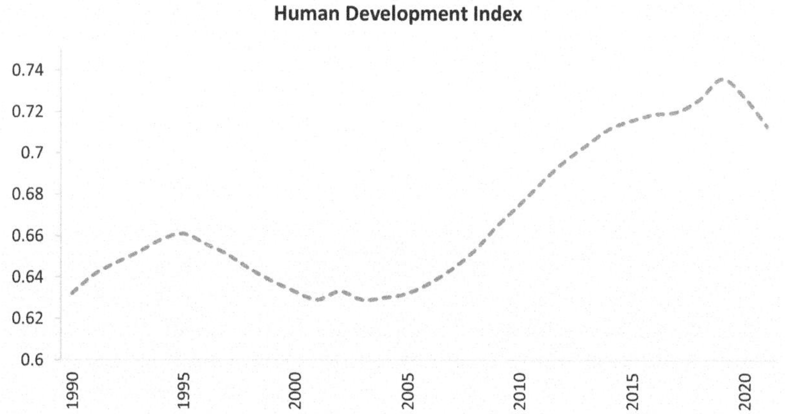

Fig. 6.9 Trend of human development in Soth Africa. (Source: Authors' computation using the UNDP)

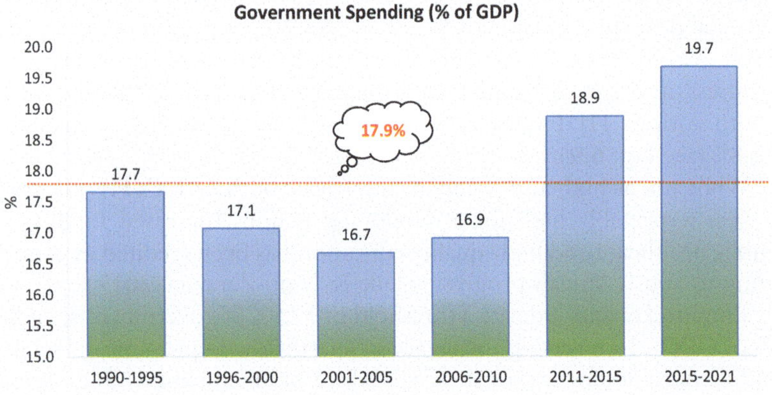

Fig. 6.10 Government spending in South Africa. (Source: Authors' computation using the World Bank datasets)

Fig. 6.10 suggest that South Africa is currently above the estimate threshold of 17.9%.

However, despite the elevated government size, South Africa remains a dual economy with one of the highest and most persistent inequality rates in the world, with a consumption expenditure Gini coefficient of 0.67 in the last ten years. High inequality is perpetuated by a legacy of exclusion and the nature of economic growth, which is not pro-poor and does not generate sufficient jobs. Inequality in wealth is even higher, and intergenerational mobility is low, meaning inequalities are passed down from generation to generation with little change over time (Fig. 6.11).

6.5 Examples from High Intervention Economies

6.5.1 Venezuela

In the 1950s, Venezuela was the fourth wealthiest country in the world. Today, Venezuela is poorer than it was prior to the 1920s, its infrastructure is deteriorating and its economy has been shrinking since the turn of the century. Hyperinflation (out of control price increases) has left the currency worthless and made it almost impossible for Venezuelans to

Fig. 6.11 Inequality in South Africa. (Source: Authors' computation using UNU-WIDER World Income Inequality Database (WIID))

afford basic necessities. Millions have fled the country's inhospitable conditions, while many blamed these economic woes on falling oil prices and U.S. sanctions. However, corruption and mismanagement were the direct result of increased government control of the economy. There are three main policies implemented by the government of Venezuela that produced the current crisis: widespread nationalisation of private industry, currency and price controls, and the fiscally irresponsible expansion of welfare programmes.

One of Chavez's first actions was to start nationalising the agriculture sector, supposedly reducing poverty and inequality by taking from rich landowners to give to poor workers. From 1999 to 2016, his regime robbed more than 6 million hectares of land from its rightful owners. Nationalisation destroyed production in affected industries because no government has the capacity to run thousands of businesses or the profit motive to run them efficiently. Instead, government officials face incentives to please voters by selling products at low prices and hiring more employees than necessary, even when that's the wrong industry decision.

6.6 Analysis of Low Intervention Economies

6.6.1 *Singapore*

The economy of Singapore is a highly developed free-market economy with dirigiste characteristics (Ministry of Trade, 2018; Central Intelligence Agency, 2012). Singapore's economy has been consistently ranked as the most open in the world (World Economic Forum, 2012), the joint fourth-least corrupt (Corruption Perceptions Index, 2018) and the most pro-business (World Bank Doing Business, 2012). The Singaporean government has remained committed to a market economy (Chua, 1995). Unlike northeast Asian developmental states (Japan, Taiwan, South Korea), the Singaporean government did not rely on the local capital class, but largely on foreign transnational corporations and the state capitalist sector during the development of the economy. The latter two have continued to propel economic growth of Singapore (Chua, 2015; Tan, 1991). The state in Singapore acts as an entrepreneur. It undertakes market risks when it establishes a company. State-Owned Enterprises operate profitably. The profitable and effective operation of the state capitalist sector offers several benefits to Singaporean citizens: low unemployment and crime rates and little social unrest; world-class infrastructure; affordable housing, education and health care, etc.

6.7 Lessons from Different Approaches

In this section, we compared the development outcomes and government size of the selected comparators with South Africa. The achievement of human development varies across the countries. South Africa's HDI score of 0.72 in the last one decade is almost at par with the selected countries and better than Nigeria. This means that South Africa is relatively doing well in terms of achievement in the human development, which includes access to education, health and income. South Africa has a relatively high level of public spending compared to the other countries in this comparison. This reflects its efforts to address historical disparities and promote social and economic development. South Africa allocates a significant portion of its budget to areas such as education, healthcare, social services and infrastructure development. However, despite the high government spending, income inequality remains high when compared to other countries. South Africa has one of the highest levels of income inequality globally. Historical factors, such as apartheid, have left a legacy of inequality (Table 6.1).

Table 6.1 Comparison of South Africa with other countries

	HDI	Gini coefficient	GDP Per capita ($)	Govt spending (% of GDP)
South Africa	0.72	67.24	6639.13	19.43
Brazil	0.75	50.25	9319.51	19.50
Malaysia	0.80	41.81	10645.63	12.59
Poland	0.87	32.76	14983.71	18.22
Nigeria	0.52	35.80	2372.86	6.26

Source: Authors' computation using World Bank, UNU-WIDER World Income Inequality Database (WIID)

South Africa needs to improve the efficiency of public spending and of the tax system to achieve an equitable society. Government exposure to State-Owned Enterprises remains high and, in terms of state guarantees, amounts to around 16% of GDP. The financial performance of SOEs worsened with the pandemic, increasing the pressure on public finances. Restoring the finances of the main SOEs and privatising those intervening in competitive markets would reduce the fiscal burden. Better enforcement of sanctions for corruption offences is needed to restore public confidence and the proper functioning of public services. Reducing the size of the government's wage bill also remains essential. Finally, even though South Africa's tax-to-GDP ratio, standing at 26% of GDP, is higher than many emerging economies, there is room to increase tax revenues, while reducing inequality and making the tax system less distortive to growth.

6.8 Identifying Optimal Government Intervention for Economic Development

In this section, we empirically determined the optimal government size in South Africa. However, before identifying the optimal government intervention for economic development in South Africa, we examined the nonlinear impact of government size. We also begin our analysis with stationarity and cointegration tests, before applying the cointegrating regressions.

Annual data for South Africa spanning 1960–2022 were employed in this study. The dependent variable is economic growth, and it is measured by real GDP per capita growth. The main explanatory variable is government spending. As in previous studies (Chen, 2020; Ghose & Das, 2013; Kimaro et al., 2017; Lin Oo, 2019; Stiglitz, 2021) government spending is measured using government spending (% of GDP). Other independent variables in the model capita stock, financial development and trade openness are measured by gross capital formation, credit to the private sector and the export plus import as percentage share of GDP, respectively. All of the variables were sourced from the World Bank's World Development Indicators.

6.8.1 *Unit Root Tests*

To ensure the selection of the appropriate estimation technique, unit root tests of Augmented Dickey-Fuller (ADF) and Phillips-Perron (PP) have been conducted on the variables. The results are presented in Table 6.2, and they reveal that all the variables (real GDP per capita, government spending, credit to private sector, trade openness, gross capital formation) are stationary at first difference.

Table 6.2 Augmented Dickey-Fuller and Phillips-Perron unit root tests

Variable	*Augmented Dickey-Fuller*		*Phillips-Perron*		*Stationarity*
	Level	*1st Difference*	*Level*	*1st Difference*	
lnRGDP	1.232	-4.888***	1.376	-4.850***	I(1)
govt	1.950	-7.687***	2.138	-7.687***	I(1)
govtsqaure	1.513	-8.025***	1.613	-8.025***	I(1)
CPS	0.255	-6.577***	0.172	-6.563***	I(1)
TO	0.348	-7.226***	0.795	-7.408***	I(1)
GCF	0.733	-4.786***	1.006	-4.825***	I(1)

Note: ** and *** indicate 5% and 1% levels of significance, respectively

6.8.2 Cointegration Test

The tests of cointegration based on the Engle-Granger is presented in Table 6.3. From the statistics of the results, we can reject the null hypothesis that the model is not cointegrated. These results demonstrate evidence of long-run association among all the variables in each of the two models.

The long-run estimates of the variables are provided in Table 6.4 via the FMOLS, dynamic OLS and canonical cointegration regression. As displayed in Table 6.4, government spending is negatively signed and statistically significant at the 5% level, which implies that government spending exerts a negative impact on the GDP per capita of South Africa in the long run. Specifically, this result demonstrates that a percentage rise in government spending is associated with a -0.1% decline in economic growth, ceteris paribus. This result suggests that government spending is an important influencer of economic growth in South Africa. However, the impact is detrimental to the growth process of South Africa. This aligns with the empirical evidence of Nuru and Gereziher (2020), Makhoba et al. (2019) and Hauptmeier et al. (2018) that government intervention crowds out domestic investment and that larger government could lead to more taxes which may reduce market incentive and growth process.

However, the coefficient of government squared is positive and statistically significant at the 5% level, indicating that government spending has a non-linear impact on economic growth in South Africa. Precisely, this result demonstrates that a percentage rise in government spending squared corresponds to a 0.3% increase in economic growth, ceteris paribus. This suggest that at the initial stage, government spending deteriorates economic growth up to a certain point before the impact is positive. This empirical outcome is characterised by the U-shape relationship between

Table 6.3 Engle-Granger cointegration

Dependent	*tau-statistic*	*z-statistic*
lnRGDP	-4.134***	-23.899***
Rho - 1	-0.385478	
Number of observations	62	

Note: ** and *** indicate 5% and 1% levels of significance, respectively. *MacKinnon (1996) p-values. Automatic lags specification based on Hannan-Quinn criterion

Table 6.4 Cointegrating regression result

	FMOLS		*DOLS*		*CC*	
Variable	*Coefficient*	*t-Statistic*	*Coefficient*	*t-Statistic*	*Coefficient*	*t-Statistic*
lngovt	-0.104***	-5.676	-0.116***	-5.634	-0.103***	-5.644
Lngovt^2	0.003***	4.784	0.003***	4.686	0.002***	4.698
lnK	0.346***	12.587	0.341***	9.494	0.346***	12.895
CPS	-0.002**	-4.857	-0.001***	-3.632	-0.002***	-4.839
TO	0.002	1.389	0.002	1.407	0.002	1.306
C	1.146***	2.091	1.323	1.862	1.130**	2.152
R-squared	0.945		0.971		0.944	
Adjusted R-squared	0.940		0.957		0.939	

Note: *, ** and *** indicate 10%, 5% and 1% levels of significance, respectively. FMOLS: Fully modified OLS; DOLS, dynamic OLS; CC, canonical cointegration

government spending and economic growth in South Africa. Studies like Pelin and Taner (2017) and Phan (2019) have reached similar conclusions. The result of capital stock enters the model with a positive and significant impact. This result implies that capital stock is a key driver of economic growth in South Africa. It also reinforces the premise of the endogenous growth theory that capital plays a key role in the attainment of long-run growth (Lucas, 1988).

Similarly, trade openness is found to exert a positive impact on economic growth in South Africa. It reveals that a percentage increase in trade openness is associated with a 0.02% increase in long-run economic growth, ceteris paribus. This result reinforces a previous finding by Loots (2003) that about 98% of South Africa's growth performance may be attributed to the dynamics of trade and globalisation. Financial development is found to be negative and statistically significant and in the model. We believe that this might be due to over-leveraging, as a highly developed financial sector like South Africa may encourage individuals, businesses and even governments to take on excessive debt, which could lead to financial stress and debt crises, as borrowers are unable to meet their obligations.

6.9 Optimal Size of Government on South African Economy

After establishing that government spending has a non-linear impact on economic growth, we proceeded by estimating the optimal threshold of government intervention on economic growth in South Africa. Table 6.5 presents the results of the threshold autoregressive model with two regimes.

The output consists of two tables. The first table reports the estimated threshold and the corresponding coefficients below the threshold, while the second table reports the estimated coefficients when the government spending is greater than the threshold. The estimated threshold of 17.9% splits the sample into two regimes. The coefficient of 17.9% is similar to the estimated threshold of 18–24% obtained by Kleynhans and Coetzee (2019) for South Africa. At the lower regime, government spending reduces economic growth, while at the upper regime the impact is not significant.

Table 6.5 Identifying the optimal government size for economic growth in South Africa

Variable	*Coefficient*	*t-Statistic*
GOVERNMENTSPENDING < 17.900599		
LNREALGDPPERCAPITA(-1)	0.745***	11.27482
GOVERNMENTSPENDING	-0.008***	-5.545987
LOG(CAPITAL)	0.058***	2.687859
CPS	0.002	1.506003
TRADEOPENNESS	0.001***	2.823042
C	0.827***	3.439201
17.900599 <= GOVERNMENTSPENDING		
LNREALGDPPERCAPITA(-1)	-0.077	-0.312823
GOVERNMENTSPENDING	-0.002	-0.241090
LOG(CAPITAL)	0.419***	4.023325
CPS	-0.001	-1.621870
TRADEOPENNESS	-0.001	-0.280219
C	-0.805	-0.831309
R-squared	0.987440	
F-statistic	357.3509	
Prob(F-statistic)	0.000000	

Standard errors in parentheses, ***$p < 0.01$, **$p < 0.05$, *$p < 0.1$

6.10 Conclusion

This chapter looked at government intervention in emerging economies, proxied by government spending as a percentage of GDP. The analysis of data shows variations, with South Africa and Brazil registering a reasonably high level of government spending, Malaysia representing a minor government footprint and Poland tumbling somewhere in the middle. Perhaps fascinatingly, Nigeria registered comparatively lower government involvement. Though expected, such variations in government involvement in these countries call attention to the importance of adapting policies to country's distinctive state of affairs for optimal economic development. Thus, government officials or those responsible for policy formulation and implementation need to ensure that there is effective government spending and configuration with long-term goals to stimulate economic growth.

The chapter also explored the important question of whether South Africa's economy can possibly attain an optimal size of government. After setting up the non-linear analysis of the impact of government spending on economic growth, it proceeded to estimate the optimal threshold for government intervention. The results indicate a threshold of 17.9% of government spending to GDP. The chapter recommends that South Africa should aim for a balanced approach between government intervention and market forces. Overreliance on either extreme can be detrimental. A mixed economy allows for essential public services while promoting economic growth. It is worth highlighting that Chap. 2 argued that government expenditure is important for the economy. Other studies also confirm that social policy is important for economic growth. Therefore, the estimated optimal size of government intervention is a guide.

References

Altunc, O. F., & Aydin, C. (2013). The Relationship between Optimal Size of Government and Economic Growth: Empirical Evidence from Turkey, Romania and Bulgaria. *Procedia-Social and Behavioral Sciences, 92*, 66–75.

Armey, R. K., & Armey, R. (1995). *The Freedom Revolution: The New Republic House Majority Leader Tells Why Big Government Failed Why Freedom Works, and How We Will Rebuild America*. Regnery Publishing.

Aznan, M. S. B. M., Goh, H. H., Koong, S. S., & Tan, S. H. (2022). Nonlinear Threshold Approach for Asymmetric Effects of Government Size on Economic Growth in an Emerging Asian Economy: The Malaysian Experience. *Heliyon, 8*(9).

Barro, R. (1989, February). A Cross-Country Study of Growth, Saving and Government. NBER Working Paper2855, National Bureau of Economic Research.

Baumol, W. J., & Oates, W. E. (1988). *The Theory of Environmental Policy.* Cambridge University Press.

Central Intelligence Agency. (2012, August 6). The World Factbook. cia.gov. Retrieved August 13, 2012, from https://www.cia.gov/the-world-factbook/countries/singapore/

Chen, J. (2020). Research on the Relationship Between Government Size and Economic Growth. *Modern Economy, 11*(2), 209–219.

Chen, S. T., & Lee, C. C. (2005). Government Size and Economic Growth in Taiwan: A Threshold Regression Approach. *Journal of Policy Modelling, 27*(9), 1051–1066.

Chirwa, T. G., & Odhiambo, N. M. (2016). Macroeconomic Determinants of Economic Growth: A Review of International Literature. *South East European Journal of Economics and Business, 11*(2), 33–47.

Chua, A. L. (1995). The Privatization–Nationalization Cycle: The Link between Markets and Ethnicity in Developing Countries. *Columbia Law Review, 95*(2), 223–303.

Chua, B. H. (2015). State-owned Enterprises, State Capitalism and Social Distribution in Singapore. *The Pacific Review, 29*(4), 499–521.

Corruption Perceptions Index. (2018). transparency.org. Transparency International. Retrieved April 21, 2019, from https://www.transparency.org/files/content/pages/CPI_2018_Executive_Summary_EN.pdf

De Soto, H. (1989). *The Other Path* (p. 17133). Harper & Row.

El Husseiny, I. A. (2011). The Optimal Size of Government in Egypt: An Empirical Investigation. *Journal of North African studies, 24*(2), 271–299.

Fendos, J. (2019). South Korea's Economic Tipping Point. The Diplomat: 20 March. Retrieved August 14, 2019, from https://thediplomat.com/2019/03/south-koreas-economic-tipping-point/

Gadinabokao, L., & Daw, D. (2013). An Empirical Examination of the Relationship Between Government Spending and Economic Growth in South Africa, from 1980 to 2011. *Mediterranean Journal of Social Sciences, 4*(3), 235–242.

Ghose, A., & Das, S. (2013). Government size and Economic Growth in Emerging Market Economies: A Panel Co-integration Approach. *Macroeconomics and Finance in Emerging Market Economies, 6*(1), 14–38.

Gnangoin, Y. T. B., Du, L., Assamoi, G., Edjoukou, A. J., & Kassi, D. F. (2019). Public Spending, Income Inequality and Economic Growth in Asian Countries: A Panel GMM Approach. *Economies, 7*(4), 115.

Gobetti, S. W., & Orair, R. O. (2017). Taxation and Distribution of Income in Brazil: New Evidence from Personal Income Tax Data. *Brazilian Journal of Political Economy, 37*, 267–286.

Haile, F., & Nino-Zarazúa, M. (2017). Does Social Spending Improve Welfare in Low-Income and Middle-Income Countries? *Journal of International Development, 30*(3), 367–398.

Hauptmeier, S., Martin, H., & Ludger, S. (2018). Expenditure Reform in Industrialized Countries: A Case Study Approach. *Journal of Economic Studies, 18*, 3–30.

Heitger, B. (2018). The Scope of Government and Its Impact on Economic Growth in OECD Countries. *Journal of Economic Literature, 22*, 38–39.

Higgins, S., & Pereira, C. (2014). The Effects of Brazil's Taxation and Social Spending on the Distribution of Household Income. *Public Finance Review, 42*(3), 346–367.

Jibao, S. S., Schoeman, N. J., & Naraidoo, R. (2012). Fiscal Regime Changes and the Sustainability of Fiscal Imbalance in South Africa: A Smooth Transition Error-Correction Approach. *South African Journal of Economic and Management Sciences, 15*(2), 112–127.

Kimaro, E. L., Keong, C. C., & Sea, L. L. (2017). Government Expenditure, Efficiency and Economic Growth: A Panel Analysis of Sub-Saharan African Low Income Countries. *African Journal of Economic Review, V No. II*, 34–54.

Kleynhans, E. P., & Coetzee, C. E. (2019). Actual vs Optimal Size of the Public Sector in South Africa. *Acta Universitatis Danubius. Administratio, 11*(1).

Lazarus, W. Z., Khobai, H., & Le Roux, P. (2017). Government Size and Economic Growth in Africa and the Organization for Economic Cooperation and Development Countries. *International Journal of Economics and Financial Issues, 7*(4), 628–637.

Le Grand, J. (1991). The Theory of Government Failure. *British Journal of Political Science, 21*(4), 423–442.

Loots, E. (2003). Globalisation and Economic Growth in South Africa: Do We Benefit from Trade and Financial Liberalisation? *South African Journal of Economic and Management Sciences, 6*(2), 218–242.

MacKinnon, J. G. (1996). Numerical Distribution Functions for Unit Root and Cointegration Tests. *Journal of Applied Econometrics, 11*(6), 601–618.

Makhoba, B. P., Kaseeram, I., & Greyling, L. (2019). Assessing the Impact of Fiscal Policy on Economic Growth in South Africa. *African Journal of Business and Economic Research, 14*(1), 7–29.

Ministry of Trade and Industry Singapore. (2018). Free Market System. mti.gov.sg. Archived from the Original on 7 October 2015. Retrieved December 11, 2018, https://www.mti.gov.sg/MTIInsights/Pages/Free%20Market%20System.aspx

Nouira, R., & Kouni, M. (2021). Optimal Government Size and Economic Growth in Developing and MENA Countries: A Dynamic Panel Threshold Analysis, Middle East. *Development Journal, 13*(1), 59–77.

Nourzad, F., & Martin, V. (2017). Public Capital Formation and Productivity Growth: Some International Evidence. *Journal of Productivity Analysis, 6*, 283–295.

Nuru, N. Y., & Gereziher, H. Y. (2020). The Effect of Fiscal Policy on Economic Growth in South Africa: A Nonlinear ARDL Model Analysis. *Journal of Economic and Administrative Sciences, 38*, 229–245. https://doi.org/10.1108/JEAS-06-2020-0088

Pearce, D. (2002). *Energy Policy and Externalities: An Overview*. https://discovery.ucl.ac.uk/id/eprint/17531/1/17531.pdf

Pearce, D., Bann, C., & Georgiou, S. (1992). The social costs of fuel cycles. A report to the UK Dept. of Trade and Industry. HMSO, London.

Pelin, V. I., & Taner, T. (2017). Government Size and Economic Growth in Turkey: A Threshold Regression Analysis. *Prague Economic Papers, 26*(2), 142–154.

Phan, T. T. (2019). The Optimal Public Expenditure Decision: A Case of Economic Growth in Southeast. Asian Countries. *Journal of Management Information and Decision Sciences, 22*(2), 25–35.

Rahn, R., & Fox, H. (1996). *What Is the Optimum Size of Government?* Krieble Foundation.

Rutkowski, J. J. (1998). Welfare and the Labor Market in Poland: Social Policy During Economic Transition. World Bank Publications, pp. 77–78. ISBN 978-0-8213-4318-0. Retrieved March 3, 2013.

Scully, G. W. (1994, November 1). *What Is the Optimum Size of Government in the United States?* National Center of Policy Analysis, Policy Report No. 188, North-Central Expressway Dallas.

Scully, G. W. (1995). The "Growth Tax" in the United States. *Public Choice, 85*(1–2), 71–80.

Stiglitz, J. E. (2021). The Proper Role of Government in the Market Economy: The Case of the Post-COVID Recovery. *Journal of Government and Economics, 1*, 100004.

Sundqvist, T. (2004). What Causes the Disparity of Electricity Externality Estimates? *Energy Policy, 32*, 1753–1766.

Tan, H. (1991). State Capitalism, Multi-National Corporations and Chinese Entrepreneurship in Singapore. In G. Hamilton (Ed.), *Business Networks and Economic Development in East and Southeast Asia* (pp. 201–216). Centre of Asian Studies, University of Hong Kong.

Tirole, J. (2015). Market Failures and Public Policy. *American Economic Review, 105*(6), 1665–1682.

Tun Lin Oo. (2019). The Effect of Fiscal Policy on Economic Growth in Myanmar. *East Asian Community Review, 2*(1–2), 101–124.

Van Horen, C. (1996). *Counting the Social Costs: Electricity and Externalities in South Africa*. University of Cape Town Press and Elan Press.

World Bank. (2019). Gini Index: Brazil. Retrieved August 19, 2019, from https://data.worldbank.org/indicator/SI.POV.GINI?locations=BR

World Bank Doing Business Report. (2012). World Bank. Retrieved May 27, 2013, from http://doingbusiness.org/reports/global-reports/doing-business-2012

World Economic Forum. (2012). Global Enabling Trade Report. Retrieved July 29, 2012, from https://members.weforum.org/pdf/GETR10/GETR10-Overall-Rankings.pdf

Zungu, L. T., & Greyling, L. (2022). Government Size and Economic Growth in African Emerging Economies: Does the BARS Curve Exist? *International Journal of Social Economics, 49*(3), 356–371.

Zungu, L. T., Greyling, L., & Sekome, M. S. (2020). Government Expenditure and Economic Growth: Testing for Nonlinear Effect Among SADC Countries, 1994–2017. *African Journal of Business and Economic Research, 15*(3), 37–69.

CHAPTER 7

The Institutional Architecture: Reorganising Government for Better Socio-economic Development

7.1 Introduction

As indicated in Chap. 3 and highlighted in the various parts of the book, the successive post-apartheid administrations in South Africa have been attempting to facilitate social and economic development among other pressing objectives. As argued in Gumede (2022), it is critical to assess the prospects of South Africa achieving its developmental goals as well as dealing with the challenge of state-building particularly as development outcomes appear to be deteriorating amidst various efforts to capacitate and reorganise the government. It is better to deal with these kinds of issues in a comparative context in order to draw lessons from countries that are known to have better development outcomes and countries that are comparable to South Africa. As a result, we compare South Africa with Malaysia, Singapore, Taiwan, Brazil, India, Mauritius, Botswana and Nigeria. These countries were carefully selected because of their relevance for the institutional architecture that can deliver commendable development outcomes. Other countries are also considered. The analysis largely makes use of a developmental state framework.

The chapter starts with a discussion of public sector reforms that have been pursued in South Africa since 1994. That is followed by analysing planning and associated critical government functions in a comparative

V. Gumede et al., *South African Economy*, African Histories and Modernities, https://doi.org/10.1007/978-3-031-54180-3_7

context. We then examine critically why have development outcomes not improved in South Africa and/or why development outcomes have been deteriorating. Before concluding, we quantify the role of government in socio-economic development particularly highlighting the role of social policy in socio-economic development. Overall, the central argument of the chapter is that government can be reorganised differently with a view of ensuring that it functions better and ensures that correct policies are in place for the advancement of wellbeing in South Africa.

7.2 Public Sector Reforms

The start of reforms in post-apartheid South Africa, besides the reorganisation of the government nationally and provincially, was with the White Paper on the Transformation of the Public Service (1996). There have been many legislative and policy interventions since 1994. The Public Service Act has continually been amended. Institutions pursuing public sector reforms have evolved since 1994.

To start with, the South African Management Development Institute (SAMDI) was the first institution that was established after the end of apartheid, to provide necessary training for the public sector. Later, SAMDI was transformed into Public Administration Leadership and Management Academy (PALAMA) whose main aim was to provide or coordinate the provision of training and management development interventions that lead to improved performance and service delivery in the public sector. PALAMA, which was established in 2006, reported to the Minister for Public Service and Administration. In 2013, the National School of Government (NSG) replaced PALAMA. The training provided has not received positive feedback in some instances.

For instance, Dastile (2018) finds that 34% who attended the training provided felt that the training was not linked to their performance development plans, but they attended the training because they were selected by their superiors to attend the training as it was deemed to be aligned to the departmental objectives. In some instances, respondents said they attended training due to late cancellation by their colleagues. Much earlier, the Public Service Commission (2008) had also found that employees either were not sufficiently trained and/or monitored by senior managers on whether they complied with some of the Batho Pele principles. These are principles that govern the behaviour of government officials and the functioning of the public sector in South Africa.

It was during the Nelson Mandela administration (1994–1999) that government undertook first steps in public sector reforms. The primary focus, arguably, of the Mandela administration was reconciliation. The administration was constrained by coalition that had to be formed resulting in the Government of National Unity. Many of the Presidential Review Commission's recommendations were implemented during the first term of the Thabo Mbeki administration. Among these are the Batho Pele principles (i.e. consultation, service standards, access, courtesy, information, openness and transparency, redress and value for money). It can be argued that the Mbeki administration implemented the public sector and public management reforms that had been initiated in the Mandela administration. The cluster system, for instance, was firmly put in place during the Mbeki administration. Further improvements in the functioning of the government were pursued earnestly during the Mbeki administration.

The Kgalema Motlanthe administration continued with that. The Jacob Zuma administration made some modifications. The Cyril Ramaphosa administration largely continued with what the Zuma administration was pursuing but it also resuscitated what the Mbeki administration had put in place. For instance, the Ramaphosa administration resuscitated the Policy Unit but in a different form. It is called the Policy and Research Services. It mainly focuses on influencing policy making, whereas the Mbeki's Policy Unit dealt with coordination, monitoring and evaluation, planning and policy thinking/advise.

As indicated earlier, the public sector reforms have been geared to making South Africa a developmental state. The terminology or phraseology has changed over time, but the focus is essentially on a democratic developmental state. Gumede (2022) concludes that there is still a long way for South Africa to become a democratic developmental state because of factors such as policy paralysis, weak leadership and absence of a sound development agenda. Although the Ramaphosa administration has been trying to steer the government and social partners back to the developmental state, the efforts have not yielded any positive results so far.

Among recent initiatives in relation to public sector reforms is the Public Service Charter. As a measure to ensure that public service officials conduct themselves in a manner that is professional, a social contract was entered into and it involved the employer and the employees, through the Public Service Charter (2013). Included in the Charter are the values that govern public administration, as they are set out in Chapter 10 of the Constitution, which also includes professional ethics, transparency, accountability and good management of human resources (PSCBC, 2013). The Charter has a context legislatively that includes the 1997 Batho Pele White Paper on Transforming Public Service delivery. Within the Public Service Charter is a Code of Conduct for Public Servants. This includes prohibitions on abusing positions of authority and a commitment to the optimal development of public servants.

In 2009, President Zuma appointed 34 ministers responsible for various portfolios, a shift from President Mbeki's Cabinet which had a composition of 26 ministers—President Cyril Ramaphosa has 28 Ministers. When the second term of office of President Zuma commenced after the general election of 2014, he reconfigured his Cabinet again on 24 May 2014 and introduced new ministries, namely, the Small Business Development; Water and Sanitation; Environmental Affairs; Telecommuni cations and Postal Services; and Communications ministries and combined a few existing ministries, namely, the Justice and Correctional Services; Planning and Performance Monitoring and Evaluation bringing the number of his Cabinet members to 35 (Koma & Tshiyoyo, 2015).

Over and above resuscitating public sector reforms started under Mbeki, the Ramaphosa administration has pursued a number of additional public sector reforms. Among the initiatives in the Ramaphosa administration is the National Implementation Framework towards the professionalisation of the Public Service. In December 2020, the then Minister for the Public Service and Administration, Senzo Mchunu, approved the publication of the draft National Implementation Framework towards the professionalisation of the Public Service for public comments. The purpose of the Framework was to develop a national implementation framework towards the professionalisation of the public service as part of creating a capable and ethical developmental state.

A high-level task team on the professionalisation framework was established in 2021. The members of the task team represent a wide array of institutions and sectors, including representation from Auditor-General South Africa (AGSA), think tanks, state-owned training academies, academia and the legal fraternity.

The Department of Planning, Monitoring and Evaluation (DPME) recently came up with a National Policy Development Framework which has been developed with the aim of regulating policy management processes in South Africa. It also seeks to develop a code of practice for policy making and entrench evidence-based policy making. It will also guide officials on analysing policy, developing policy, policy authorisation, implementing policy and on policy reviews. The framework further gives clarity on how to approach intra/inter-departmental consultation (policy coordination) and external stakeholder consultations during the process of policy management.

The District Development Model (DDM) is an operational model for improving Cooperative Governance aimed at building a capable and ethical Developmental State. It embodies an approach by which the three spheres of government and state entities work in unison in an impact-oriented way and where there is higher performance and accountability for coherent service delivery and development outcomes. Essentially, it is a method of government operating in unison focusing on the municipal district and metropolitan spaces as the impact areas of joint planning, budgeting and implementation.

All the initiatives discussed above confirm that institutional capacity of the South African government has been increasing overtime. The number of public sector employees has increased faster since 2009/10. It is therefore not surprising that the compensation of public servants as a share of gross domestic product (GDP) has increased from about 12% in 2009/10 to about 16% in 2019/20. This is higher than USA, Japan, UK, China, Malaysia, Singapore, Brazil, Mauritius and Botswana. In addition, public servants per 100 economically active people or public servants per 100 people in South Africa compare well with other countries. For latest data available (2019 or 2020), public servants per 100 economically active people in South Africa is 7.43. In Malaysia it is 7.47, it is 7.76 in Brazil and 9.81 in USA (see Gumede, 2022).

7.3 Planning, in a Comparative Context

Development plans presuppose that there are clear developmental goals or a clear developmental agenda driven by the developmental elite that is guided by a developmental ideology. In other words, the outlook of those leading society and government has to be developmental—at the core, the desire to advance the wellbeing and welfare of society or a particular group or groups in a society. Development is largely understood as the improvements in wellbeing and welfare. In the context of this book, the focus is on social and economic development: higher levels of human development and economic performance.

In a comparative context, per capita incomes (signifying standard of living) measured in US dollars are much higher in Singapore (followed by

Malaysia). India has the lowest per capita incomes among the countries that South Africa is compared with in this particular context. This is to be expected—that Singapore leads—because, as will be illustrated, Singapore has venerated bureaucratic planning capacity and a robust development plan. This, however, does not take away that the East Asian Tigers developed quicker because of geo-political and geography-related factors as well as under authoritarian regimes. The proximity to markets and the agenda of the West to 'defeat' communism played important roles in the speedy industrialisation of some Southeast Asian countries.

Per capita incomes for Botswana and South Africa have been similar from 2000 to 2012. In fact, during the same period, there were years when South Africa's GDP per capita was higher than that of Botswana. From 2013, South Africa's GDP per capita has remained stagnant; in fact, it has actually been declining for some years before the Covid-19 pandemic (see Gumede, 2020). South Africa's GDP started declining from around 2007/8. It seems to be an anomaly that South Africa is the only country in the selected countries (i.e. Singapore, Malaysia, Mauritius, Brazil, Botswana, India and Nigeria) with a declining GDP per capita over the period under study (2000–2019). Although GDP per capita for India and Nigeria is low, the numbers have been increasing throughout the same period. It is also insightful that South Africa's GDP per capita was approximately equal to that of Brazil until about 2005. With all its challenges, Brazil's GDP per capita has continued to grow over the years leaving South Africa far behind.

Regarding human development—a comprehensive measure of wellbeing considering access to healthcare, education and income—Singapore has the highest level of human development followed by Malaysia. The Human Development Index (HDI)—a composite indicator consisting of life expectancy, literacy and per capita income—for all the countries being compared to South Africa has been improving as shown by an upward trend. Nigeria has the lowest index in the selected countries and it has not improved much: the HDI for Nigeria has been standing still since 2015. The same can be said about South Africa's HDI: it has not improved much since 2000 and it has remained constant since 2015. Compared to Botswana, South Africa's HDI was higher during 2000–2010; however, Botswana has since overtaken South Africa's HDI (see Table 7.1).

There appears to be a relationship between per capita incomes of the selected countries and their indices of human development. This is unsurprising since HDI is calculated using per capita incomes. It would also

Table 7.1 Human Development Index, 2000–2019

	2000	*2010*	*2013*	*2015*	*2016*	*2017*	*2018*	*2019*
Singapore	0.818	0.909	0.923	0.929	0.933	0.934	0.935	0.938
Malaysia	0.724	0.773	0.787	0.797	0.801	0.802	0.804	0.810
Mauritius	0.674	0.748	0.775	0.786	0.790	0.793	0.796	0.804
Brazil	0.684	0.726	0.752	0.755	0.757	0.760	0.761	0.765
Botswana	0.578	0.660	0.699	0.714	0.719	0.724	0.728	0.735
India	0.497	0.581	0.607	0.627	0.637	0.643	0.647	0.645
Nigeria	–	0.484	0.520	0.527	0.528	0.533	0.534	0.539
South Africa	0.629	0.662	0.683	0.699	0.702	0.704	0.705	0.709

Source: United Nations Development Programme (UNDP), various sources

Table 7.2 Human Development in South Africa (1990–2019)

	Life expectancy at birth	*Expected years of schooling*	*Mean years of schooling*	*GNI per capita (2017 PPP$)*	*HDI value*
1990	63.3	11.4	6.5	9588	0.625
1995	61.6	13.0	8.2	9023	0.652
2000	56.0	13.0	8.8	9498	0.629
2005	53.4	12.9	8.9	10,798	0.620
2010	57.7	12.8	10.2	11,723	0.662
2015	62.6	13.8	10.1	12,052	0.699
2016	63.2	13.7	10.2	11,908	0.702
2017	63.5	13.7	10.2	11,864	0.704
2018	63.9	13.7	10.2	11,756	0.705
2019	63.87	13.8	10.2	12,129	0.709

Source: United Nations Development Programme (2021/22)

seem that the two Asian Tigers perform far better than the rest of the selected countries. Looking at South Africa more closely, the 2019 Human Development Report suggests that South Africa's Human Development Index (HDI) has effectively been stagnant, though it has been marginally increasing in the past few years. As Table 7.2 shows, the 2010 HDI for South Africa was 0.662 and 0.629 in 2012—an insignificant change. Table 7.2 also illustrates that both per capita incomes and life expectancy have been stagnant, especially in the recent period. Other useful numbers in the 2019 Human Development Report relate to schooling: data implies that South Africans, on average, school five years less than expected.

As a result, there have been insignificant improvements in the HDI and associated factors. In fact, from 2016 it seems all indicators given in Table 7.2 are dormant. Of concern is that the average number of years for school remains unchanged while the expected years of schooling have increased. The gap/shortfall has increased to four years. By implication, the level of human development would decline further as a result of Covid-19. In fact, development outcomes and the performance of the South African economy have worsened ever since Covid-19 came to South Africa in March 2020.

As indicated earlier, the HDI is a composite index consisting of three main dimensions: a long and healthy life, the ability to acquire knowledge and the ability to achieve a decent standard of living (see Gumede, 2016). Using the NIDS data to calculate the HDI, the level of human development in post-apartheid South Africa has not improved much: 0.649 in 2010; 0.685 in 2014 and 0.69 in 2017 as shown in Table 7.3. The 2018 Human Development Report was used because the 2019 Human Development Report did not have certain figures, particularly those corresponding with the waves of the NIDS for analysing similar years and similar periods; hence, no data for some years for the Inequality-adjusted Human Development Index (IHDI) and the Gender Inequality Index (GII). It is important to indicate that the HDI is determined based on two calculations, as undertaken for this chapter. First, before computing the overall HDI, each dimension is transformed into indices of between 0 and 1 by setting their minimum and maximum values, which is followed by aggregating the dimensional indices to produce the HDI.

Table 7.3 also shows the Inequality-adjusted Human Development Index (IHDI) which combines a country's average achievements in health, education and income with how those achievements are distributed among the country's population by discounting each dimension's average value according to its level of inequality (UNDP, 2019). The IHDI seems to have been increasing relatively faster than the normal HDI in South Africa:

Table 7.3 Human Development (2008–2017)

	2008	*2010*	*2012*	*2014*	*2017*
HDI	0.633	0.649	0.664	0.685	0.699
IHDI	–	0.411	–	0.428	0.467
GII	–	0.635	0.462	0.407	0.389

Source: Gumede (2021)

0.411 in 2010 and 0.467 in 2017. Although this is commendable, the IHDI is generally low. It is not unreasonable to expect that the IHDI should have been at least 0.50 if government was vigorously pursuing interventions aimed at improving wellbeing. It is, however, worth highlighting that the Gender Inequality Index (GII), a measure of gender disparity, has been declining with relative significance since 2010: 0.635 in 2010 and 0.389 in 2017. This means that the country is doing relatively well in addressing the gender gap.

It appears that countries with clear development plans perform better than those with inarticulate development plans. Indeed, countries with effective capacities in place for implementing development plans appear to perform better in terms of social and economic development. How governments are organised in the selected countries also plays a role for socio-economic development. Planning commissions for countries such as Malaysia and Singapore have necessary technical capacities and work closely with government departments or ministries and various agencies of the government.

In addition, or more importantly, as Table 7.4 shows, Malaysia and Singapore have crisp (and ambitious) plans. An examination of their plans over the decades suggests that these countries have had very clear intentions about goals and objectives. Also, their plans come across as realistic although quite ambitious—ambition in planning works if the track record supports it and if requisite capacities are in place to accomplish the plan. Lastly, most of the plans under study are relatively brief.

Table 7.4 Country by country vision statements or objectives

Country	*Vision or overarching national objective*
Malaysia	To become a high-income country by 2024
Nigeria	To become one of the world's 20 largest economies by 2020
Brazil	To reduce poverty and grow the middle class
India	Aspiring for developed country status
Mauritius	To become a high-income country
Botswana	To raise the standard of living for its population
South Africa	To eliminate poverty and reduce inequality by 2030
Singapore	To become a developed country in the first league
Taiwan	To become a Green Silicon Island

Source: Summary from plans of selected countries

With some exceptions, all the countries compared with South Africa have relatively short long-term/development plans and relatively clear focus. The South African NDP is by far the longest in terms of the number of pages. In addition, for countries compared with South Africa that have higher development outcomes, there are requisite capacities to plan, monitor and evaluate as well as implementation. The planning commissions are relatively independent and influential. All these countries have either tweaked existing long-term plans or came up with comprehensive interventions to deal with the negative impact of Covid-19. Taiwan, for instance, developed a plan aimed at increasing Taiwan's global visibility and influence taking into account Covid-19.[1]

7.4 Social and Economic Transformation

Much has been achieved regarding the implementation of the government's priority on addressing the lack of access to basic social services. However, as the discussion will show, there is still a long way to go in ensuring a 'Better Life for All'. Statistics South Africa (Stats SA) data and government records indicate impressive progress has been achieved in ensuring that people have access to basic services such as clean water sources despite numerous more people still being piped (tap) water.[2] The service delivery challenges remain unabated. Progress has varied: some areas show improvements while others are deteriorating. For instance, as Table 7.5 illustrates, there has been an increase in access to form"l dw'lling and a decline in informal and traditional dwelling although these improvements are not that significant particularly from 2011.

There remain significant backlogs. For instance, approximately 18% of households do not have access to a flush toilet and about 14% of the households do not have a toilet at all as shown in Table 7.5. Table 7.5 provides apt reasoning for the increased public protests that have increased significantly post 2007. It is also worth highlighting South Africa's social assistance programme—the cash transfer system. Table 7.6 indicates that

[1]Taiwan National Development Council, 2021, *National Development Plan (2021–2024)*, Taipei.

[2]According to the 2011 Census there were about 1,265,907 people without access to piped water, of which 1,234,087 were Africans—this supports the point that most of the socio-economic challenges confronting South African society remain predominantly problems of Africans.

Table 7.5 Access to services and type of dwelling in South Africa (1996–2019)

Type of main dwelling	*1996*	*2001*	*2011*	*2018*	*2019*
Formal	65.1	68.5	77.6	81.1	81.9
Informal	16.2	16.4	13.6	13.1	12.7
Traditional	18.3	14.8	7.9	5.0	4.1
Other	0.4	0.3	0.9	0.8	0.3
Household basic services					
Piped water (tap)	80.3	84.5	91.2	89.0	88.2
Electricity (lighting)	58.2	51.4	84.6	84.7	85
Toilet facilities					
Access to a flush toilet	82.9	82.3	90.6	83.0	82.1
Bucket toilet	4.7	4.1	2.1	2.8	2.4
No toilet	12.4	13.6	7.3	14.2	–

Source: Compiled from various Stats SA surveys

Table 7.6 Number of social grants per grant type, 2012/13–2019/20

Grant type	*2013/14*	*2014/15*	*2015/16*	*2016/17*	*2017/18*	*2018/19*	*2019/20*
Old age	2,969,933	3,086,851	3,194,087	3,302,202	3,423,337	3,553,317	3,676,791
War veterans	429	326	245	176	134	92	62
Disability	1,120,419	1,112,663	1,085,541	1,067,176	1,061,866	1,048,255	1,042,025
Grant in aid	83,059	113,087	137,806	164,349	192,091	221,989	273,922
Care dependency	120,632	126,777	131,040	144,952	147,467	150,001	154,735
Foster child	512,055	499,774	470,015	440,295	416,016	386,019	355,609
Child support	11,125,946	11,703,165	11,972,900	12,081,375	12,269,084	12,452,072	12,787,448
Total	15,932,473	16,642,643	16,991,634	17,200,525	17,509,995	17,811,745	18,290,592
Annual growth	-1.08%	4.46%	2.10%	1.23%	1.80%	1.72%	2.69%

Source: Compiled from South African Social Security Agency's Annual Reports

South Africa has an extensive social assistance programme that has helped cushion households from extreme hardship.

In 2012/13 approximately 16 million people received social grants which constituted 3.1% of GDP. By 2018/19, grant recipients were 17.8 million in total. The 12.5 million child support grant recipients constituted 70.2% of the total grant recipients in 2018/19. This grant is provided to children in need until the age of 15 years. It is expected that children under 18 years will, over time, also receive the child support grant as per the means test. The age requirement for the old age pension for men was also reduced to 60 years.

The challenge with the social assistance programme is its financial sustainability and possible unintended consequences. Although it was stabilising as a share of the GDP, it is still remarkably high (over 3%). As for the unintended consequences, the fundamental issue relates to the kind of the society South Africa aspires towards. Ideally, as in Brazil and India, more people should be gainfully employed than on social assistance.

The grants however, especially in the context of a small informal sector, play an important role in mitigating severe hardship endured by those in need. As some findings on poverty suggest, the grants may have cushioned the poor against the global economic recession.

With regard to economic performance, South Africa's economic growth has not been commensurate to the size of its economy. Looking at comparable countries such as Botswana, India, Brazil and Malaysia, South Africa's economic performance has been low. The low GDP growth rate, compared to similar countries, supports the point that it is not only the global economic recession that has lowered SA's economic performance, but that GDP appears to have begun to decline after its highest point in the post-apartheid dispensation, in 2006.

There were no significant economic policy reforms undertaken for effectively ten years (1996–2006). Macroeconomic stabilisation was achieved, through Growth, Employment and Redistribution (GEAR), around the year 2000. The obvious next policy or strategy would have been the one focusing on accelerating GDP growth, which has happened around 2002. There was, arguably, a significant policy reform lag because AsgiSA began in 2005. And because it takes a while for any policy to gain traction, AsgiSA would have started to deliver optimally around 2008. However, there was state of flux and relative instability in the public sector due to the recall of former President Mbeki in 2008, the immediate resignation of former vice president, Phumzile Mlambo-Ngcuka, and others who championed AsgiSA.

There was an exodus of critical technocrats and policy gurus such as Joel Netshitenzhe who left government in 2009. The researcher left the presidency in 2009 but returned for a year as a special advisor in the State-Owned Enterprises portfolio of the Department of Public Enterprises. The caretaker administration of Kgalema Motlanthe during mid-2008 to mid-2009 maintained relative stability and continuity, but the politics of that specific period made governing a challenge. It was always understood in the African National Congress (ANC) that Kgalema Motlanthe was temporarily holding the reigns for Jacob Zuma (who became president of the ANC, replacing Thabo Mbeki, in December 2007 in Polokwane).

7.5 Why Have Development Outcomes Not Improved?

The fundamental issue requiring addressing is what could be causing a deterioration in development outcomes when capacity seems to have been increasing since 1994. We have examined this issue because it is critical for the South African economy. This should be instructive for the further public sector reforms that are being pursued. It might very well be that public sector reforms implemented since 1994 have not addressed the correct problem. Part of the challenge might have been that the reforms pursued were aligned to the neoliberal agenda. The New Public Management approach for instance that was followed in the 1990s in South Africa had been critiqued by those who felt that it was akin to neoliberal reforms that had not worked well in other countries. Similarly, GEAR was criticised as it was seen as akin to the Washington Consensus.

The analysis in this chapter suggests that what matters most is the kind of capacity that the government has and how the government is organised. Countries with which South Africa is compared placed significant technical capacities at the centre of the government. There were attempts to do this in the late 1990s to the late 2000s. That capacity, largely centralised in the Mbeki's policy unit, was not sufficient and it was destroyed during the Zuma administration. Zuma created fully-fledged long-term planning as well as monitoring and evaluation, but development outcomes started deteriorating. He also inaugurated a national planning commission.

Given the experience of countries that South Africa is compared with, the organisation of the government seems to matter greatly. Requisite capacities should be at the highest level in the government. The planning commission should not only have necessary technical capacity, but it must also be part of the government. In South Africa, the national planning commission was constituted more as a political structure made up of different social partners. This might not be a major problem, but the capacity of the national planning commission and its secretariat should be sound. There have been various attempts at this, but it might be that the capacity building has not been appropriate. Arguably, there are specific skills set that are needed at local government level that might differ from the expertise required at the provincial and national levels. This point has implications for the professionalisation of the public service that is being pursued. It would be important that the professionalisation addresses the correct problem.

As Mkandawire (2001) explained, a country's 'circumstances' shape the kind of a developmental state a country can be or can become. It is largely in this context that I argue that the notion of a developmental state should be viewed as a framework instead of attempting to copy the developmental state 'model' of another country. In fact, developmental state as a framework guides the work of a government that is serious about development—if a government can achieve the various attributes of what is perceived to be a developmental state that government would have achieved what any society hopes for and thereby ensure inclusive development. As Mkandawire put it, deciding on universalism versus targeting is about "the choice of instruments for redistributing resources in society and for determining levels of social expenditure" (Mkandawire, 2005: 12). Linked to this is what Mkandawire called a shift from development to poverty reduction (Mkandawire, 2005: 7). Overall, Mkandawire provides evidence that social policy has been universalistic while targeting was used to make universalism more effective in the countries that have been able to reduce poverty—Theda Skocpol's "targeting within universalism" notion.

7.6 Government's Role in Socio-economic Development

Although there are those who argue that governments must not intervene in economy, evidence confirms that governments can play important roles in socio-economic development (see Gumede, 2022). Among the important policies that can advance inclusive development is social policy. As explained in Gumede (2019), social policy has to do with policy interventions in the public sector aimed at directly improving wellbeing in a society—it can be thought of as a series of public policies that ensure that the quality of life in a society improves. It is also worth highlighting that social policy has various roles/functions (i.e. production, distribution, reproduction, protection and social cohesion/nation building). Leading scholars of social policy emphasise social policy's transformative role; that social policy must transform society, societal relations, the economy, etc. For estimations, several input variables (i.e. expenditures on education, health, social development, art and culture as well as water and sanitation) were used to come up with policy scores for the social policy variable.

Because of many advantages associated with the autoregressive distributed lag (ARDL) econometric method, the ARDL model is used to assess the role of the government in society (based on 1996–2020 time period). For instance, there is no need to worry about the order of integration and ARDL can be used even with a limited number of samples (Pesaran et al., 2001).

The equations estimated are:

$$HDI_t = \beta_0 + \beta_1 lnGDP_t + \beta_2 \ln GSP_t + e_t \tag{7.1}$$

and

$$HDI_t = \beta_3 + \beta_4 \text{Social Policy}_t + \beta_5 \text{Institutions}_t + u_t \tag{7.2}$$

HDI in both equations refer to Human Development Index which is a composite index consisting of three main dimensions: long and healthy life, the ability to acquire knowledge and the ability to achieve a decent standard of living (as explained earlier). In Eq. 7.1, *GDP* is gross domestic product (measured in constant price) and *GSP* is government spending (measured as a percentage of GDP). In Eq. 7.2, *social policy* denotes the scores of the PCA (principal component analysis) index and the ***institutions*** variable is measured by regulatory quality. Like social policy, institutions are critical for socio-economic development but are often not sufficiently accounted for. For this chapter, analysing the institutional architecture, it is necessary to include institutions in the equation that estimates socio-economic development.

The subscript t indicates a certain variable at time t while e and u in Eqs. 7.1 and 7.2 denote the error terms, respectively. Equations 7.1 and 7.2 are extended in order to depict the ARDL approach and include lag operators for dependent variable p and the regressors ($q1, q2, q3$ *and* $q4$). The ARDL models are then shown as:

$$\Delta HDI_t = \beta_6 + \beta_7 \sum_{i=1}^{p} \Delta HDI_{t-1} + \beta_8 \sum_{i=0}^{q1} \Delta \ln GDP_{t-i} + \beta_9 \sum_{i=0}^{q2} \Delta \ln GSP_{t-i} + \alpha_1 \ln GDP_{t-i} + \alpha_2 \ln GSP_{t-i} + e_t \quad (7.3)$$

and

$$\Delta HDI_t = \beta_{10} + \beta_{11} \sum_{t=i}^{p} \Delta HDI_{t-1} + \beta_{12} \sum_{i=0}^{q1} \Delta Social\ Policy_{t-i} + \beta_{13} \sum_{i=0}^{q2} \Delta Institions_{t-i} + \alpha_3 Social\ policy_{t-i} + \alpha_4 Institutions_{t-i} u_t \quad (7.4)$$

Δ depicts the first difference and β_6, β_7, β_8, β_9, β_{10}, β_{11}, β_{12}, β_{13} indicate the short-run elasticity given a 1% increase in the control variables, while α_1, α_2, α_3 ***and*** α_4 denote the long-run elasticity.

Table 7.7 gives the summary statistics of the variables.

Gumede (2022) estimated the relationship between government spending, economic growth and socio-economic development and found that economic growth does not necessarily translate to socio-economic development although government spending does. Essentially, the findings supported the view that governments should be active in facilitating social and economic development. As Table 7.8 shows, estimates for this chapter suggest that, apart from the initial conditions, both social policy and institutions have a positive impact on socio-economic development.

As shown in Table 7.8, in addition to the fact that a 1% increase in the previous values of the HDI leads to an increase of the current HDI for about 0.92%, results also show that a 1% increase in social policy and institutions is significantly responsible for an increase of HDI (0.01% and 0.07%, respectively). In addition, the social policy estimation also seems to have a long-run relationship as demonstrated by bound test result. The vector error correction (VEC) model and its long-run results indicate that social policy as well as institutions both have a long-run impact. With regard to social policy, for instance, a 1% increase in social policy leads to 0.07% increase in HDI in the long run as shown in Table 7.8.

Table 7.7 Summary statistics

Variable	*Mean*	*Std. Dev*	*Min*	*Max*	*Variable*
HDI	0.6665	0.0384781	0.611	0.727	Human Development index
GDPac	3.10189982371	4.28758563	2.276776	3.5871244	Gross domestic product
GSP	18.09188	1.4130	15.8607	20.6502	Government spending
Social Policy	0.0000000206	2.1865	-3.1689	3.5738	Social policy scores
Institutions	0.3887817	0.2881	-0.0731	0.8196	Institutions

Table 7.8 The impact of social policy and institutions on human development

	ARDL		*ECM*		*Long-run estimates*	
	Coef.	*SE*	*Coef.*	*SE*	*Coef.*	*SE*
D.HDI (-1)	0.9161**	0.2187	-0.3129	0.1136		
D.HDI(-2)	0.3129	0.2317		0.0440		
D.Social Policy	0.0100**	0.0030	0.0100**	0.0013	0.0652**	0.0436
D.Social Policy(-1)	-0.0045	0.0027	-0.0094**	0.0014		
D.Social Policy(-2)	0.0094	0.0094				
Institutions	0.0591	0.0236	0.0591**	0.0516	0.9405**	0.5257
Institutions(-1)	0.0713**	0.0181	-0.0849**	0.0515		
Institutions(-2)	0.849**	0.0169				
Con	-0.2180	0.0913			0.9519**	0.1539
CointEq(-1)*			-0.2290**	0.0232		
R-squared	0.9985		0.9595			
Adj R-squared	0.9924		0.9190			
F-Bounds Test		Null Hypothesis		No levels relationship		
Test statistic	Value	Signf.	I(0)	I(1)		
F-statistic	9.7581	10%	2.63	3.35		
K	2	5%	3.1	3.87		
		2.5%	3.55	3.38		
		1%	4.13	5		

Standard errors in parentheses, *** denotes significance at 1%, ** at 5% and * at 10%

7.7 Conclusion

Examining the post-apartheid development experience implies that many mistakes have been made regarding the development approach pursued so far. Arguably, the country has not had a clear development agenda which would have taken into account perspectives and insights from research and advise from other. For instance, the role of social policy would have been more pronounced in such a development agenda as well as an important issue of the link between social and economic policies. The research presented in this chapter further confirms the critical role of social policy for inclusive development.

Fundamentally, the manner in which the South African government is organised and capacitated has affected socio-economic development. This does not mean that other factors (e.g. corruption) have not had a negative impact on development outcomes. Lastly, the assessment of the role of the government in the economy confirms that the South African government can play an important role in socio-economic development. Among the critical policies that should be in place and should be properly implemented is social policy.

References

Dastile, F. (2018). Analysing Performance Management Training Interventions in The Public Service: A Case of the National School of Government. Masters thesis, University of Pretoria.

Gumede, V. (2016). *Post-Apartheid South Africa: Social & Economic Inclusion.* Cambria Press.

Gumede, V. (2019). Social Policy in Post-apartheid South Africa. *Journal of Public Administration, 54*(5), 499–511.

Gumede, V. (2020). Elusive Pursuit of Reconciliation and Development in Post-apartheid South Africa. *Strategic Review of Southern Africa, 42*(2), 129–154.

Gumede, V. (2021). Revisiting Poverty, Human Development and Inequality in Democratic South Africa, *Indian. Journal of Human Development, 15*(2), 183–199.

Gumede, V. (2022). *South Africa: State and Development.* South African Association of Public Administration and Management (SAAPAM).

Koma, S., & Tshiyoyo, M. (2015). Improving Public Service Delivery in South Africa – A Case of Administrative Reform. *African Journal of Public Affairs, 8*, 30–42.

Mkandawire, T. (2001). Thinking About Developmental States in Africa. *Cambridge Journal of Economics, 25*, 289–313.

Mkandawire, T. (2005). Targeting and Universalism in Poverty Reduction. *UNRISD Paper Number 23*, December 2005, UNRISD, Geneva.

Pesaran, M. H., Shin, Y., & Smith, R. J. (2001). Bounds Testing Approaches to the Analysis of Level Relationships. *Journal of Applied Econometrics, 3*, 289–326.

Public Service Commission. (2008). *State of the Public Service Report 2008.* Government Printers.

Public Service Co-ordinating Bargaining Council. (2013). *Public Service Charter.* Government Printers.

United Nations Development Programme. (2019). *Human Development Report: Beyond Income, Beyond Averages, Beyond Inequality: Inequalities in Human Development in the 21st Century.* UNDP.

United Nations Development Programme. (2021/22). *Human Development Report: Uncertain Times, Unsettled Lives: Shaping our Future in a Transforming World.* UNDP.

CHAPTER 8

Conclusion

8.1 Introduction

The book has dealt with many aspects pertaining to the South African economy. Having discussed various economic policies that have been pursued during the post-apartheid dispensation so far and having examined economic performance as well as an assessment of socio-economic development and the government-market interface and the institutional architecture for better economic development, this concluding chapter revisits economic policies with a view of recommending the critical aspects of an economic policy that could work better for South Africa. As indicated in the introductory chapter, the focus is on macroeconomic policies and the national development plan. Although the national development plan (viz. Vision 2030) is not an economic policy per se, it cannot be ignored because it has some aspects of economic policy. The same can be said about the Reconstruction and Development Programme (RDP). In addition, the chapter synthesises main issues that the book covers, and we discuss prospects for the South African economy. We start this concluding chapter with a synthesis of key issues.

V. Gumede et al., *South African Economy*, African Histories and Modernities, https://doi.org/10.1007/978-3-031-54180-3_8

8.2 Economic Policies

In the early years of democracy, policy focus was mainly on correcting past imbalances and growing the economy through redistribution. Although economic policies that have been implemented since democracy have yielded some positives, the daunting challenges of low economic growth, high unemployment and high inequality support the need to relook into these economic policies. Particularly, it is important to reflect and identify the shortcomings of the policies and frameworks for the economy that have been implemented.

The first policy framework immediately at the dawn of democracy was the RDP. According to Terreblanche (1999) the African National Congress (ANC) was uncertain to make critical decisions about RDP policies. Moreover, Terreblanche (1999) argued that another possible explanation of the RDP's failure and the reason why the RDP was abruptly abandoned can be attributed to lack of manpower to implement the policy. The RDP was therefore seen as overly ambitious given the economic conditions of that time. The democratic government inherited large fiscal deficits and public debt. It was an obstacle on its own to have a Keynesian policy plan, with enormous government debt. Terreblanche (1999) further raised challenges in tax collection and tax base as one of the contributing factors to the failure of the RDP. The government did not set out clear plans on how they would broaden the tax base and improve tax collection. Given the 'skewness' of the apartheid government spending and the redistribution plans of the democratic government it was a tedious exercise to implement the RDP.

The RDP was also constrained by several economic challenges. The growth rate of that time was relatively low to achieve the RDP set objectives. This created a question on whether the RDP wanted to achieve growth through redistribution or to achieve redistribution through a growing economy. Perhaps one of the main reasons why the RDP short fall in achieving its objectives was focusing on distribution, without a thorough plan on growing the economy. The set objective of achieving 4–6% growth rate was unattainable in 1994. The government was faced with many challenges that required conflicting solutions. For example, the government did not have a strategy on how it would simultaneously lower unemployment, lower tax burden, reduce high income inequality, lower inflation and increase public provision of welfare services (Masters, 2019; Blumenfeld, 1996). Terreblanche (1999) stated that the economic woes during the RDP tenure required a robust and a comprehensive economic policy.

In 1996, the Growth, Employment and Redistribution (GEAR) policy framework was introduced to grow the economy sufficiently to attract foreign investment and to achieve other macroeconomic objectives beyond redistribution. The GEAR strategy was conservative, advocating for privatisation, elimination of exchange controls and fiscal prudence (Tregenna, 2011). Some scholars believe that GEAR was a successful policy framework as it met most of its target and even exceeded expectations. For example, Streak (2004) and Masters (2019) commended the achievements of GEAR of lowering inflation from 7.35% in 1996 to 5.34% in 2000, narrowing the budget deficit as a share of gross domestic product (GDP) from 4.5% in 1996 to 1.9% in 2000, consecutively recording a surplus of 0.6% in 2006. Horton (2005) praised the GEAR strategy for improving fiscus stance, broadening tax base yet reducing tax burden and stabilising the exchange rate. The government cut corporate taxes from 35% to 30%, while providing tax incentives for small business. The government introduced the capital gains tax and taxed personal income on a worldwide basis (Ibid.). The macroeconomic stability brought by the GEAR strategy was received well by the business and international community.

The GEAR policy however was criticised for failing to meet its growth targets. The GEAR had aimed to grow the economy by an average of 6% per annum (Department of Finance, 1996). During the GEAR tenure (1996–2005) the economy grew by a modest 3.2%. COSATU was the outspoken critique of the GEAR policy framework and viewed the GEAR as a neoliberal policy, carrying out the International Monetary Fund mandate to capitalise the economy (Le Roux, 1997; Masters, 2019). Moreover, COSATU viewed GEAR as a policy decided on panic after the dramatic depreciation of the rand (COSATU, 1996). Streak (2004) is of the view that GEAR failed to put South Africa in a positive growth trajectory and to reduce unemployment. This is due to GEAR's heavy reliance on economic growth to reduce poverty and inequality (Ibid.). The sentiments of Le Roux (1997) are that GEAR was not necessarily criticised based on merits or shortcomings, but it did not get the political approval from the other ANC alliance members. Its drafting was based on orthodox economics and the process was not transparent (Le Roux, 1997). By the end of 2005, GEAR had failed to achieve its set objectives (Streak, 2004; Masters, 2019) and a much comprehensive strategy that will tackle past imbalances and grow the economy simultaneously was required (Streak, 2004).

In 2006, AsgiSA (Accelerated and Shared Growth Initiative for South Africa) was introduced to replace GEAR, with an aim to fast-track infrastructure backlogs and to address poverty and inequality through shared growth. AsgiSA aimed halve poverty by 2014 to reduce unemployment from 30% in the year of its inception to 15% in 2006 and achieve the annual growth rate of 6% per year. AsgiSA also aimed to improve skills of the labour force to enhance labour productivity. However, AsgiSA fell short of its targets and in fact unemployment increased, inequality remained high, while poverty rates worsened. Reflecting on what might have transpired for AsgiSA not to bear the intended fruit, the government sited lack of sufficient funds to finance AsgiSA programmes. Another challenge to hinder performance of AsgiSA was the complexity of implementation of the policy which resulted in coordination failure (The Presidency, 2007).

AsgiSA was abandoned and in 2010 the New Growth Path (NGP) was introduced under the presidency of Jacob Zuma. The NGP was criticised for lacking detail on implementation (Meyer, 2013). Furthermore, the NGP was seen as a plan, rather than a policy which has a recipe for implementation (Ibid.). Prinsloo (2011) critiqued NGPs over reliance on government to create jobs, rather than strengthening economic institutions to enable the private sector to thrive. This was a challenge considering the large public wage bill. The NGP was also criticised for biting more than it can swallow when it came to job creation. The NGP targeted to create 5 million new jobs by 2020, which was even impossible to achieve during the commodity boom of 2002–2008—only 300,000 jobs were created (Nattrass, 2011; Meyer, 2013).

In 2011, the government introduced the National Development Plan (Vision 2030). Since the National Development Plan (NDP) was adopted, the economy is still taking an unfavourable growth trajectory. Unemployment has increased significantly, while South Africa remains the most unequal society. Among other things, the NDP promised to reduce unemployment from 26% to 6% in 2030. It appears highly unlikely that this target and others will be met, hence our suggestions of what a better economic policy could look like for South Africa.

Table 8.1 shows economic performance in South Africa since 1994 against the different economic policies pursued. We use per capita growth rate as it also captures the standard of living. Table 8.1 confirms the

Table 8.1 Average per capita growth rate under RDP, GEAR, AsgiSA and NDP

Macroeconomic framework	*Period*	*Average per capita growth rate (%)*
RDP	1994–1996	1.4
GEAR	1996–2005	1.58
AsgiSA	2006–2010	1.76
NGP and NDP	2013–2022	–0.44

Source: Based on South African Reserve Bank data

argument we have made that the South African economy has performed poorly since 1994 although there were years—the Mbeki years—when the economy performed better. The average per capita growth rates for the RDP and GEAR policy years are respectful given that the economy was emerging from a deep recession and the new democratic government was implementing many reforms to undo the ramifications of apartheid (and colonialism).

The average per capita growth rate for the RDP period (between 1994 and 1996) was 1.4%. This led to the introduction of GEAR in February 1996. During the GEAR period the economy grew by 1.58%, slightly higher than the RDP period. The economy was favourable due to higher commodity prices which put South Africa at an advantage. The international business community as well as the local markets received the results of GEAR of stabilising the economy well.

The AsgiSA period recorded the highest average per capita growth of 1.76. Although AsgiSA grew per capita income, it failed to reduce unemployment, poverty and inequality. Even though unemployment reduced slightly during the AsgiSA tenure, the strategy created many jobs, but not creating skilled labour. The strategy therefore did not live up to its promise to ensure that growth was enjoyed equally. After the National Planning Commission's *Diagnostic Report*, it was established that the economy was still faced with several major challenges including high unemployment, poor quality education for black people, overreliance of the economy on primary commodities, poor health services and high levels of corruption in government. In 2013 the implementation of the National Development Plan commenced in 2013 to tackle economic and social challenges that persisted despite several economic strategies. The NDP (and the National Growth Path) period recorded the worst growth rate of -0.44. This period somehow gives an image of economic performance outside commodity booms. This is the problem which was already identified by the Planning Commission that outside commodity booms, the economy will be stagnant.

As a response to Covid-19, the government unveiled an Economic Recovery and Reconstruction Plan (ERRP) which was aimed at mitigating the effects of Covid-19 on the economy and other challenges. What stands out from the ERRP are the eight key elements: localisation, infrastructure development, energy reform, gender equality, job creation, business support, economic reform and agriculture enhancement. This was a commendable intervention on the part of the government. Various funds were committed to some of the key elements of the ERRP. We touch on the ERRP because it has economic aspects. However, it is not an economic policy. In addition, although the ERRP provides information on the economic impact assessment it does not provide sufficient detailed metrics or computable data to measure the effectiveness of the plan. The ERRP also mentions the identification of structural constraints to growth and aspires for a re-imagined industrial strategy. However, there is limited detail on specific structural reforms and the envisaged re-imagined industrial strategy, which are crucial for sustainable economic growth.

Acknowledging the economic challenges that the country continues to face, the National Treasury proposed an economic strategy that aimed at various reforms that support labour-intensive growth, promote economic transformation and create a globally competitive market for South Africa. It is also from the same perspective that the National Treasury's economic strategy deals with what it terms 'fundamental building blocks' for the long-run growth. The following are the issues covered as building blocks to undo binding constraints and unleash sustainable and pro-poor growth:

1. **Modernising network industries to promote competitiveness and inclusive growth**

   Under this theme, the National Treasury highlights interventions to be prioritised in order to address challenges such as lack of efficient regulation, poorly managed SOEs and lack of access of quality services and some of those interventions include:

   For electricity, transparent electricity tariffs management and correction of the over-alliance of the municipality budget on the electricity revenue. For telecommunication, open access requirements should be implemented to reduce needless duplication of telecommunications infrastructure, and rapid deployment rules that expedite the installation of telecommunications infrastructure should be finalised. For transport, encouraging the switch from road to rail where it is practicable and efficient, as well as enhancing communication and cooperation between shippers and transportation providers. For Water, the Treasury recommends that a nationwide programme to conserve water can be put into place to lessen urban water demand and waste.

2. **Lowering barriers to entry and addressing distorted patterns of ownership through increased competition and small business growth**

   To ensure that entry barriers are lowered, and monopolistic structure is addressed the National Treasury suggests the implementation of the following: the consideration of the competition and market structure-related issues when drafting a new legislation, regulations or policies; development finance should be accessible to the new and small entrants and government support should be widely and effectively communicated.

3. **Prioritising labour-intensive growth in sectors such as agriculture and services, including tourism**

   Prioritising labour-intensive growth in the agriculture and services sectors is strategic because these sectors in most of the cases absorb low skill labour and have higher multiplier effects as well as linkages to different economic sectors, therefore policy makers should focus on improving access to financing for farmers; improving extension services for smallholder and emerging farmers in the agriculture sector. In the service sector, due to its resiliency in downturns relative to other sectors, overcoming challenges such as vulnerability to currency fluctuations, immigration regulation is an imperative. To address this, the Treasury recommend a greater budgetary support from tourism agencies, tourism support by the department of tourism and the amendment of the visa regulations.

4. **Implementing focused and flexible industrial and trade policy**

   Under the industrial policy theme, one can see that the Industrial Policy Action Plan (IPAP) covers about 13 sectoral areas broadly with various interventions under each area, this lowers the policy effectiveness. Therefore, a more precise and focused IPAP should be considered in order to increase its impact. Moreso, it is important to adopt and increase the piloting and experimentation of industrial policy options, this would allow limited implementation of fiscal benefits to a wide economy that at the end erodes fiscal revenue through the tax redundance.

5. **Promoting export competitiveness and harnessing regional growth opportunities**

   As the export sophistication and diversification increase the economic resilience, especially post shocks, policies such as improving the promotion of competition and private sector participation in infrastructure, implementing a specific sector export marketing and investment assistance scheme as well as coordination between government and private sector to set up an automated licensing system for key export documentation and reviewing border control procedures, plant and animal health standards are encouraged.

While the Treasury's economic policy outlines various reforms for South Africa's economic challenges, there are a few key areas of concern that need to be well thought-out. The Treasury's economic policy sketches a number of reforms across different sectors, but it would be beneficial to discuss potential challenges and obstacles in the implementation process. One of the possible challenges and obstacles in the implementation process would include political resistance from various stakeholders who may consider the changes as a threat to their interests, leading to potential obstructions. Another potential challenge is bureaucratic difficulties and slow decision-making processes within government institutions which can delay the rapid and effective implementation of proposed reforms. Finally, insufficient expertise and capacity within government agencies may pose challenges in executing complex reforms, requiring investments in skill development and capacity building. Addressing these challenges upfront could contribute to a more realistic assessment of the feasibility of the proposed reforms. In addition, the Treasury's economic policy does not comprehensively deal with environmental sustainability—how economic reforms might impact the environment.

8.3 Synthesis

The book, besides the background and its scope in the introductory chapter, has six chapters. Chapter 2 unpacked the nature and the performance of the South African economy with a focus on the post-apartheid period. Chapter 3 assessed social and economic development in post-apartheid South Africa. Chapter 4 deals with emerging markets of which South Africa is one of those markets and macroeconomic resilience. Chapter 5 discusses the interface between the market and the government. Chapter 6 examines the government role in the economy. Chapter 7 deals with the institutional architecture that could be effective in the pursuit of socio-economic development in South Africa. The chapter draws lessons from countries (which are comparable to South Africa) that are said to be having institutional architectures that have resulted in wellbeing improvements. An institutional architecture should result in economic growth and better development outcomes. The chapter also supports the view that the government has an important role in the economy and it confirms that social policy is critical for socio-economic development.

Chapter 6, to say more, examines the role of government size in the South African economy by learning from the perspective of Poland, Malaysia, Brazil, Nigeria, Venezuela and Singapore. The empirical results indicate that the relationship between government size and economic growth is characterised by a non-linear relationship (i.e. a U-shape). This suggests that at the initial stage, government intervention deteriorates economic growth up to a certain point before the impact is positive. Our analysis further suggests a threshold of 17.9% of government spending to GDP. We believe that while it is important for government to intervene in the economy in order to direct and regulate to act as catalyst for economic prosperity, social justice and ecological sustainability, too much of government intervention may be detrimental to the economy. South Africa can learn from the experience of Singapore, which is a highly developed free-market economy with dirigiste characteristics.

With regard to Chap. 5, the chapter argued that the size of the government in South Africa is big, looking at the government as an employer, a consumer and a producer. The direct intervention of the government in the economy as a producer became widespread during apartheid era as the government advocated for a protectionist approach. Several SOEs were formed during apartheid era and were later inherited by the democratic government. Although these SOEs played a significant role in bringing development, they are currently in a dire financial state. They have become a burden to the country's fiscus as they depend on government bailouts. The state of SOEs also poses a risk on economic growth. The Bayesian vector autoregressive (BVAR) results found that domestic debts of SOEs have negative impact on the economic growth in the short run but exert a positive impact in the long run.

In Chap. 4, different shocks that hit South Africa and its counterparts Brazil, Nigeria, Malaysia and Poland are outlined. Furthermore, the chapter investigated shocks transmission mechanisms and the results indicate that among all the compared samples, Poland appeared to be much more resilient, which was proved by the number of negative growth rates registered by this country. Moreso, different from Poland, South Africa experienced different shocks, but it was also found to be resilient because it was able to bounce back, although in a smaller rate. Something that also deserved an attention was that although Nigeria seemed to have bounced back to its usual steady state, still, this was considered to be less resilient due to its high volatility overtime, which may be explained by its high reliance on commodity exports. Regarding transmission mechanisms, the chapter found that although most of the indicators played some role, consumption was found to be a high transmission factor of the shock and the most plausible explanation for this is that most of these economies are driven by consumption, accounting on average for 60% of the total GDP. Nonetheless, export was in many cases found to be shock buffer/absorber, other shock absorbers included diversification.

As far as Chap. 3 is concerned, the chapter analysed socio-economic transformation since 1994. Like other chapters that assess the economy, Chap. 3 confirms that economic development has been in decline since the mid-2000s. Similarly, social development has not improved of late (at least since 2015 or so). This is largely because of lack of appropriate policies and inefficiencies in the public sector.

Regarding Chap. 2, the chapter assessed the nature and the performance of the South African economy and empirically employed the autoregressive distributed lag (ARDL) and vector error correction (VEC) to test what drives growth in the economy. Findings indicate that South Africa is still battling with some socio-economic problems such as high levels of inequality, poverty and unemployment, which persists with over 30% of the workforce being officially unemployed, with black youth experiencing much higher rates of unemployment. Modern infrastructure in the nation facilitates a rather effective transportation of products to significant metropolitan centres throughout the area, although unpredictable electrical supply impedes development. Empirically, the chapter also observed consumption, government spending as well as export key determinants of economic growth.

8.4 Towards an Economic Policy for South Africa

There is sufficient ground to argue for a new economic policy for South Africa. It is also important that there is a comprehensive social policy that can work in tandem with an economic policy. In addition, it is also important to relook at South Africa's labour market policy to ensure that there is job creation.

An economic policy that could be ideal for a country with a history that South Africa has should prioritise socio-economic transformation. Put differently, as this book implies, there is a need for an inclusive economic development policy. At the centre of such a policy should be the restructuring of the South African economy. This point has been made by many and the government has tried since 1994 to address this challenge with little success. The economic reforms, both at macro- and micro-economic levels, have largely been an attempt at restructuring of the South African economy. Fiscal policy and tax reforms have also been, arguably, part of attempts at restructuring of the South African economy. The interventions to change the mineral-energy-complex character have been part of attempts at restructuring of the South African economy. All these efforts have had minimal successes and Covid-19 reversed some of the gains. Similarly, the poor management of public finances and inefficiencies in the public sector have compromised the efforts that government has been making in restructuring of the South African economy.

While focusing on the restructuring of the South African economy, there are specific areas that we view as critical aspects of an inclusive economic development policy. In particular, the small, micro- and medium enterprises (SMMEs) as well as the informal sector have potential to grow the economy while ensuring inclusive development. Another area that we believe has great potential for economic growth and inclusive development is agricultural development and the associated sub-sectors and agrarian reforms that contribute to economic development. Thirdly, needless to say, an inclusive industrial development strategy will go a long way in facilitating economic development for South Africa. Such a strategy has to take into account climate change implications and the envisaged energy transition. We use a phrase 'inclusive industrial development strategy' because we think such a strategy (not a policy per se) would have to encompass various aspects of industrial development that can ensure economic growth and inclusive development. For all associated interventions—be it for SMMEs or for agricultural development—Black African youth and women should be prioritised, given the political history that the book explains in its introductory chapter.

It is also important to emphasise that we are not convinced that economic policy alone will ensure inclusive development that South Africa needs. It is in this context that we make a point that social policy should be comprehensive and work in tandem with economic policy to ensure inclusive development. Similarly, there is a role for labour market policy because the creation of jobs should be part of economic development endeavour particularly for a country with as high unemployment as South Africa has. In any case, labour market policy would need to be tailored for the energy transition because many people would lose jobs through decarbonisation and new (green) industries would require a different set of skills. Lastly, South Africa should be playing a role in economic development of the southern African region and leverage through the African Continental Free Trade Area (AfCFTA) for the inclusive socio-economic development of the country.

All the various interventions, including dealing with weak public sector productivity and reversing corruption, are important but we are emphasising that economic policy (and a comprehensive social policy) will play a more effective role in socio-economic development.

8.5 Conclusion

We have tried to cover what we consider to be critical issues for the South African economy. The book has compared South Africa with similar countries in the context of emerging market economies. Among the key findings is that South Africa must come up with a robust economic policy that is ideal for a country with the history that South Africa has and that the structure of the South African economy needs special attention. In addition, a comprehensive social policy will help in sound socio-economic transformation. The book contributes to a better understanding of the South African economy, its path so far and its possibilities.

Our research, published in various platforms and in this book, supports the argument for a more robust role of the government on the economy. Our research also makes a convincing case for social policy that would work in tandem with economic policy for socio-economic transformation. Fundamentally, as this book argues, our research concludes that South Africa needs an appropriate economic policy. Our argument is that an economic policy is very important for socio-economic development. In other words, economic reforms and other initiatives are not enough.

References

Blumenfeld, J. (1996). Pragmatists Versus Populists in the 'new' South Africa. *The World Today: Chatham House Review, 52*(7), 185–189.

COSATU. (1996, November). A Draft Programme for the Alliance, Presented to Exco. Unpublished, Discussion Paper.

Department of Finance. (1996). Growth, Employment and Redistribution: A Macroeconomic Strategy. Republic of South Africa.

Horton, M. (2005). Role of Fiscal Policy in Stabilization and Poverty Alleviation. In M. Nowak & L. A. Ricci (Eds.), *Post-Apartheid South Africa. The First Ten Years*. IMF.

Le Roux, P. (1997). The Growth, Employment and Redistribution Strategy (GEAR): A Critical Discussion. *Africanus, 27*(2), 45–66.

Masters, D. M. (2019). *Policy-Oriented Learning and Policy Change in South Africa Between 1994–2006: An Assessment of South Africa's Economic Policies* (RDP, GEAR AND ASGISA). Masters Thesis, University of Johannesburg.

Meyer, D. (2013). *The New Growth Path (NGP) for South Africa: Can the Policy be Applied in the Local Government Sphere?* Department of Public Management: North West University.

Nattrass, N. (2011). The New Growth Path: Game Changing Vision or Cop-Out? *South African Journal of Sciences, 107*, 103–104.

The Presidency. (2007). ASGISA Annual Report 2007, Republic of South Africa, from https://www.gov.za/sites/default/files/gcis_document/201409/asgisa-2007.pdf

Prinsloo, L. (2011). *Economists Lay into SA's New Growth Path (NGP) Framework*. http://engineeringnews.co.za

Streak, J. C. (2004). The Gear Legacy: Did Gear Fail or Move South Africa Forward in Development? *Development Southern Africa, 21*(2), 271–288.

Terreblanche, S. J. (1999). *The Ideological Journey of South Africa from the RDP to the Gear Macroeconomic Plan*. Stellenbosch University.

Tregenna, F. (2011). *Manufacturing Productivity, Deindustrialization, and Reindustrialization*. WIDER Working Paper Series wp-2011-057, World Institute for Development Economic Research (UNU-WIDER).

Index[1]

[1] Note: Page numbers followed by 'n' refer to notes.

V. Gumede et al., *South African Economy*, African Histories and Modernities, https://doi.org/10.1007/978-3-031-54180-3

The manufacturer's authorised representative in the EU is Springer Nature Customer Service Centre GmbH, Europaplatz 3, 69115 Heidelberg, Germany. If you have any concerns regarding our products, please contact ProductSafety@springernature.com

Printed and bound by CPI Group (UK) Ltd, Croydon, CR0 4YY
01/10/2026
02225898-0002